# MAGILL'S HISTORY
## OF
# NORTH AMERICA

# Magill's History
# of
# North America

# Volume 1

*Edited by*
FRANK N. MAGILL

Grolier Educational Corporation
Danbury, Connecticut

LIBRARY OF CONGRESS

Library of Congress Cataloging-in-Publication Data

Magill's History of North America / edited by Frank N. Magill—Rev. ed.

ISBN 0-7172-8204-X (set)
1. North America—History.  I. Magill, Frank Northen, 1907-
II. History of North America.
E18.M2 1988
970—dc19                                                    88-16506
                                                                   CIP


REVISED EDITION


First Printing


Published 1988 by
Grolier Educational Corporation
Danbury, Connecticut, 06816


Printed in the United States of America

# PREFACE

MAGILL's HISTORY OF NORTH AMERICA begins with the arrival of the Indians, the first Americans, from Asia and ends with the signing of a trade agreement between the United States and Canada in 1988. Between these two noteworthy happenings, more than four hundred additional events are studied in depth through the literature they have inspired.

The events are presented chronologically in twelve volumes, enabling one to examine the beginning and development of a brand-new society from point zero — a societal *tabula rasa*, so to speak. Furthermore, this development may be examined through contemporary sources not flawed by myth and information gaps, as well as through scholarly retrospect. Nowhere in human history has such an opportunity on so large a scale presented itself, where the record is there without guesswork — the social development as clear as an ant colony behind glass. It is a remarkable story that unfolds.

The style of the articles is consistent throughout all series. Each article consists of four sections: reference material at the beginning showing type of event, time, locale, and principal personages involved if applicable; the Summary of Event, a journalistic account of the occurrence describing the basic facts of what took place and some of the causes and effects; the Pertinent Literature, wherein two or more original essay-reviews of scholarly works written about the event are presented; and an Additional Recommended Reading list which annotates several other works that the student or researcher might profitably examine if interested in an in-depth study of the event. The critical evaluations referred to above provide a review of the immediate and long-range effects of an occurrence and should enable the reader to view objectively the forces that sparked the event.

The primary objective of the editor has been to present an individual discussion and analysis of significant happenings whose consequences have changed the course of history in the Western world. Events considered in addition to the conventional political and military groups include those dealing with intellectual, scientific, literary, sociological, and cultural achievements as well as various other civilizing forces. A major purpose also has been to make available, along with the narrative summaries of the occurrences themselves, scholarly evaluations of representative literature dealing with the events.

All the material was written by history professors and scholars from campuses throughout the United States. Reports of the events themselves average more than one thousand words in length while individual reviews of the literature run about six or eight hundred words each. Events are presented in chronological order.

At the beginning of each volume there appears a chronological list of events for that volume. Volume Twelve includes these four indexes: Alphabetical List of Events, Key Word Index, Category Index, and an alphabetized listing of Principal Personages. Since, unlike book titles, not all events lend themselves to a specific title universally applied, as do "Battle of . . ." or "Establishment of . . ."

articles, the Key Word Index should enable the user to locate many events more readily than would an alphabetical index of events whose first word was arbitrarily assigned by the editors.

FRANK N. MAGILL

# INITIALS IDENTIFYING CONTRIBUTORS OF SIGNED ARTICLES

| | | | |
|---|---|---|---|
| *A.C.L.* | Anne C. Loveland | *F.N.M.* | Frank N. Magill |
| *A.C.R.* | Anne C. Raymer | *F.P.P.* | Francis P. Prucha |
| *A.G.G.* | Alan G. Gross | *G.J.F.* | George J. Fleming |
| *A.O.B.* | Anita O. Bowser | *G.L.S.* | Gustav L. Seligman |
| *A.T.* | Anne Trotter | *G.M.R.* | Germaine M. Reed |
| *B.A.* | Bryan Aubrey | *G.Q.F.* | George Q. Flynn |
| *B.F.* | Barry Faye | *G.R.M.* | George R. Mitchell |
| *B.H.W.* | Bennett H. Wall | *H.C.* | Howard Cody |
| *B.K.* | Burton Kaufman | *J.A.B.* | James A. Berlin |
| *B.L.N.* | Burl L. Noggle | *J.B.L.* | James B. Lane |
| *B.S.* | Beatrice Spade | *J.C.C.* | John C. Carlisle |
| *C.B.R.* | Courtney B. Ross | *J.C.G.* | John C. Gardner |
| *C.E.C.* | Charles E. Cottle | *J.D.* | John Duffy |
| *C.L.E.* | Cecil L. Eubanks | *J.D.R.* | John D. Raymer |
| *C.W.J.* | Charles W. Johnson | *J.E.F.* | James E. Fickle |
| *C.W.T.* | Carol Whyte Talabay | *J.F.F.* | James F. Findlay, Jr. |
| *D.B.* | Dan Barnett | *J.G.C.* | John G. Clark |
| *D.F.P.* | Doris F. Pierce | *J.G.U.* | Jonathan G. Utley |
| *D.H.* | Donald Holley | *J.H.D.* | John H. DeBerry |
| *D.H.C.* | David H. Culbet | *J.J.B.* | James J. Bolner |
| *D.K.P.* | Donald K. Pickens | *J.J.H.* | James J. Herlan |
| *D.L.A.* | David L. Ammerman | *J.K.* | Jeffrey Kimball |
| *D.M.* | Daniel Murphy | *J.L.C.* | Jack L. Calbert |
| *D.R.G.* | Don R. Gerlach | *J.L.L.* | John L. Loos |
| *D.W.T.* | David W. Talabay | *J.M.F.* | Jonathan M. Furdek |
| *E.A.Z.* | Edward A. Zivich | *J.R.H.* | John R. Hanson, II |
| *E.E.* | Ernesto Encinas | *J.R.P.* | John R. Phillips |
| *E.F.* | Elizabeth Fee | *J.R.S.* | Jane R. Shoup |
| *E.G.D.* | E. Gene DeFelice | *J.S.A.* | J. Stewart Alverson |
| *E.J.M.* | Edward J. Maguire | *J.W.P.* | James W. Pringle |
| *E.M.T.* | Emory M. Thomas | *K.A.R.* | Karl A. Roider |
| *E.P.K.* | Edward P. Keleher | *L.P.S.* | Lewis P. Simpson |
| *F.J.D.* | Fredrick J. Dobney | *L.S.* | Leon Stein |
| *F.M.S.* | Fredrick M. Spletstoser | *M.A.* | Michael Adams |

| | | | |
|---|---|---|---|
| *M.A.P.* | Mark A. Plummer | *R.O.M.* | Rex O. Mooney |
| *M.D.C.* | Michael D. Clark | *R.R.* | Richard Rice |
| *M.E.R.* | Merl E. Reed | *S.B.* | Scott Bouvier |
| *M.G.* | Manfred Grote | *S.E.A.* | Stephen E. Ambrose |
| *M.L.W.* | Major L. Wilson | *S.L.* | Saul Lerner |
| *M.O.D.* | Merle O. Davis | *S.L.C.* | Sidney L. Cohen |
| *M.S.S.* | Margaret S. Schoon | *T.A.B.* | Terry Alan Baney |
| *M.T.D.* | Maurice T. Dominguez | *T.A.W.* | Theodore A. Wilson |
| *M.W.B.* | Meredith William Berg | *T.D.* | Tyler Dierhoi |
| *N.S.C.* | Norman S. Cohen | *T.D.C.* | Thomas D. Crouch |
| *P.A.* | Paul Ashin | *T.J.C* | Terrill J. Clements |
| *P.D.M.* | Paul D. Mageli | *T.L.S.* | Terry L. Seip |
| *P.R.P.* | Philip R. Popple | *T.M.S.* | Thomas M. Smith |
| *R.A.B.* | Robert A. Becker | *T.R.K.* | Thomas R. Koenig |
| *R.A.G.* | Roger A. Geimer | *W.G.H.* | William G. Haag |
| *R.D.H.* | R. Don Higginbotham | *W.I.H.* | William I. Hair |
| *R.F.E.* | Robert F. Erickson | *W.J.C.* | William J. Cooper, Jr. |
| *R.H.C.* | Richard H. Collin | *W.L.R.* | William L. Richter |
| *R.H.S.* | Richard S. Sander | *W.M.B.* | Warren M. Billings |
| *R.J.C.* | Ronald J. Cima | *W.M.T.* | William M. Tuttle |
| *R.M.* | Russell Magnaghi | *W.T.J.* | W. Turrentine Jackson |
| *R.N.S.* | Ronald N. Spector | | |

# List of Events in Volume One

# ARRIVAL OF THE INDIANS, THE FIRST AMERICANS

*Type of event:* Sociological: prehistoric migration
*Time:* Unknown
*Locale:* The North American continent

## Summary of Event

America's native populations have been the objects of centuries of speculation and investigation. From Europe's discovery of the American "Indian" at the end of the fifteenth century to the present, the question of who the Indians are and how they came to the Western Hemisphere has intrigued scholars, poets, clergymen, and laymen. The answers to these questions range from intricate and scholarly theories to arrant nonsense.

When it became apparent that Columbus had not reached India in 1492 but had instead found a new continent, Europeans sought to explain the existence of the New World's indigenous people. Some, especially clergymen, theorized that the Indians descended from the ten lost tribes of Israel. Others maintained that the Indians' ancestors were Welshmen whom Prince Madoc had led to America. Still others insisted that the natives came from the fabled lost continents of Atlantis and Mu. Periodically, from the sixteenth to the twentieth century, each of these notions held sway and none was entirely satisfactory. But the advent of anthropology as an academic discipline at the end of the nineteenth century promised to provide more prosaic interpretations based upon careful and scientific analyses of available data. Modern techniques such as dendrochronology, the dating of organic matter by means of carbon 14 tests, and the hydration of obsidian finds have enhanced the development of sophisticated theories to answer the questions Europeans first posed half a millennium ago.

Regarding the Indians' ancestral identity, anthropologists seem to agree on only one point—that the Indians did not arise *sui generis* in North America. As proof of this contention they note that no skeletal remains of a human physical type earlier than *homo sapiens* have yet been found in the Americas. This fact also makes possible the tentative dating of man's arrival on the continent because *homo sapiens* emerged from the evolutionary process about fifty thousand years ago, but there is disagreement over whether one or several archaic genetic stocks of *homo sapiens* populated the New World. The resolution of that controversy depends on one's conception of the manner in which early man arrived in the Western Hemisphere.

At present, many scholars believe that Asians came to America during two periods: the first, between 50,000 and 40,000 B.C.; and the second, between 26,000 and 8,000 B.C. They are believed to have come by way of a great land bridge between Asia and North America which existed at the Bering Strait. This causeway was covered by water from about 40,000 to 26,000 B.C. because of a melting episode in mid-Wisconsin glacial time.

Because of the many different early cultural remains which have been

1

found, it is generally held that there were several discrete, and perhaps isolated, movements of various peoples from Asia to America, rather than one steady flow for a short period of time. It is speculated that this migration was caused by an increase in population of the tribes of central Asia which impelled them to move eastward in quest of additional sources of food. As hunters, they had to follow the game in order to support life. So, as the animals retreated into North America, primitive man followed.

Once they arrived in the New World, these early men did not have to make many significant cultural adjustments to survive, for the resources and climates of North America and Asia are believed to have been similar. Generation by generation, however, population pressure urged them ever farther southward toward the margins of the two continents, so that by 8,000 B.C. there were primitive hunters even in Tierra del Fuego. Around 5,000 B.C., the disappearance of large game animals in both North and South America produced a series of regional developments in certain areas which culminated in the emergence of several great civilizations, such as those of the Inca and Aztec. At the same time, remnants of the old hunting cultures survived in some isolated areas such as California and the tip of South America.

## Pertinent Literature

Josephy, Alvin M., Jr. *The Indian Heritage of America.* New York: Alfred A. Knopf, Inc., 1968.

Studies of the Indians' origins are voluminous. Frequently such studies require an understanding of anthropology and archaeology in order to render them intelligible. For the uninitiated but curious nonspecialist, Josephy's book is a good place to begin investigation of the subject.

Josephy's long acquaintance with contemporary Indians and their affairs has led naturally to a deep appreciation of the first Americans and the writing of two other books about Indians. This feeling is apparent in *The Indian Heritage of America,* for like other people concerned with the present condition of the red man, Josephy often seems to be pleading a case. He tries to penetrate white stereotypes about the Indian, to emphasize cultural and physical diversity among Indians, and to suggest how much white America has depended upon the Indian throughout its history.

Drawing widely from historical, archaeological, anthropological, and ethnographic sources, Josephy attempts to portray the Indian as he was and as he is. He describes concepts of society which were fundamentally different from those of Europe, and he argues that these basic distinctions account for the rise of the stereotypic Indian in American folklore. His reconstruction of pre-Columbian Indian societies demonstrates the great variety of cultural syntheses which existed before 1492. In examining the impact of Indian culture upon European culture, Josephy also shows the debt contemporary white America owes to the Indian. Then he moves into a discussion of the modern Indians' ancestral

2

origins.

Josephy presents a balanced, brief reading of available evidence and modern scholarship without advancing any new theory of his own. He does not load his discussion with technicalities, yet he manages to convey the essentials of present knowledge. He touches lightly on pre-twentieth century theses, while giving some attention to suggestions like Thor Heyerdahl's belief that some South American Indians had contacts with natives from the Pacific islands. His general conclusion is that the Americas were populated by successive waves of prehistoric Asians who crossed the Bering Strait land bridge during the latter stages of the Wisconsin glaciation. Over a twenty to thirty thousand year period, these immigrants diffused throughout the hemisphere, developing distinct cultures, languages, and social customs. In developing these conclusions, Josephy relies mostly upon the recent work of an archaeologist named Alex D. Kreiger.

In seeking to explain the variant manifestations of culture, language, and physical types which the pre-Columbian Indian displayed, Kreiger has postulated a series of staged developments through which early man has passed. According to Kreiger's theory, these stages occurred at periodic intervals and for varying lengths of time in different parts of the Americas. The occurrence of the development was uneven throughout the hemisphere, and the stages were marked by numerous local and regional variations. Within this conceptual framework, Kreiger has formulated three stages: Pre-Projectile Point, Paleo-Indian, and Protoarchaic. These stages make possible the relation of available archaeological data to a spatial sequence, and help to account for the known cultural flowerings of prehistory.

Josephy does not maintain that Kreiger's typology provides a final solution to the questions of who the Indians' ancestors were and how they came here. He believes that new finds will continue to shed light on these matters.

Jennings, Jesse D. *Prehistory of North America.* New York: McGraw-Hill Book Company, 1958.

The study of the modern American Indians' origin indicates how history and other academic disciplines working in concert can gain new knowledge. Since the prehistoric Indian has left none of the types of data which historians ordinarily employ in their reconstruction of the past, they must, as Alvin Josephy has done, turn to the work of other scholars. In this instance, anthropologists and archaeologists have produced most of the best recent work about the Indians of prehistory. Consequently, those persons who seek a wider perspective on the matter than is offered by Josephy's book should go to the vast corpus of literature which anthropology and archaeology provide. An excellent introduction to this literature is Jesse Jennings' *Prehistory of North America.*

Professor Jennings has written a basic, but sophisticated, study of North American Indian archaeology. Jennings' book is designed to acquaint the student with the mysteries of archaeology. Jennings imparts the flavor of field work and the "exciting order, consistency, and unbelievable efficiency of the many American cultures or tradi-

3

tions" which the field techniques have revealed.

Drawing upon the work of numerous scholars, Jennings concludes that man probably arrived in successive waves on the North American continent from Asia during the latter stages of the Wisconsin glaciation. As the glacier retreated, the land bridge was submerged, and the men were trapped forever. Furthermore, Jennings accepts the idea that this prehistoric man had attained a high level of evolutionary development. None of these facts explains, however, why "the Indians were more nearly homogeneous and like one another than they were like any other population segment in the rest of the world." This question cannot be answered definitively on empirical grounds, but Jennings theorizes that the homogeneous Indian population probably derived from one or more primitive Asian populations between ten thousand and forty thousand years ago, who when isolated from Asia by the retreating glacier, became the genotype for the modern Indian. Some of the known skeletal remains tend to confirm such a view, but too many links are missing to make this concept a certainty.

The tentative nature of Jennings' conclusions focuses attention on a major problem about the attempt to obtain a precise view of the Indians' origin. Such data as have been discovered are so fragmentary that any theory based upon them is suspect and subject to revision pending new discoveries. Reference to Jennings' bibliography, which is extensive, demonstrates how often new discoveries have forced revisions of old ideas and theses. — *W.M.B.*

## Additional Recommended Reading

Underhill, Ruth M. *Red Man's America: A History of Indians in the United States.* Chicago: University of Chicago Press, 1960. A standard introductory study of the North American Indian emphasizing anthropological and archaeological, rather than historical, evidence.

Martin, Paul S., *et al. Indians Before Columbus: Twenty Thousand Years of North American History Revealed by Archaeology.* Chicago: University of Chicago Press, 1947. This brief summary stresses the diversity of the Indians' racial origins and maintains that prehistoric men migrated to America in successive waves across the land bridge.

Bushnell, G. H. *The First Americans: The Pre-Columbian Civilizations.* New York: McGraw-Hill Book Company, 1968. Provides useful data on the Indians' origins.

Heyerdahl, Thor. *Kon-Tiki.* Chicago: Rand-McNally & Company, 1950. Advances the thesis that some of the Indians may have established contact with people on the Pacific Islands by sailing across the Pacific in balsa rafts.

Gladwin, Harold S. *Men Out of Asia.* New York: Whittlesey House, 1947. Accepts the Asian migration thesis while positing the assumption that the high culture areas were populated by Alexander the Great's soldiers.

Kreiger, Alex D. "Early Man in the New World," in *Prehistoric Man in the New World.* Edited by Jesse D. Jennings and Edward Norbeck. Chicago: University of Chicago Press, 1964. This article contains a complex discussion of the typology described in Alvin Josephy's *The Indian Heritage of America.*

# THE MAYAN CALENDAR

*Type of event:* Technological: chronological invention
*Time:* c.350 B.C.
*Locale:* Southern Mexico and Guatemala

## Summary of Event

Throughout meso-America during the period A.D. 300 to 1500, there were several related calendrical systems in use. Those of the Maya were undoubtedly the equal or superior of any others in completeness and internal relations. Compared to the Julian calendar, the Mayan system appears complex and difficult to understand, but actually it is relatively simple. Although the origin of the Mayan calendar is unknown and lost in antiquity, the Maya developed several devices through the centuries. The one usually meant in references to the calendar is the interrelated solar year of 365 days and the sacred year of 260 days.

Basic to all Mayan calendrics is the day. All reckoning was in single days or multiples of days. The 260-day scheme, now called the *tzolkin* or "count of days," is conceived of as an interrelationship of twenty named days through a cycle of thirteen numbers (20 x 13 = 260). This scheme has no astronomical basis and seems to be an arbitrary development of unknown origin. Although independent of movements of celestial bodies, undoubtedly it was an "astrological" guide to the fates of the Maya. The life of every individual was predetermined by the portent of the day upon which he was born. Each of the twenty days in the name cycle was controlled by a deity who was either benevolent or malevolent. Not only were the fortunes, and even the names, of individuals at the mercy of the gods, but the whole country was downcast on days ruled by dangerous gods, and cheerful on the days of benign spirits.

These twenty days marched inexorably through time one after another but they were geared to a succession of thirteen numbers. Their names and numbers beginning with each sacred year were as follows: (1) *Imix,* (2) *Ik,* (3) *Akbal,* (4) *Kan,* (5) *Chicchan,* (6) *Cimi,* (7) *Manik,* (8) *Lamat,* (9) *Muluc,* (10) *Oc,* (11) *Chuen,* (12) *Eb,* (13) *Ben;* (1) *Ix,* (2) *Men,* (3) *Cib,* (4) *Caban,* (5) *Eznab,* (6) *Cauac,* (7) *Ahau,* (8) *Imix,* (9) *Ik,* and so on. It will be noted that after (13) *Ben,* the numbers revert to (1) but the names continue; after (7) *Ahau,* the names revert to the first, *Imix.* Hence, (1) *Imix* would not appear again to inaugurate a new sacred year until after twenty cycles of thirteen days or thirteen cycles of twenty days, making up 260 days.

The Maya also recognized a year (the *haab*), roughly equivalent to the solar year. It consisted of eighteen months of twenty days each and a period of five days of uncertainty and foreboding. These nineteen "months" were called the "vague year," meaning that it approximated the true solar year. It has been supposed that the Maya realized the sacred year would not serve for marking the times of planting or harvesting, or for activities related to the annual changes in the sun. It is also evident that the astron-

5

omer-priests knew that this vague year did not correspond exactly to a solar or tropical year (365 days, 5 hours, 48 minutes, and 46 seconds). To have corrected the discrepancy by adding a day every four years, as is now done, would have played havoc with the interrelationships of the *haab* and the *tzolkin*.

The nineteen month names are *Pop, Uo, Zip, Zotz, Tzec, Xul, Yaxkin, Mol, Chen, Yax, Zac, Ceh, Mac, Kankin, Muan, Pax, Kayab, Cumhu,* and *Uayeb* (the five-day period). Each of the first eighteen were twenty days long, but they were numbered from 0 to 19, for the Maya thought it more important to indicate a day that was "seating" the month before beginning that month's day count. The last month, *Uayeb,* counted (0) *Uayeb* through (4) *Uayeb.* This last day of the solar year was followed by (0) *Pop.*

The Maya moved in a world of these two important chronological systems, recognizing that their relationship wound through time in such a way that the coincident New Year's day for the sacred calendar and the vague year calendar could only be repeated when the two had gone through a cycle of years that brought (0) *Pop* and (1) *Imix* to fall again on the same day. For a 260-day and a 365-day period this would be fifty-two vague years or 18,980 elapsed days. This time interval is called the "calendar round." It is unknown what the Maya called it.

It may be seen from the foregoing that in the fifty-two-year calendar round, each day had a dual designation, one for the *tzolkin* and one for the *haab.* Thus, a given day might be (3) *Cib* and (17) *Pop.* This day would not reappear in the same combination for fifty-two years.

As indicated above, the Mayan priests were cognizant of the difference between the vague year and the solar year. Each calendar round departed from fifty-two true solar years by thirteen days. In a few centuries the conjunctions of various cycles would be greatly different from the priestly calculations. This seems to have led directly to the evolution of a simple notational positional vigesimal number system remarkable for involving a zero concept. This mathematical system enabled the Maya to make corrections in their observations and note discrepancies between astronomical events and calendrical calculations. It does not mean that the *tzolkin* or *haab* were corrected or shifted, but rather that the ceremonial days were shifted from certain times to others as necessary.

The growing sophistication of astronomy and of mathematics produced other calendrical inventions for the Maya: the *tun,* an approximate year of 360 days, and the *katun* of 20 *tuns* or 7,200 days. Both these periods formed important permutational cycles with the *tzolkin.* In addition, the Maya devised a 584-day cycle for the planet Venus, and some lesser cycles based on the moon and solar eclipses.

Several meso-American peoples borrowed their calendars from the Maya, but none utilized year counts greater in length than the calendar round of the Maya. The Maya, however, took the remarkable step of devising a count that began from a fictitious starting point in the distant past, determined to be 3113 B.C. by some modern scholars. This count is now referred to as the "long count" or "initial series" calendar. The latter designation stems from the position of six glyphs at the beginning of each inscription carved on commemorative monuments. When another four are added, the glyphs give a total for the number of days that have elapsed since the beginning of recorded time. The long count made possible calculations of the dates of events far in the future and millions of years in the past. So accurate were the astronomer-priests with the long count calculations that any given event could be noted in the chronology not to recur for 374,440 years.

The classic period of Mayan culture is defined as the interval during which the long count was used. It was gradually phased out during the closing centuries of that period and was replaced by a shortened form of notation that enabled a given day to be indicated by only three glyphs instead of the ten necessary for the long count. Nonetheless, this cycle was accurate to within one day in nearly nineteen thousand years. Still later, further curtailment brought the count down to an accuracy of only one day in 256 years, a system called the "short count" by modern students.

## Pertinent Literature

Thompson, J. Eric. *Maya Hieroglyphic Writing: An Introduction.* 2nd ed. Norman: University of Oklahoma Press, 1960.

This monographic study is truly monumental, definitive, and exhaustive. The first edition, entitled *Maya Hieroglyphic Writing: An Introduction,* was published in 1950 by the Carnegie Institution of Washington. The 1960 edition is an offset process reproduction with a new preface by the author. Although much research had been done in Mayan writing in the intervening decade, Thompson comments on these new efforts only briefly in the preface. The fact that the volume was reproduced in facsimile is indicative of its fundamental value to modern students. It will remain for some decades the essential source for studies on this subject. The new edition is part of the *Civilization of the American Indian* series, published continuously since 1932, by the University of Oklahoma Press on the aboriginal cultures of North, South, and Central America.

Thompson is not only a fine scholar but also a great artist, a craftsman in love with his work. His intimate knowledge of the whole range of available source materials—carved stelae, altars, building features, codices, and artifacts—gives an almost incontrovertibly authoritative ring to his treatment, although Thompson would be the first to admit that future students are almost certain to bring great changes to our present understanding of Maya hieroglyphs.

The introductory material in Thompson's work is largely devoted to a short sketch of the history of the Mayan civilization in its tropical rainforest setting. Particular emphasis is given to the religious beliefs of the Maya, for many hieroglyphs are concerned with religion and nearly all are representations or conventionalizations of deities. A description follows of glyphic texts such as are to be found on altars, monolithic stone monuments, door lintels, walls, ceilings, pyramid stairways, façades, ball courts,

7

artifacts, and codices. This description justifiably merits special attention. So also do the paragraphs on the history of research on Mayan glyphs and the disclosure of many still untranslated sources such as some of the books of the *Chilam Balam,* which are manuscripts written in Yucatec with European characters by native Maya during the colonial period.

Mayan writing is hieroglyphic in principle, and it is as complex and perplexing as ancient Egyptian. In the chapter entitled "Principles of Maya Glyphic Writing," Thompson sets forth the characteristics of the glyphs. Hieroglyphic writing generally involves the use of homophones, that is, words of similar sound but having different meanings, such as "fly" (an insect) and "fly" (process of flight). The word *xoc* in Yucatec is a mythical fish but the word also means "to count." In Mayan the head of a fish is the main glyph which means "to count forward to" or "count back to" depending upon prefixes or suffixes attached as part of the glyph. There are several other well-established homophonic glyphs that function in a similar manner.

Not all glyphs are homophonic. Many are purely pictorial or even ideographic. "The hieroglyph for 'west' is the back of a partly opened hand over the sun symbol. The hand in that position symbolizes 'completion' or perhaps 'ending.' 'End of sun' is an ideographic sign for 'west.' " This example demonstrates that decipherment of the glyphs is fascinating work.

The most important element in the panoply of calendric devices used by the Maya was the sequence of twenty days with their associated numbers. Together they constituted a unit; separately they meant nothing. Each day was named for some deity, represented in writing by his specific glyph. The origin of these symbols and the names associated with various Maya languages constitute an engrossing detective story. Thompson discusses the several explanations for the 260-day sacred year, but he discounts an astronomical basis for its origin. Similarly, the 365-day year was inspired by agricultural activities, but each of its nineteen months had a "bearer" who tirelessly furthered the "burden of time" through eternity.

The Mayan calendar called the "calendar round" served certain purposes in itself, but the Maya were not content to stop there. Further progress was limited until a good notational system was evolved. When and where numbers were first used in meso-America is unknown, but it was probably among peoples marginal to the Maya. Thompson documents the development of a mathematical system with a base of twenty. A dot for a unit (four dots in a row meant "four") and a bar for five enabled notation up to nineteen. Twenty had a separate symbol, the moon. All these numbers could be written in more than one way. Of great significance was the use of a symbol for zero.

The mathematical base was necessary before the long count cycle could be developed. The Maya were, perhaps, more interested in the past than in the future, and a counting system that enabled them to go beyond the calendar round of fifty-two years gradually came into use. Although counting was by days, the year of 360 days, called a *tun,* entered into these lengthy calculations. In keeping with the vigesimal base of twenty, the following calculations were

8

meaningfully employed by the astronomer-priests:

| | |
|---|---|
| 20 tuns | = 1 katun (7,200 days) |
| 20 katuns | = 1 baktun (144,000 days) |
| 20 baktuns | = 1 pictun (2,880,000 days) |
| 20 pictuns | = 1 calabtun (57,600,000 days) |
| 20 calabtuns | = 1 kinchiltun (1,152,000,000 days) |
| 20 kinchiltuns | = 1 alautun (23,040,000,000 days) |

The long count is obviously appropriately named.

Thompson devotes the remainder of his monograph to techniques for noting distances forward and backward through time (sometimes called "secondary series" when used with initial series). Minor cycles involving Venus, the moon, and eclipses are described. The final chapter is entitled "Aids to Decipherment," and several appendices expand certain problems in the study.

De Landa, D. *Landa's* Relación de las Coasas de Yucatan: *A Translation*. Translated by Alfred M. Tozzer. Papers of the Peabody Museum of American Archaeology and Ethnology, Harvard University, Vol. XVIII. Cambridge: Harvard University Press, 1941

No studies of the Mayan calendar seem possible without an acquaintance with *Landa's Relación de las Coasas de Yucatan*. In this translation there is special emphasis on passages that give the first exact knowledge of Mayan hieroglyphic writings. No other source offers so grand a view of Mayan life and none dwells so thoroughly on the religion of these people.

Tozzer's is the eighth translation of this famous manuscript discovered in Madrid in the nineteenth century. Its value surpasses that of all other translations because of the accompanying notes. The manuscript on which the translation is based was itself a copy and probably dates from about A.D. 1616. Tozzer believes that it is an incomplete copy of the original. Nonetheless, the two hundred pages of text and Tozzer's notes give great insight into the daily life of the Maya.

Four other short manuscripts are included in the volume. Each is an extract from a longer account by a Spanish *conquistador*. Fray Landa was Bishop of Yucatan from 1572 until his death in 1579. The *Relación de las Coasas de Yucatan* was written about 1566. He undoubtedly had access to other written accounts, such as Oviedo's *Historia* published in 1550, and he seems to have drawn freely from various manuscripts which are appended to this edition.

Although Tozzer's translation is scholarly and may look uninviting to the lay reader, it is intriguing and fascinating. The serious student and the desultory searcher alike will find this volume indispensable for understanding Maya life. — *W.G.H.*

**Additional Recommended Reading**

Coe, Michael D. *The Maya*. New York: Frederick A. Praeger Publishers, Inc., 1966. One of the *Ancient Peoples and Places* series, this up-to-date volume is a comprehensive treatment of the whole Mayan civilization. It is scholarly but readable. It has a wealth of illustrations, mostly artifacts of the classic period, but drawings of glyphs make the calendar easily understood.

Morley, Sylvanus G. *The Ancient Maya.* 3rd ed. Revised by George W. Brainard. Stanford: Stanford University Press, 1956. Morley was one of the great scholars of the Maya who often differed from other students. This volume is extensively illustrated and is one of the most widely read concerning ancient civilizations of meso-America. Its exposition of the Mayan calendar and mathematics is excellent.

Thompson, J. Eric. *The Rise and Fall of Maya Civilization.* Norman: University of Oklahoma Press, 1954. An interesting and lively account of Mayan history directed to the general reader without factual evidence being modified or distorted. Not only is the daily life of the prehistoric Maya compared with that of colonial Maya, but a description of the living Maya is included.

# NORSEMEN DISCOVER THE NEW WORLD

*Type of event:* Sociological: voyages of discovery
*Time:* c.990-1015
*Locale:* Labrador and Newfoundland

> *Principal personages:*
> ERIK THE RED (fl. 982-986), founder of the Greenland settlement
> BJARNI HERJOLFSON (fl. 985), first European to sight American shores
> LEIF THE LUCKY (fl. 999-1000), son of Erik the Red, who organized the first Norse expedition to America
> THORVALD ERIKSON (fl. 1000-1010), Leif's brother, who was killed in battle with Indians and was the first Christian to be buried in North America
> THORFINN KARLSEFNI (fl. 1002-1015), Icelander who tried to found a permanent settlement in America

## Summary of Event

Much of our information about the discovery of America by the Norsemen is contained in the Icelandic sagas, histories which were written to glorify and preserve the traditions of a particular family. As such they have to be used with caution. If it were not for independent verification of the voyages, such as in the account written about 1075 by Adam of Bremen, a German monk, and other mostly ecclesiastical sources, one could justifiably doubt the truth of the saga material. What now is open to question is the location of the Norsemen's landfall on the North American continent; the extent of their exploration and colonization; and the centuries during which Norsemen from the Greenland colony continued to visit America's shores.

The two sagas which deal with the Norse voyages to America are *The Greenlander's Saga,* written perhaps as early as the twelfth century and preserved as part of a fourteenth century manuscript known as *Flateyjarbok* (*The Annals of Flatey,* an island); and *Eirik the Red's Saga,* known from *Hauksbok* (*Book of Hauk Erlendsson,* c.1330) and in another version, *Skalholtsbok,* written in the second half of the fifteenth century. *Skalholtsbok* (the book from Skalholt, the seat of Iceland's bishop), though later in date, is generally regarded as the more reliable of the two versions of *Eirik's Saga.* But the saga itself appears to have been based in part on the *Greenlander's Saga* and to have added details about the motives of the Norsemen which do not have the ring of authenticity. *The Greenlander's Saga* almost certainly represents a more genuine tradition, and the six voyages it describes are the basis for the following summary.

Bjarni was the son of Herjolf, an Icelander who had migrated to Greenland about 985 along with Erik the Red. Bjarni returned to Iceland from a visit to Norway and learned that his father

11

had sailed west to the newly discovered Greenland. He set out from Iceland with a crew and sailed west for seventy-two hours until the land disappeared. Thereafter he sailed "many more days" until land was sighted. It was a land of woods and low hills. His crew asked Bjarni if this was Greenland, and Bjarni replied that he did not think it was Greenland. So the ship departed and sailed for two more days. A second land was sighted, flat with white sandy beaches and covered with forest, and Bjarni knew that this was not Greenland either. So the ship departed again and sailed northwest for three days and reached a third land of mountains and glaciers. Bjarni still did not believe that he had reached Greenland because the land "appeared to be worthless." So the ship set out again, and after four days came to a fourth land, which Bjarni declared to be Greenland. He landed near the very spot where dwelt his father. If Bjarni had sailed to a fifth land, one may reasonably suppose that the saga would have reported a trip of five days.

Bjarni made no attempt to follow up his discoveries, but the news of what he had found provoked great interest in the Greenland colony, and after some years (certainly after A.D. 1000), an expedition was fitted out under the leadership of Leif, the son of that Erik the Red who had founded the Greenland colony and who was its chief citizen.

Reversing Bjarni's sailing directions, Leif, with a crew of thirty-five men in Bjarni's old ship, first discovered a land covered by huge glaciers and which looked like a single slab of rock. He named it Helluland, or Flat Stone Land, after the first impression he had

received of it. Thereafter Leif found a second land which was flat, covered with forests, and had wide, sandy beaches. Leif called this land Markland, after the forests which he had first observed. After two more days of sailing, Leif sighted a third land and went ashore on an island which lay to the north of it. Here Leif and his men observed a fresh meadow with dew on the grass. They tasted the dew and it was sweeter than anything they had ever tasted before.

Leif and his men decided to winter in this third land at a place on the mainland where a river flowed out of a lake. Both river and lake were full of salmon, a fact suggesting New England or points north, as salmon do not usually occur south of the Hudson river. No frost occurred that winter, and the Norsemen noted that the length of day at mid-winter was much longer than in either Greenland or Iceland. Moreover, one of Leif's men, perhaps his first mate, Tyrkir the German, accidentally discovered vines and grapes.

The following spring, Leif and his men departed for Greenland, and Leif named the land in which he had wintered "Vinland." Offshore from Greenland, Leif rescued fifteen people shipwrecked on a reef. For this deed he was thereafter known as "the lucky."

The following spring, Leif's brother Thorvald decided to explore Vinland with a crew of thirty men. After arriving there, he used houses which Leif had built as a base, and attempted to explore the coast west of this point. The men remained in Vinland all that summer and the following winter. In the spring they sailed to the east of Leif's houses. They ran aground in a storm and their ship was wrecked.

12

After considerable delay while the ship was repaired—on a promontory which they named Kjalarness, the (ship's) keel's point—they continued their voyage eastward. Eventually they came to a promontory between two fjords, or inlets. Because of the beauty of the place, Thorvald decided to settle permanently on the site.

Shortly thereafter, Thorvald and his men discovered three skin boats, with three men under each. The Norsemen killed eight of these *Skraelings,* a name of uncertain derivation possibly meaning "wretch" and designating the aboriginal inhabitants of North America, but one escaped. Thus ended the first confrontation of white men and Indians in North America.

The saga then reports that Thorvald and his men were overcome with drowsiness, but were awakened by a magic voice which urged them to flee. The *Skraelings* returned to the Norse camp and flailed them with arrows. The crew fled to the ship, and eventually the *Skraelings* withdrew. But Thorvald had been mortally wounded in the armpit, and by his request he was buried on the promontory by his men. They put crosses at his head and feet and called the place Krossaness. Thorvald was thus the first white man and the first Christian to die and be buried in North America. The date must have been sometime after the conversion of Greenland to Christianity in the first decade after the year 1000.

When Thorvald's crew returned home, still another brother, Thorstein, attempted to sail to Vinland to fetch back his brother's body. But the sea was stormy, and after some weeks of tossing about, the ship landed in the western (or northern) settlement of Greenland.

About a year later a ship arrived in Greenland from Norway captained by Thorfinn Karlsefni. He settled near the farm of Leif Erikson and fell in love with Gudrid, Leif's sister-in-law and the widow of Thorstein, who had died of disease.

After the marriage was celebrated, Gudrid urged Karlsefni to explore Vinland. Extensive preparations were made, with provisions for a crew of sixty men and five women. After an uneventful crossing, the mariners arrived at Leif's houses in Vinland, and passed the first season successfully. There was plenty of food, as the men captured a whale which had been stranded on the beach, and they were able to hunt game and gather grapes.

The following summer the *Skraelings* appeared. They came out of the woods one day, but a bull which the settlers had brought with them terrified the aborigines, and they attempted to hide in the Norsemen's houses. Karlsefni and his men, however, barred the way. The Skraelings then set down packs which they carried containing furs, and tried to barter. Karlsefni decided to offer them milk, and the *Skraelings* were willing to exchange all their furs for milk. Thereafter Karlsefni ordered his men to build a stockade around their homes.

During the same summer Gudrid, Karlsefni's wife, gave birth to a son, who was named Snorri. He was the first white child, so far as is known, to be born in North America.

The subsequent winter the *Skraelings* returned and again traded furs for milk. But they also tried to steal the Norsemen's weapons. Fighting broke out, many of the *Skraelings* were killed,

13

and the survivors fled the scene. Karlsefni thereupon decided to return to Greenland the following spring.

The *Greenlander's Saga* tells of a final voyage led by two Icelanders, Helgi and Finnbogi, and by Freydis, a daughter of Erik, but the story deals mainly with Freydis' treachery, and it is probably unhistorical.

*Eirik's Saga,* our other literary tradition, provides additional details of the voyages which may originally have been part of the *Greenlander's Saga* but were lost before that saga was written down. Or they may have come from another source. We may assume, however, that there were continuing Norse contacts from Greenland to the North American coast until the fourteenth century, when the Greenland colony itself was extinguished. But after the failure of Karlsefni's expedition, no extensive or permanent settlement was undertaken by the Norsemen on American shores.

## Pertinent Literature

The literature on the Norse exploration of North America is vast. Much of it belongs to the realm of fancy rather than fact. There are learned treatises and the lunatic fringe. Both kinds of books have been produced in quantity for more than one hundred years.

Vinland has been found, or probably could be, in anyone's backyard. At least Emil Horsfjord thought that he had found Leif Erikson's house in his backyard on Cape Cod, a belief he described in a work published in the late nineteenth century. Others have located Vinland in one of four principal places: Newfoundland, the St. Lawrence Estuary, Cape Cod, and Chesapeake Bay. Part of the problem is the meaning of the word "Vinland." With a short "i," the name could mean "meadow land," and thus Leif might have named Vinland after the first quality that he noted there, a meadow of sweet grass, as he had named Helluland and Markland after the rocks and forests which he saw there first. Most scholars are of the opinion, however, that "vin" with a long "i" means "wine." At least Adam of Bremen called the place "Wineland" in 1075, and that is a nearly contemporary source.

But grapes do not grow in Newfoundland, where remains of houses which appear to be eleventh century Norse have recently been uncovered. Thus some writers have suggested that "vin" means "wine berries," such as currants.

Another problem concerns the observations of the length of day made in Vinland by Leif Erikson and his men. Basing his assumption on a description in the sagas that the position of the sun at the time of the evening meal in Vinland could be determined, a Norwegian mathematician (who assumed that the evening meal was at four o'clock) calculated that Vinland must have been on Chesapeake Bay. And an Italian geographer insisted that *Eirik's Saga* told of Niagara Falls ("they entered a river where the sea fell down from the land") and located Vinland north of Lake Ontario.

Still other books have dealt with the finding of ninth century Norse artifacts in Canada; the Runic (Germanic alphabet) inscription found or manufac-

14

tured at Kensington, Minnesota, in 1898 and dated 1362; and the stone mill (probably built around 1675) at Newport, Rhode Island, which strongly resembles medieval Swedish architecture. All of these books attempt to relate their archaeological materials to the Vinland problem, while, if anything, they should connect them with the extinction of the Norse colony on Greenland in the fourteenth century.

The pre-Columbian map, now in the possession of the Yale University Library, which was drawn in the 1440's and which shows a stylized Vinland, has done little to provide corroboration for the truth of the sagas or the location of Vinland, and it is without value as a historical source. It is probable that the name "Vinland" was applied to a rather large region, and any attempt to localize it to a single province or state is doomed to failure.

There are two recent treatises on the Vinland problem which are most worthy of consideration.

Ingstad, Helge. *Westward to Vinland: The Discovery of Pre-Columbian Norse House-Sites in North America.* New York: St. Martin's Press, 1969.

The archaeologist has long been able to make stones speak, and they usually tell him what he wants to hear. Thus Ingstad has been able to transform a site at L'Anse aux Meadows (the Bay of Meadows) on the Northwest coast of Newfoundland from a settlement which appears to be Norse, made perhaps as early as the eleventh century, into the site of Vinland itself, established in the year 1000. Or perhaps he is overstating the case. Ingstad at least admits that other places could have been the Vinland of the sagas. But other scholars have not been so cautious. Samuel Eliot Morison, for example, in a book published in 1971, states definitively that L'Anse aux Meadows and Vinland are one and the same.

Ingstad and his wife, Anne Stine, both Norwegian archaeologists, searched the coasts of Labrador, Newfoundland, and New England as far south as Narragansett Bay in search of likely landfalls for the Norsemen. The ruins of houses of Norse type were uncovered in 1960 at L'Anse aux Meadows, and from 1961 to 1968, systematic excavations were undertaken there. Five houses were unearthed at first, and later on, a smithy. Charcoal in the hearths gave a carbon 14 dating of A.D. 1080, plus or minus seventy years. The year 1010 would do well for dating the Vinland voyages, but the year 1150 would not do so well.

The Norse character of the buildings was inferred from the discovery of iron slag, rusty nails, a needle whetstone, and a stone lamp. Much, also, has been made of a spindle-hole of Greenland type.

Ingstad has also compared old maps of Vinland, which show that medieval geographers believed it to be a promontory to L'Anse aux Meadows site. It must be admitted that, in general, L'Anse aux Meadows does conform to the geographical details given in *The Greenlander's Saga* and *Eirik the Red's Saga.*

However, Ingstad is at a loss to identify the grapes of Vinland because grapes simply do not grow so far north. He therefore is willing to believe that berries are meant, even though elsewhere he does not insist that New-foundland is Vinland. In other words, despite the difficulty posed by the

philological evidence, Ingstad wants to believe that he has found Vinland.

Wahlgren, Erik. "Fact and Fancy in the Vinland Sagas," in *Old Norse Literature and Mythology, A Symposium.* Edited by Edgar C. Polome, pp. 19-80. Austin: University of Texas Press, 1969.

Professor Erik Wahlgren is a philologist specializing in runology and folklore. His most notable book is a study of the Kensington Rune Stone of Minnesota (*The Kensington Stone, A Mystery Solved,* Madison, Wisconsin, 1958), which he believes he has shown to be a forgery. On the basis of largely philological evidence, Wahlgren in the present essay examines the question of the prior authority of *The Greenlander's Saga* versus *Eirik's Saga,* and shows fairly convincingly the greater trustworthiness of the former. He takes up the question of "vin" meaning meadow, wine, or berries, and votes unequivocally for wine. He argues, moreover, that while the L'Anse aux

Meadows site is doubtlessly authentic, "it is probably not the Wineland of the Sagas."

Wahlgren's treatise must be regarded as the most judicious assessment of the Vinland problem yet published. It is improbable that a precise location of Leif's houses in Vinland will be made without extensive archaeological discoveries by competent observers under controlled conditions. But discoveries of this sort are usually made by amateurs, if not publicity seekers or treasure hunters.

One fact is certain: the Norsemen did get here, but precisely where or when is still very much a mystery. — *S.L.C.*

## Additional Recommended Reading

Magnusson, Magnus and Hermann Palsson. *The Vinland Sagas: The Norse Discovery of America.* New York: New York University Press, 1966. A translation of *The Greenlander's Saga* and *Eirik's Saga,* with a long introduction which emphasizes the prior authority of the *Greenlander's Saga.*

Oleson, Tryggvi J. *Early Voyages and Northern Approaches, 1000-1632.* Vol. I: *Canadian Centenary* series. London: Oxford University Press, 1964. The Vinland problem is dealt with briefly and sanely, with Vinland itself located on Cape Cod.

Jones, Gwyn. *The Norse Atlantic Saga: Being the Norse Voyages of Discovery and Settlement to Iceland, Greenland, America.* London: Oxford University Press, 1964. A highly readable account by a historian of literature who expresses no firm opinion on the location of Vinland but who is mostly in favor of Newfoundland.

Morison, Samuel Eliot. *The European Discovery of America: The Northern Voyages, A.D. 500-1600.* New York: Oxford University Press, 1971. A dashing account, written by a master of prose, but uncritical, assigning without foundation dates for the various voyages and ignoring controversy of any sort.

# COLUMBUS LANDS IN THE NEW WORLD

*Type of event:* Sociopolitical: discovery and exploration of the Western Hemisphere
*Time:* 1492
*Locale:* The Caribbean Sea

*Principal personages:*
CHRISTOPHER COLUMBUS (c. 1451-1506), Italian navigator in Spanish service who discovered America in 1492
ISABELLA I, QUEEN OF CASTILE (1451-1504), who was patroness of the Columbus venture

## Summary of Event

At 2:00 A.M. on October 12, 1492, three Spanish ships sailing under the command of an Italian navigator named Christopher Columbus made a landfall off a small coral island in the Caribbean. Soon after daybreak Columbus landed, named the island San Salvador, and took possession of it in the name of the Spanish Crown that had subsidized his voyage. Thus was the "New World" discovered.

This land, in fact, had been discovered many times before. The first discoverers were ancestors of the American Indian tribes who followed migrating game across the land bridge between Asia and North America that existed during the ice ages. Then came the Norsemen sailing west across the Atlantic from Scandinavia and Iceland at least five hundred years before Columbus; remnants of a Viking settlement dating from A.D. 1000 have been discovered on the coast of Newfoundland. They were followed by Basque and later other European fishermen in search of whales, and later cod on the Grand Banks. A century before Columbus sailed, they may have coasted Newfoundland and Nova Scotia and come ashore occasionally to find fresh food, to make repairs, and to trade with the natives.

What sets Columbus apart is the fact that he did not sail as a common fisherman who returned home to sell his catch and then perhaps to gossip in some seaport tavern about strange lands he had seen. Columbus sailed as an agent of the Spanish Crown, and on his return he reported his discoveries to the highest levels of Spanish government, and ultimately to Europe's most learned geographers and navigators. Almost as important as his rediscovery of the Americas was the fact that Columbus made that discovery generally known in Europe and thus spurred curiosity about, and interest in, what he had found.

But what had he found? There was considerable doubt. Much of the New World would be explored by men searching for what was not there—passages to India or golden cities—and Columbus was no exception. As he sailed west in the autumn of 1492, he was not looking for a new world, but for a short water route to the riches of the East Indies, and as he waited for dawn off San Salvador on October 12, he thought he had found it. Columbus made a second voyage in 1493-1494, coasting Puerto Rico, Jamaica, and

17

Cuba, but it was not until his third voyage in 1498, when he touched the South American mainland at present-day Venezuela, that he understood he had stumbled across a new continental land mass. Even then he remained convinced to his death that the islands in the Caribbean Islands and the new continent were but a short sail from Asia and the East Indies. After a brief, disastrous term as a colonial Governor on the island of Hispaniola (from which he was sent back to Spain in chains), he made one final attempt, in 1502, to find a water route to Asia. He failed again and spent the rest of his life unsuccessfully badgering the Spanish Crown for the honors and rewards he thought were his due.

Columbus' voyages typified later explorations in many other ways. The three elements that underlay almost all efforts at discovery and colonization —God, gold and glory—underlie his expeditions as well. Spain agreed to finance his explorations in part to convert Indians to Christianity, in part from hopes of rich profits (hopefully from gold), and Columbus sailed in part at least for glory, planning through his discoveries to win entry for himself and his descendants into Spain's nobility.

Through the years, Columbus' voyages have become almost as shrouded in myth as the lands he discovered were cloaked in mystery and ignorance. Columbus did not, for example, have to argue against scholars who thought the world was flat before Queen Isabella agreed to subsidize his trip. By 1492, Europe's learned men knew the world was round. Columbus did spend several years convincing Isabella that the trip was feasible, and a council of experts did recommend to the Crown that his proposals be rejected. Ironically, the experts were in some respects right and Columbus wrong. They argued, for example, that Asia was much too far away to be reached by simply sailing west from Europe. Columbus insisted that Japan would be found no more than 2,400 nautical miles west of the Canary Islands—in other words, he expected to find Japan about where the Virgin Islands are. Thus he underestimated the distance between Europe and where he wanted to go by about three hundred percent.

However wrong his theory was, Columbus' voyages nevertheless marked the beginning of general awareness of the New World. European attitudes toward the new-found islands were not always favorable. The first response was sometimes annoyance, and the Americas were occasionally looked upon as an obstacle to be sailed around rather than a resource to be developed. But with the discovery of gold in Central and South America, attitudes changed rapidly. Thanks to Columbus, the leading nations of the Old World found a new arena for competition and conflict. As news of his discoveries spread across Europe, the history of the Western World became increasingly the history of the Old World interacting with the New—an interaction that continues to shape world history today.

# Columbus Lands in the New World

## Pertinent Literature

Morison, Samuel Eliot. *Admiral of the Ocean Sea: A Life of Christopher Columbus.*
Boston: Little, Brown, and Company. 1951.

There are many biographies of Columbus, but Samuel Eliot Morison's *Admiral of the Ocean Sea* is certainly the best known, and in many ways most unique. Most biographers content themselves with describing the life and significance of their subjects from printed or manuscript sources, but Morison went further. He tried to recreate (as much as was possible) Columbus' experiences as a navigator so that he might better understand and describe his four voyages. Morison chartered a sailing ship of roughly the size Columbus used and retraced a good deal of the explorer's route. Morison's first-hand knowledge of what it is like to travel under sail gives his biography a richness of detail and an aura of authenticity not found in other accounts. Thus Morison makes vividly clear the difficulties and dangers of sailing west into unknown waters in the fifteenth century that are often overlooked by modern readers for whom rapid transatlantic crossings in powered ships are a common occurrence.

One of Morison's most interesting chapters is entitled simply "A Day at Sea." In it he describes the common routine of sailing ships during Columbus' time, and he recounts some of the problems mariners faced. Take for example the simple matter of telling time. There were no clocks on board the *Niña, Pinta,* and *Santa Maria* except for sand-filled hourglasses. It took the sand thirty minutes to run from one section of the glass to another, and then one of the ship's company had to be ready immediately to reverse the glass

in order to keep even a roughly accurate account of the time. The sand clocks had to be checked constantly against the stars and the position of the sun to keep them even remotely accurate. Since time reckoning was important for accurate navigation, Columbus' accomplishments as a sailor are all the more impressive.

Besides the hourglass, Columbus had only the most rudimentary instruments (compass and quadrant) to work with, and navigating by the stars was a relatively new art, known and practiced by a few mathematicians, astronomers, and cartographers, but not by ordinary sea captains. Columbus did not understand, nor did he have the instruments necessary to carry out, celestial navigation on his voyage to the New World. He navigated largely by dead-reckoning; that is, by using the compass and by glancing over the side to watch debris float by in order to estimate the speed and to guess roughly how much progress his fleet made on any given day.

Morison notes that the fifteenth century was a deeply superstitious and religious age. Sailors, who risked their lives against the uncertainties of wind and tide and storm, and against the horrors of presumed sea monsters, were prone to invoke all the divine assistance they could on every voyage. The normal routine of Columbus' ships included a daily series of religious rituals, normally common prayer or singing, conducted sometimes as often as every hour.

Another particular strength of Morison's biography is the direct manner in which he deals with certain commonplace stories about Columbus, many of which are pure myth. Furthermore, Morison does not manufacture evidence or make loose guesses merely to flesh out his story. Where the evidence on a point is nonexistent or contradictory, Morison says so clearly, whether the issue is minor ("Who did the cooking? I do not know.") or more substantive ("For fifteen years the records tell us nothing of the Colombos").

There are some drawbacks to *Admiral of the Ocean Sea*. Morison, unfortunately, fell into the trap that catches many biographers who tend to develop too close a familiarity with their subjects and too great a liking for them. As a result, they sometimes credit them with more importance than may be justified. However courageous Columbus was, however brilliant a seaman and explorer, it is doubtful that he did "more to direct the course of history than any individual since Augustus Caesar," as Morison claims. And Morison makes only a few off-hand references to pre-Columbian discoverers, and then only to debunk what he calls the "Nordic Myth"—that Columbus may have learned of the New World during a voyage to Iceland that he made in 1477.

Despite these drawbacks, *Admiral of the Ocean Sea* remains among the best biographies of Columbus. Morison wrote from his own experiences as well as from documentary sources, and his book offers the kind of insight into the experience of crossing the ocean under sail five hundred years ago that is available in no other account.

Parry, J. H. *The Age of Reconnaissance: Discovery, Exploration, and Settlement, 1450-1650. History of Civilization* series. London: Weidenfeld and Nicholson, 1963.

J. H. Parry's *The Age of Reconnaissance* is a useful volume for putting Columbus' voyages in historical perspective. Rather than concentrate on one man, as did Morison, Parry takes a broader view and surveys the causes, events, and consequences of two centuries (1450-1650) of discovery and exploration. He points out that Columbus' effort was but one incident in a continuing pattern of exploration that began long before he sailed and that pushed outward the limits of Europe's geographic knowledge in other areas than the Americas. European sailors had been working south along the West African Coast, and even west into the Atlantic to discover and settle new islands long before the *Niña, Pinta,* and *Santa Maria* set sail.

But what caused this burst of exploration? What made it possible? And why did it occur at this particular time in history? Parry deals with these and related questions in the first part of his book, "The Conditions for Discovery". The two most common motives for exploration and colonization, he explains, were the two most commonly admitted by contemporaries—religious zeal and the desire for profit. They were well summarized by a Conquistador named Bernal Diaz, who explained that he went to the New World "to serve God and His Majesty, to give light to those who were in darkness, and to grow rich as all men desire to do." Those who did not go themselves were often willing to subsidize those who did, and for the same reasons. By the middle of the fifteenth century, for example, Portuguese and Spanish merchantmen began actively seeking some way to break into the virtual monopoly on the rich East Indies trade in spices, silk, ivory, and gold, held by Italian merchantmen from Venice and Genoa. Since that trade moved through the Levant and then the Mediterranean, the Portuguese, perched on the western flank of the Iberian Peninsula, sought an all-water route to the Indies that might give them a competitive advantage of their own. As Parry notes, they never found one, for even after Africa had been rounded, the voyages involved were so long and uncertain that Italian and other Mediterranean merchants retained much of their favored position. Monarchs, too, were sometimes willing to risk their funds in order to find new lands to conquer, new resources to exploit, and new sources of wealth to tap. Out of the search for these things came Columbus' voyages.

And behind all the commercial motives or the hope of personal wealth there lay the sanction of religion. Expansion south into Africa might be profitable, but it could also be justified as a crusade of sorts against Islam. Parry notes, for example, that under Isabella, Spain was caught up in a wave of religious crusading zeal in the fifteenth century that culminated in the final expulsion of the Moors from the Iberian Peninsula in the same year that Columbus sailed. Farther south, profit and piety combined again and the search for gold and colonies also included the search for converts among Black Africans. Commerce and converts together motivated more and more explorations of the African Coast, and once the New World was discovered the same motives combined in the same way to promote exploration and colonization there.

These motives may explain, at least in part, why men were willing to risk their lives or their money on voyages of discovery or on colonizing schemes, but they fail to explain why they were willing to do so at this particular time in history. Many historians seek to relate the Age of Discovery to the Italian Renaissance. The general expansion of knowledge and the growing curiosity about the world in general that marked the Renaissance, they argue, sparked renewed interest in geography and a new determination to fill in the blank areas on maps. They suggest, in fact, that the Age of Discovery was a direct outgrowth of the Renaissance. Parry, however, warns that the connection between the Renaissance and the Age of Discovery has been emphasized too much, that the relationship is more complex than is sometimes suggested. "Portuguese captains" he explains, "were sailing on tentative voyages of Atlantic discovery long before the Italian Renaissance had seriously affected Iberian culture," and Columbus himself "embarked on his famous enterprise with an intellectual equipment which was mainly medieval and traditional." Thus, for Parry, the Age of Discovery was only a partial reflection of the Renaissance; it was instead an age of transition that stretched across the declining years of feudalism to the Renaissance and the emergence of early modern Europe.

The remaining portions of Parry's book deal with the events of the great Age of Discovery and their consequences. Parry provides brief accounts of the major voyages, including those of Columbus, not only in the Atlantic and the South Seas but also for Africa and the Indian Ocean. The final section of the book, "The Fruits of Discovery" deals with various European nations' efforts to organize, govern, and exploit the lands their explorers had found by accident or design.

The particular value of *The Age of Reconnaissance* is that it is not only a history of discovery and European colonization; it is those things and more. It is a history of European expansion, of the impact Europeans had on the new lands they discovered, and the impact those new lands had on them. The book's wide focus and broad range allowed the author to treat Europe's thrust into the New World and Africa and Asia not as a series of disconnected events or isolated voyages, but as complex, integrated processes that involved two centuries, five continents, and many nations. — *S.L.C.*

## Additional Recommended Reading

Columbus, Christopher. *The Journal of Christopher Columbus, (During His First Voyage, 1492-1493) and Documents Relating to the Voyages of John Cabot and Gaspar Corte Real.* London: The Hakluyt Society, 1960, translated by Cecil Jane. The Hakluyt Society is the foremost source for published explorers' journals, letters, and other first-person accounts of discovery and exploration. Columbus' *Journal* is the source for much of what is known about his voyages.

Crone, G. R. *The Discovery of America. Turning Points in History* series. London: Hamish Hamilton & Co., Ltd., 1969. A broad survey of New World explorations from the pre-Columbian period to the sixteenth century. Nearly one-third of the chapters deal with Columbus.

Elliott, J. H. *The Old World and the New, 1492-1650.* Cambridge: Cambridge University Press, 1970. Concentrates on the impact the discovery of America had on European thought about geography, history, religion, and the nature of man.

Oleson, Tryggvi J. *Early Voyages and Northern Approaches, 1000-1632.* Vol. I: *Canadian Centenary* series. Toronto: McClelland and Stewart, 1963. Part of the Canadian Centenary series, this volume is a good source for pre-Columbian explorations in the North Atlantic.

Penrose, Boies. *Travel and Discovery in the Renaissance, 1420-1620.* Cambridge: Harvard University Press, 1955. One of the better surveys of Renaissance exploration. Includes an informative chapter on the classical and medieval background to the Age of Discovery.

Wright, Louis B. *Gold, Glory, and the Gospel: The Adventurous Lives and Times of the Renaissance Explorers.* New York: Atheneum Publishers, 1970. A popularly written account of the New World exploration which contains an especially good discussion of the motives for exploration and colonization.

# THE VOYAGES OF JOHN CABOT

*Type of event:* Sociopolitical: early exploration of North America
*Time:* 1497-1498
*Locale:* Bristol, England, and the coast of Newfoundland

*Principal personages:*
JOHN CABOT (GIOVANNI CABATA) (1450-1498), Italian explorer in the service of England
SEBASTIAN CABOT (1476?-1557), his son, a "genial and cheerful liar"
HENRY VII (1457-1509), King of England

## Summary of Event

The late fifteenth century was an age of intense, increasingly national rivalry. When, therefore, the news went around that Christopher Columbus by sailing west had landed on a hitherto unknown coast, all the nations fronting on the Atlantic became interested in exploring the new world and laying claim to some of the lands which Spain and Portugal planned to reserve for themselves. England, now at peace after the Wars of the Roses, with a strong government headed by that canny monarch, Henry VII, had no intention of being left out. To us, accustomed to thinking of the English as the great seafaring nation of Western Europe, it may seem strange that Henry should have turned to a foreign mariner to begin his outreach for a piece of the new world. But so he did; his choice fell on an Italian, John Cabot. Like other monarchs of the era, Henry was willing to use the services of such seamen whenever they were available.

Actually, we know very little about John Cabot. "No portrait, no personal description of him, no letter, no scrap of his handwriting, not even a signature has been found." The assiduous researches of several scholars have, however, turned up a few facts. It is reasonable to conclude that Cabot was born in Genoa, nursery of seamen, possibly in 1450, a year before Columbus. In 1484 he was married and living in Venice, where he had resided the fifteen years required to gain Venetian citizenship. Between 1490 and 1493, a John Cabot, possibly the navigator, resided in Valencia, Spain. We know that in 1495 he was in England trying to interest Henry VII in trans-Atlantic explorations.

It is significant that Cabot, with his wife and three sons, was then living in Bristol. Bristol, with its good harbor on the Avon river, was the second largest port in England. It faced the Western Ocean, carried on a large trade in spices, and was the headquarters of a large fishing fleet. It is little wonder that many of its inhabitants were deeply interested in western exploration.

Cabot was successful in his attempt to engage the King's interest. On March 5, 1496, Henry granted him letters patent to sail east, west, and north with five ships. As the King's lieutenant, he was to govern all lands he might

23

find, but the King was to have one-fifth of all profits. Cabot was not to venture south, for Henry wanted no trouble with Spain or Portugal.

On or about May 20, 1497, Cabot set sail from Bristol. Instead of five ships, he had only one, the *Mathew,* a vessel of fifty tons burthen, with a crew of eighteen men. It was the equivalent of a fair-sized modern yacht. Going around the south end of Ireland, he last sighted land at Dursey Head. His plan, a favorite one with westbound mariners in that age, was to follow a parallel of latitude straight west. Dursey Head is in latitude 51° 33'.

At 5 A.M. on June 24, Cabot came in sight of land again. He had made the Atlantic crossing in thirty-one days. The exact spot where he first saw the coast of North America has been much disputed, and the dispute has been made foggy by local patriotism, various places trying to be "firsts." Samuel Eliot Morison, whose account is one of the best, concludes that what Cabot saw was Cape Dégrat on the northeast tip of Newfoundland (latitude 51° 37' —only 4' off the Dursey Head latitude). If that is true, he had performed a real feat of navigation, having come almost straight west from the Irish coast. Furthermore, he was only five miles from where it is believed Leif Erikson had landed in 1001. Turning south, Cabot entered Griquet Harbor, where he made his only landing. Here he formally took possession of the country in the name of Henry VII. Continuing his southward course, he skirted the whole east side of the island and rounded its southern tip into Placentia Bay. From Placentia he turned about, retraced his course to Cape Dégrat, and on July 20 left for home. After a fast passage of

fifteen days, he made landfall at Ushant on the coast of Brittany, headed north, and on August 6 was in Bristol. Cabot had not found the way to Japan or China, and he had brought back neither gold nor spices, but he had found a coast teeming with codfish—a most important fact.

Cabot wasted no time in Bristol, but hurried to London to make his report to Henry. The King gave him £10, and on the thirteenth of the following December, settled on the explorer a pension of £20 per year. That, for Henry VII, was liberality.

On February 3, 1498, Henry issued new letters patent giving Cabot authority to impress six ships for a second voyage to the new world. Cabot was now to explore more thoroughly the coast he had touched, and when he had reached the source of the spice trade, to set up a trading factory with the intent of funneling that desired commodity to English ports. Cabot succeeded in obtaining five ships with which he sailed from Bristol at the beginning of May, 1498. One ship turned back, but Cabot and the other four disappear from the pages of history. To this day, no one knows what happened to any of them.

The Cabot story does not end with the disappearance of John. Much more is known about his son Sebastian. Sebastian may, as a boy of fifteen, have accompanied his father on the first voyage. He said that he did, but his statement is not particularly good evidence. He also claimed to have made in 1508 a voyage to discover the fabled Northwest Passage, but as he was a "genial and cheerful liar," we do not know that this is true. He certainly knew how to feather his own nest. He set up as an

24

# The Voyages of John Cabot

expert adviser to would-be explorers and was paid by the kings of both England and Spain for his advice. He died in England about 1557. Eventually, John's name was practically forgotten, and historians took Sebastian to be the discoverer of North America.

The one voyage of John Cabot, for all the gaps in the story, may seem a small thing in the history of American exploration. But it had great results, for on Cabot's voyage was laid the British claim to North America. After a long interval, it became one of the foundation stones of the first British empire.

## Pertinent Literature

Morison, Samuel Eliot. *The European Discovery of America: The Northern Voyages, A.D. 500-1600.* New York: Oxford University Press, 1971.

This is the best starting place for anyone who wants to know about the exploratory work of John Cabot. Samuel Eliot Morison is one of the best of living American historians, and this book is up to his high standards. As its title indicates, it is a comprehensive work, telling the story of the explorations of the North American coast from the mythical voyages of St. Brendan through the Virginia expeditions of 1585-1587. One chapter is devoted to John Cabot, and part of a second to his son Sebastian. Thus the Cabots are placed in their proper relation to the whole process of northern exploration.

It is one of Morison's great merits as an historian that he is able to combine qualities not often found in one writer. His narrative style is excellent. He makes good use of the historical imagination; but back of it lies thorough research. Thus at the end of the chapter on John Cabot, which is told as a straightforward story, he has eighteen pages of bibliography and notes. This is a critical bibliography in which Morison lists with comment the principal modern works dealing with Cabot, discusses with humor the various theo-

ries as to where Cabot's explorations actually led him, and adeptly uses and reproduces early maps.

One of the most valuable features of these notes is the inclusion of the complete text of the recently discovered John Day letter. Day was an English merchant, resident at times in Bristol and Seville, who wrote a letter to Columbus in the winter of 1497-1498 in which he described at some length Cabot's first voyage. This is the only contemporary account of that event of which we know.

Morison has a particular advantage over all other historians who have dealt with the early explorations of North America. He is himself a practical seaman who has handled sailing ships. As a result, his chapter on "English Ships and Seamen, 1490-1600" is one of the best features of the book. Furthermore, the historian himself has sailed the coast of Newfoundland and has a first-hand acquaintance with its fogs and icebergs. These facts make for lively narrative. The book is superbly illustrated with reproductions of old maps and with modern photographs of the Newfoundland coast.

# The Voyages of John Cabot

Williamson, James A. *The Cabot Voyages and Bristol Discovery Under Henry VII, with the Cartography of the Voyages by R. A. Skelton.* Cambridge: Published for the Hakluyt Society at the University Press, 1962.

This is in many ways the best single book on the Cabots for students who want to dig deeper than in Morison. Williamson was a Cabot specialist who devoted years to thorough and painstaking research of his subject. The result is a volume of over three hundred pages. Samuel Eliot Morison obviously depends on Williamson for many of his facts and makes suitable acknowledgment. On the other hand, Williamson frequently cites earlier works of Morison on exploration.

In spite of their interdependence, however, Morison and Williamson sometimes come to quite different conclusions. Williamson cites considerable evidence to prove that, after 1480, Bristol mariners were reaching out into the Atlantic in quest of something new, and he is sure, on what seems to be slim evidence, that in 1494 Nicholas Thorne and Hugh Elyot, both sailing from Bristol, anticipated Cabot and discovered a "New found Land." This opinion, of course, affects Williamson's whole estimate of Cabot's method and his achievement. Williamson is probably on safer ground when he discusses Cabot's second expedition, maintaining that it was very unlikely that all four of the ships in that expedition were lost. And, unlike Morison, Williamson is by no means certain where Cabot actually landed. He debates all the possibilities and votes at times for Cape Breton, and at other times for Maine. Otherwise, the two writers are in close agreement on the facts of the narrative.

Morison and Williamson, however, differ widely in their method of presenting those facts. Morison writes straightforward narrative. Bibliography, documentation, and scholarly argument are all placed together at the end of each chapter; the reader may take them or leave them. Williamson, on the other hand, might be said to incorporate his footnotes (and they are many) in his text. This makes his work far more difficult reading than Morison's. But these are two different kinds of books, and each writer uses the method suitable to his purpose.

One of the most interesting features of *The Cabot Voyages* is the long chapter on the career of Sebastian Cabot, in which the writer makes the point that until well into the nineteenth century John Cabot was practically forgotten, and the historians invariably treated Sebastian as the discoverer of North America.

Williamson's volume has two concluding sections which add greatly to its usefulness. More than one hundred pages are taken up by quotations from forty relevant documents, some of which are given in their entirety. Also, R. A. Skelton has contributed thirty pages on the cartography of the Cabot voyages. — *D.R.G.*

## Additional Recommended Reading

Beazley, Charles R. *John and Sebastian Cabot: The Discovery of North America.* London: T. F. Unwin, 1898. This is a competent and documented study by an Oxford specialist in historical geography, and it is easier reading than Williamson. Beazley concludes,

26

against all other modern scholars, that John Cabot returned from his second voyage.

Biddle, Richard. *A Memoir of Sebastian Cabot, with a Review of the History of Maritime Discovery.* Philadelphia: Carey and Lea, 1831. Republished at Freeport, New York: Books for Libraries Press, 1970. Originally published anonymously, this book has historical importance as the first attempt to apply serious scholarship to the Cabot story.

Hakluyt, Richard. *Divers Voyages Touching the Discovery of America and the Islands Adjacent.* Edited by John W. Jones. New York: Ben Franklin Press, 1963. A reprint of the famous Elizabethan collection of source material, first published in 1582 and a best seller in the years following.

Harrisse, Henry. *John Cabot: The Discoverer of North America and Sebastian Cabot, His Son, a Chapter in Maritime History of England Under the Tudors, 1496-1557.* London: B. F. Stevens, 1896. Written by the foremost French expert in the history of American discovery, this book is notable for its attack on the fictions and inflated reputation of Sebastian Cabot.

Winsor, Justin. *Narrative and Critical History of America.* Boston and New York: Houghton, Mifflin Co., 1884-1889. 8 vols. Vol. III, ch. I, by Charles Deane, consists of a brief narrative followed by a long discussion of authorities and is an excellent summary.

Weare, George E. *Cabot's Discovery of North America.* London: John Macqueen, 1897. A very discursive but thoroughly documented account, this work holds that Cabot landed on Cape Breton.

# CARTIER AND ROBERVAL SEARCH FOR A NORTH-WEST PASSAGE

*Type of event:* Politico-economic: establishment of French claims in the New World
*Time:* 1534-1543
*Locale:* Gulf of St. Lawrence and the St. Lawrence river

*Principal personages:*
JACQUES CARTIER (1491-1557), master mariner
JEAN-FRANÇOIS DE LA ROQUE, SIEUR DE ROBERVAL (fl. 1544), soldier, courtier, colonizer
FRANÇOIS I (1494-1547), King of France 1515-1547
PHILIPPE DE CHABOT, SIEUR DE BRION (1480-1543), Admiral of France

## Summary of Event

From 1492 to about 1534, the exploration of the New World was almost the exclusive domain of Italian seamen. When England and France contested the Spanish and Portuguese monopolies, they employed Cabot and Verrazano, both Italians. During the third decade of the new century, however, Italian explorers were replaced by other nationals.

As soon as John Cabot's report of the marvelous shoals of fish he had observed off the coast of Newfoundland reached the mainland of Europe, fishing boats from Brittany, Normandy, and Portugal began to brave the hazardous crossings of the North Atlantic to reap the harvest of these new and teeming waters. From these fisheries sprang the beginnings of New France.

Jacques Cartier was born probably in 1491 in Saint-Malo, one of the most notable of French fishing ports. He went to sea early and became an experienced navigator, being awarded the coveted title of master pilot. Before he appeared in the clear light of history, he evidently visited the Newfoundland fisheries and voyaged to Brazil. He was apparently well-esteemed in his native community, for it is recorded that he acted as a sponsor at no less than twenty-seven baptisms.

In 1534, when he was forty years old, Cartier was commissioned by the King of France to head an expedition across the Atlantic in search of a Northwest Passage to the Orient. Setting out on April 20 from Saint-Malo with two ships of about sixty tons burden each, Cartier made his landfall on May 10, at Cape Bonavista on the eastern coast of Newfoundland. After exploring the island, he crossed the Gulf of St. Lawrence to Cape Breton and the Prince Edward Island, landing on the Gaspé Peninsula. Here, upon the pledge of returning them, he was given two sons of a Huron chief to take to France. From Gaspé, Cartier sailed north to Anticosti Island. Returning to Newfoundland on August 15, he set sail for home and arrived at Saint-Malo on September 5. Although he had not found the Northwest Passage, Cartier had explored extensively the Gulf of St. Lawrence and its islands, and he was enthusiastic about the new country.

As a result of his favorable report, the French leaders began to think of planting outposts of the kingdom in these new lands. By royal command the Admiral of France commissioned Cartier Commander in Chief of a second expedition of three ships which was to sail beyond Newfoundland and discover and occupy lands for France. The little flotilla left Saint-Malo on May 19, 1535. This time the crossing was imperiled by severe storms, but Cartier reached Blanc Sablon, Newfoundland, on July 15; not until July 26, however, did all three ships assemble there. He had with him the two Indian boys he had taken from Gaspé the previous year. They had learned to speak French, and they told him of the great river which poured into the Gulf of St. Lawrence. Steering west and north of Anticosti Island, he entered the great river, the first white man to travel that highway into the North American interior.

As Cartier progressed up the St. Lawrence river, piloted by his two Huron guides, he was welcomed by natives from the shore. Passing the Island of Orleans, in mid-September he came to the Indian village of Stadaconé, the magnificent site of the future city of Quebec. Here he was greeted by Chief Donnaconna, who welcomed the return of his two sons but tried to dissuade Cartier from further ascending the river. Donnaconna feared the loss of his French ally to the chief of Hochelaga. But ambition and curiosity drove the Frenchman on; he set out on September 19 with the smallest of his vessels, a pinnace, and on October 2 came to Hochelaga (now Montreal) the metropolis of the Indians on the St. Lawrence. Here the Hurons feasted Cartier and tempted him with hints of a rich kingdom to the west called Saguenay. But from the top of Mont Royal Cartier saw that the rapids beyond blocked further travel inland, and he returned to Stadaconé, above which his men had built a fort. There they wintered rather than risk an unseasonable Atlantic passage. Autumnal brilliance gave way to months of ice and deep snow, and scurvy became rampant but was conquered with an Indian bark remedy. Musing upon the fabled riches of Saguenay, Cartier and his men resorted to treachery. In May, 1536, they kidnaped Donnaconna and four other Hurons as evidence to convince King François that further exploration would be profitable. With five other Indians, who apparently went without force, they set sail for France on May 6. The Atlantic crossing was speedy, and on July 15 Cartier was back at Saint-Malo. On this voyage he had opened the way for penetrating North America and had mapped out the principal sites of the future New France.

The King, impressed by Cartier's Huron captives, his samples of ores which promised diamonds and gold, and the reports of a land of spices and other abundant resources, determined to develop a colony in the New World —a New France. War between France and Spain interfered with his plans until 1538. Then followed three years of elaborate preparations and diplomatic difficulties. In 1540 Cartier received a royal commission to help lead the undertaking with a grant from the treasury. But in January, 1541, Jean-François de la Roque, Sieur de Roberval, was given command of the venture, and Cartier's authority could be exerted only in Roberval's absence. They procured and equipped five vessels, and on May 23, 1541, Cartier sailed from Saint-Malo on his third voyage. Roberval was to follow later. Settlement was now the main aim, though Christian missionary efforts and the search for Saguenay were also important objectives. After a rough Atlantic crossing, the expedition entered the Gulf of St. Lawrence and then proceeded up the river and on August 23 arrived at Stadaconé (Quebec). Welcomed by the Hurons despite his earlier kidnaping exploits, Cartier proceeded to settle his colonists beyond Quebec at Cape Rouge for an easier approach to Saguenay. Two of his vessels were sent home with news and samples of spurious minerals. They reached Saint-Malo on October 3. Leaving the Vicomte de Beaupré' in command, Cartier proceeded to Hochelaga (Montreal) and explored the rapids above it. The events of the winter of 1541-1542 are unknown except for sailors' gossip later of Indian attacks, scurvy, and misery.

On April 16, 1542, Roberval with three ships and perhaps two hundred colonists sailed from La Rochelle for New France. On June 7 the expedition entered the harbor of what is now St. John's, Newfoundland. Meantime, the winter in Canada had been too much for Cartier, and he had abandoned the

settlement at Cape Rouge in June and struck out for Newfoundland. At St. John's he found Roberval's reinforcements. In spite of Roberval's order, he slipped out into the Atlantic and returned to Saint-Malo. Roberval pushed on, ascended the St. Lawrence, and rebuilt Cartier's abandoned settlement. He sent two ships home for reinforcements in September. A difficult winter followed in which Roberval was forced to resort to drastic disciplinary measures to maintain order. In June, 1543, Roberval began his search for the riches of Saguenay, but stopped when his boat was wrecked.

By mid-September, 1543, Roberval was back in France, so he probably gave up the settlement in New France by late July. His return marked the end of the first attempt of the French to settle Canada. François I died in 1547, and his son Henry II was uninterested in American exploration. The outbreak of religious wars in France prevented any further colonizing efforts for half a century. Cartier bought a manor near Saint-Malo where he lived, respected by all his neighbors, until his death in 1557. He had revolutionized cartographical knowledge by his well-recorded findings, but for the moment neither his nor Roberval's exploits were promising enough to overcome France's European preoccupations.

## Pertinent Literature

Baxter, James P. *A Memoir of Jacques Cartier.* New York: Dodd, Mead and Co., 1906.

This is the best single book in English on Cartier and his explorations. Baxter was a bank president and several times mayor of Portland, Maine, but he made himself into a competent historical scholar, specializing in early American explorations in Maine and Canada. The scholarship of this volume is both massive and thorough. It includes, besides Baxter's own narrative, a mass of primary material for the study of the Cartier and Roberval voyages. There are several hundred pages of translated documents. Of these the most fascinating is an account of Cartier's first voyage, written in the first person. Baxter concluded that this was not, as some over-enthusiastic scholars maintained, written by Cartier himself, but that Cartier's evidence is in back of it. There are also early narratives of the second and third voyages, a collection of what Baxter calls "collateral documents," a bibliography containing fifty-eight entries, and an itinerary of the three expeditions, given almost day by day. And there are maps, both early and modern. All the material for a

thorough study of the subject is here within the covers of this one volume.

But to write good history one needs something more than careful research and accurate documentation. One needs historical imagination. This Baxter also has. Of the writers considered in this survey, he is the only one who formed a clear mental picture of what manner of man the explorer was: brave, calm, self-reliant, but most of all depending upon the "support of an overruling Providence." Living in nearby Maine, Baxter had the opportunity of following the Canadian tracks of Cartier and Roberval. He, therefore, describes their voyages with a graphic pen that reminds one of Francis Parkman; and there can be no higher compliment. This is good history.

Parkman, Francis. *Pioneers of France in the New World.* 4th ed. Boston: Little, Brown, and Company, 1912.

Of all that group of historians who participated in the flowering of New England—Bancroft, Palfrey, Hildreth, and others—Parkman seems to have best stood the test of time. He is still read, not out of curiosity, but by people who want to know the story and to enjoy it. The volume under consideration first appeared in 1865. It was the beginning of that noble series of works which traced the fortunes of New France from the beginning to their end with the decisive defeat of the French by the English on the Plains of Abraham.

The scholarly labor involved in this work was enormous. It was almost a virgin field, and the bibliographic aids available to the modern scholar were not in existence in the middle of the nineteenth century. Parkman ransacked the libraries of Canada, made

several trips to France, and became a master of the sources. Since his time, new materials have come to light, but none of them seems to have disturbed his conclusions.

The results of Parkman's labors are meticulous scholarship set forth in magnificent prose. A sample will indicate how completely he visualized the scenes of his narrative and how vividly he pictured them for the reader. Cartier is here seeing the site of Quebec: "As he drew near the opening of the channel, the Hochelaga again spread before him the broad expanse of its waters. A mighty promontory, rugged and bare, thrust its scarped front into the surging torrent. Here, clothed in the majesty of solitude, breathing the stern poetry of the wilderness, rose the cliffs now rich with heroic memories, where the fiery Count Frontenac cast defiance at his

31

foes, where Wolfe, Montcalm, and Montgomery fell." In one respect, Parkman's narrative is better than that of Baxter. Baxter allowed himself to be swamped by detail. At times, to follow his narrative of Cartier's explorations, one must have before him a detailed map. Parkman accomplished his result by giving only the detail which a reader may easily carry in his mind.

In two other respects Parkman's work is superior. Unlike some historians, he was always aware of the European background of the story and constantly related American events to this background. And being singularly free from Puritan prejudice, he gave due credit to the Catholic missionary motive in French exploration and settlement. — *D.R.G.*

## Additional Recommended Reading

Biggar, H. P. *The Voyages of Jacques Cartier.* Ottawa: Public Archives of Canada *Publications,* No. 11, 1924. Not a narrative, but a source book, giving the principal documents in French, with an English translation and copious notes. This and Biggar's *Collection of Documents Relating to Jacques Cartier and the Sieur de Roberval,* Public Archives of Canada *Publications,* No. 14 (Ottawa, 1930), contain all that is known of the Cartier-Roberval voyage.

Morison, Samuel Eliot. *The European Discovery of America: The Northern Voyages, A.D. 500-1600.* New York: Oxford University Press, 1971. In three superbly packed chapters, the exploits of Cartier and Roberval are summarized in considerable detail. A combination of fine scholarship, detailed bibliographical commentary, and attractive narration.

Pendergast, James F. and Bruce G. Trigger. *Cartier's Hochelaga and the Dawson Site.* Montreal and London: McGill-Queen's University Press, 1972. Analysis of archaeological data and ethno-history concerning the size and location of the Indian town visited by Cartier in 1535.

Pope, Joseph. *Jacques Cartier, His Life and Voyages.* Ottawa: A. S. Woodburn, 1890. This small volume of 168 pages is a popular essay, without documentation, but a good example of its type.

Winsor, Justin. *From Cartier to Frontenac: Geographical Discovery in the Interior of North America in Its Historical Relations, 1534-1700.* New York: Houghton, Mifflin Co., 1894. An excellent brief summary, with Winsor's usual good scholarship, especially valuable for its maps and illustrations.

Wrong, George M. *The Rise and Fall of New France.* 2 vols. New York: The Macmillan Company, 1928. This, perhaps the best general history of New France, contains an excellent chapter on Cartier, with a critical bibliography.

# DE SOTO'S EXPEDITION AND THE FOUNDING OF ST. AUGUSTINE

*Type of event:* Sociopolitical: exploitation of Spanish conquests in the New World
*Time:* Sixteenth century (c.1539)
*Locale:* Southeastern United States

*Principal personages:*

JUAN PONCE DE LEÓN (1460?-1521), discoverer of Florida in 1513

ALONZO ALVAREZ DE PINEDA (fl. 1519), explorer of the Florida Gulf Coast in 1519

LUCAS VASQUEZ DE AYLLÓN (?-1526), explorer of the Atlantic Coast of Florida and the Carolinas as far as Cape Fear in 1526

PÁNFILO DE NARVÁEZ (1480?-1528), leader of the expedition which landed at Tampa in search of gold

HERNANDO DE SOTO (1500?-1542), principal Spanish explorer of the southeastern United States between Tampa Bay and the Arkansas river in 1538

GASPARD DE COLIGNY (1519-1572), French Admiral who promoted Huguenot settlements along the Atlantic Coast of Carolina and Florida in 1562-1564

JAN RIBAULT (1520?-1565), and

RENÉ GOULAINE DE LAUDONNIÈRE (fl. 1562-1586), who led the first French settlers to the area

PEDRO MENÉNDEZ DE AVILÉS (1519-1574), Spanish officer who drove the French out of Florida and who founded St. Augustine in 1565

## Summary of Event

Juan Ponce de León, the discoverer of Florida, came to the New World in 1493 with Christopher Columbus' second expedition to the West Indies. Ponce settled on Hispaniola (Haiti and the Dominican Republic), but rumors of gold on neighboring Puerto Rico caused him to conquer it in 1508. Although Ponce de León was made Governor of Puerto Rico, he was soon removed from office because his appointment had been made without consulting Don Diego Columbus, the Governor of Hispaniola. The dejected Ponce then sought new fame and for-

tune by searching for the island of Bimini, which, according to the Indians of Hispañola, had a fountain whose waters turned men young again.

In 1513 Ponce de León sailed from Puerto Rico to seek his magic fountain, and when he came to a flower-covered coast, he named the area "La Florida." Ponce first anchored near the St. Johns river, then sailed south to the Florida Keys and some distance up the Gulf Coast. Ponce's party suffered three Indian attacks after the warriors tempted the Spaniards to land with false tales of rivers filled with gold. Beating off the

33

attackers Ponce sailed back to Puerto Rico, discovering the Bahama Channel which was used later by treasure fleets returning to Spain from Mexico, and which would ultimately necessitate the founding of St. Augustine to protect it.

Shortly after Ponce de León's voyage, Alonzo Alvarez de Pineda sailed northward looking for the strait between Florida and the mainland. Exploring the Gulf Coast extensively in 1519, Alvarez de Pineda sighted the mouth of the Mississippi river and later concluded that Florida was not an island as Ponce had believed, but a peninsula and part of the mainland. In 1520, an exploring party sent up the Atlantic Coast by Lucas Vasquez de Ayllón reached the same conclusion about the "island" of Florida. In addition the explorers brought back several Indians who proved to have fertile imaginations: they swore the land was full of gold and silver.

Encouraged by tales of riches, Ponce de León again set sail for Florida in 1521. His party included two ships, two hundred men, fifty horses, and several priests. The Indians proved to be hostile, however, and Ponce's settlement at Charlotte Bay was destroyed by war parties. In one of the attacks, the valiant seeker of the Fountain of Youth was mortally wounded. Deprived of their leader, the settlers abandoned Florida and sailed back to Puerto Rico. In 1526, Vasquez de Ayllón established San Miguel de Guadalupe on the Pee Dee river in South Carolina. Again the Indians refused to assist the Spaniards. Provisions soon gave out, sickness spread, Vasquez de Ayllón died, and the disheartened settlers abandoned the project. Thus, the first attempts to settle Spanish Florida ended in failure.

The next man who attempted to settle Florida was the new governor of Cuba and *adelantado,* or military commander, of Florida, Pánfilo de Narváez. Unlike the former expeditions which had originated in the West Indies, Narváez sailed from Spain in 1527 with six hundred colonists. When he reached Santo Domingo, one fourth of his party deserted and two of his ships were wrecked in a hurricane. The following spring, however, he sailed to Florida and landed at Tampa Bay, where he split his party into two sections. One group was to search inland for the rumored cities of gold, while the other was to sail northward and find a good harbor where both groups could rendezvous at a future date.

Narváez led the first party deeply inland searching for the golden cities. Each Indian village appeared poorer than the last, but the inhabitants all told of richer cities to the north, a ruse which coastal tribes soon learned would rid them of the greedy *conquistadores.* Narváez moved on seeking a town called Apalachen, near present-day Tallahassee. Instead of the promised wealth, all he found there were a few clay huts. By this time, Narváez realized that there was no gold in Florida, and he decided to move southward to the coast to find his ships.

Reaching the sea at Apalachee Bay, Narváez failed to find the expected ships, which had already gone back to Cuba. The marooned adventurers built several small boats and set sail for Mexico, which they erroneously believed was close at hand. With his men continually dying from starvation, disease, drowning, and occasional Indian attacks, Narváez sailed along the Gulf

Coast to Galveston Island. Here several of the ships sank and Narváez disappeared at sea. The survivors, led by Nuñez Cabeza de Vaca, were captured by Indians and passed from tribe to tribe until finally, with three companions, Cabeza de Vaca escaped his captors and completed the journey to Mexico City by land in 1536. These four men were the only survivors of the three hundred who followed Narváez inland at Tampa in 1528.

The Narváez expedition did not dampen the spirits of those who followed, especially after Cabeza de Vaca arrived in Mexico filled with the new tales of wealth he had garnered during the eight years he lived among the Indians. The next governor of Cuba and *adelantado* of Florida, Hernando de Soto, set sail from Havana for Florida in 1539. He, too, landed at Tampa Bay where he defeated the local Indians in a short battle. Leaving a base camp, de Soto and five hundred and fifty men marched inland seeking wealth and fame.

As de Soto's expedition advanced, they found that word of their defeat of the Indians at Tampa had preceded them and caused Indians to abandon their villages to hide in the woods. As Cortes had done before him, de Soto seized the chief of any inhabited town and held him to insure the peaceful conduct of each tribe. Only the village of Caliquen resisted, for which the inhabitants were enslaved in chains. The first winter found de Soto at Apalachen, the town visited by Narváez. Here the Spaniards rested until spring while smaller exploration parties visited Pensacola and Apalachee Bays. In 1540, de Soto moved northward searching for his golden cities, a task

which lasted four years during which the expedition traveled through the present-day states of Georgia, Alabama, Mississippi, Louisiana, and Arkansas. De Soto and his men were the first white men to identify the five civilized tribes (Choctaw, Chickasaw, Creek, Cherokee, and Seminole), to see the Great Smoky Mountains, and to chart and locate parts of the Mississippi and Arkansas rivers. During the arduous journey, the Spanish treated the Indians with great cruelty, resulting in many battles and casualties on both sides. Each conquered tribe promised the conquistadors that the Indians farther to the west possessed much gold and silver but, to the Spaniards' disappointment, little of the precious metals was found. Where the Arkansas river joins the Mississippi, de Soto fell victim to disease and died on May 21, 1542. To keep his body from the Indians, he was buried in the middle of the Mississippi river.

Upon de Soto's death, Luís de Moscoso assumed command of the expedition, which then wandered westward into Texas before returning to the Mississippi. Building small ships, de Moscoso's men floated down the Mississippi river to the Gulf. They followed the coast westward to Panuco (Tampico) in Mexico where, on September 10, 1543, the three hundred survivors disembarked and ended their journey.

These various expeditions established that Florida was a formidable wilderness, hard to penetrate, and teeming with plant and animal life. In addition, unlike the other areas conquered by Spain, the Florida Indians were extremely difficult to subdue and uncoöperative with exploration parties. There were few, if any, caches of gold or silver to attract future conquistadors. While the land was rich in natural vegetation, agriculture was extremely difficult in the sandy coastal soils. Finally, the region was plagued by severe storms and hurricanes during certain seasons of the year, which made shipping hazardous. These facts caused the Spaniards to ignore Florida for the next twenty years.

Spanish interest in Florida was rekindled when Jan Ribault, a Huguenot, established a French colony at Port Royal, South Carolina, in 1562. Although Ribault's settlement failed, the French government was impressed with its strategic location: it was close to the Bahama Channel used by the Spanish treasure fleets. To explore its possibilities as a base for French corsairs, Admiral Gaspard de Coligny of the French navy sent a second expedition to Florida led by René de Laudonnière, who founded Fort Caroline on the St. Johns river deep in Spanish Florida. Laudonnière, however, proved

to be a poor leader. He offended the nearby Indians and could not discipline his men. Coligny quickly sent Jan Ribault and three hundred additional colonists to stabilize the new settlement.

Philip II, King of Spain, had no intention of allowing the French to take over his lands. He ordered Pedro Menéndez de Avilés, along with a dozen ships and 2,646 men, to expel the French and secure Florida for Spain. On August 28, 1565, Menéndez's fleet dropped anchor at his new settlement site, which he named San Augustín for the saint whose festival was celebrated on that day. Menéndez then sailed northward to Fort Caroline, ultimately capturing the fort and scattering its garrison. Returning to St. Augustine, Menéndez supervised the construction of the first building, a fortified Indian house, which he surrounded by a trench and a log wall—a rather modest beginning for the first permanent European settlement in the United States.

## Pertinent Literature

Maynard, Theodore. *De Soto and the Conquistadores.* New York: Longmans, Green, and Co., 1930.

The Spanish conquistadors are frequently thought of as having been motivated in their conquests by the trinity of gold, glory, and God—often in that order. Theodore Maynard disagrees with this analysis. He does not deny the importance of gold in stimulating Spanish exploration of the New World, but he finds this was not the chief motive. Instead, Maynard asserts that the reason Spain became the first major colonial power (after tiny Portugal) is related to the *reconquista*—the eight-hundred-year war against the

Moslems that culminated in the siege of Granada at the same time that Columbus set sail. In effect, Spain had driven the infidel from its land and now sought to turn its vast missionary enthusiasm into saving new worlds for God and the Church. Spain sought a special glory, the glory of God. To conquer the heathen, one must despoil them; hence, the significance of the search for wealth.

De Soto was one of the crusaders who went forth convinced that Spain had a divine mission in the world. This conviction helped to make him and the other explorers fearless men, terrible in battle and harsh in justice, who preserved the faith by the use of arms. The Spanish gave the Indians two simple choices: conversion and submission, or death. To the Iberians this was not cruelty but the truest form of kindness.

Although de Soto is best known for his lengthy journey in the southeastern United States, he had a long record as a good soldier under Pizarro, the conqueror of Peru. He brought the reinforcements that made that conquest possible, and continually led dangerous scouting expeditions. De Soto was always in the vanguard, a leader from the beginning. According to Maynard, de Soto opposed Pizarro's treachery and the execution of Inca leaders, preferring honorable treatment of the Indi-

ans instead. Yet de Soto was not above committing massacres on his Florida expedition or burning an Indian alive to extort information from other captives.

One of the most important factors which caused de Soto to continue his Florida expedition, in spite of the known fate of Narváez before him and in the face of hostile Indians, was his incredible ambition and stubbornness. De Soto refused to give in. His spirit alone kept the expedition moving westward long after his men had given up all hope of success. When de Soto died in 1542, his comrades were grieved but, at the same time, they rejoiced at their good fortune because they could go home at last. Only death could have defeated de Soto; he was too proud to have failed and lived.

Chatelain, Verne E. *The Defenses of Spanish Florida, 1565-1763.* Washington: Carnegie Institution of Washington, 1941.

The failures of Ponce de León and Vasquez de Ayllón, coupled with the disastrous Pánfilo de Narváez expedition and the negligible results of de Soto's search for wealth, made Florida one of the toughest challenges faced by Spaniards in the New World. Because of Florida's liabilities, its settlement had to be forced by political considerations. The Bahama Channel, discovered by Ponce de León and used regularly by the treasure fleets from Mexico and South America, attracted enemies who wished to plunder the great wealth of New Spain. Thus, protection from imperial rivals necessitated a settlement in Florida, both as an advanced naval base and to keep other powers from setting up their own bases.

The first attempt to set up a permanent naval base to protect the Bahama

Channel was made by Tristan de Luna y Arellano in 1559. Although Luna was supposed to settle Santa Elena (Port Royal) in Carolina, he landed at Pensacola. Before Luna could unload his ships, they were destroyed by a hurricane, forcing the survivors to live a harried existence until Angel de Villafañe arrived and relieved Luna of command. Villafañe loaded the colonists on his ships and set sail for the Carolina coast. Exploring as far north as Chesapeake Bay, Villafañe found no suitable site for his colony and abandoned the project to return home. Disappointed because these men had failed to establish a settlement in Florida, Philip II declared the entire area off limits to settlers in 1561.

The founding of Fort Caroline by Laudonnière changed the whole strategic position of Florida. Philip sent Pedro Menéndez de Avilés to secure the area for Spain. Establishing St. Augustine in 1565, Menéndez then ruthlessly exterminated the French colony to the north. As he marched by land on Fort Caroline, Jan Ribault led a sea expedition on St. Augustine. A storm scattered the French, and Fort Caroline's reduced garrison soon fell to the Spanish army. Menéndez then massacred several hundred shipwrecked survivors of the French fleet located in two groups at Las Matanzas (the Massacres) south of St. Augustine.

Although St. Augustine was an ideal naval base, the area had liabilities as a growing colony. It was surrounded by swamps and sloughs which prevented extensive agriculture, as did the jungle-like forests that had to be cut back regularly. The colony also suffered from the idealistic view of the Indians taken by the Spanish Crown, and the Church, which prevented private ownership of land in Florida.

Chatelain has written a superb volume covering the period from the founding of St. Augustine to the British take-over of Florida in 1763. He goes into great detail in describing the Spanish colonial system, Florida's place in it as its northernmost bastion, and the role of Menéndez in establishing St. Augustine. Chatelain is especially concerned with the military significance of the town and describes the environment, terrain, mission system, political organization, social conditions, early military defenses, and the construction of the Castillo San Marcos. A well-illustrated volume making use of both maps and photographs, Chatelain's book is worthwhile for the student or the general reader. — *W.L.R.*

## Additional Recommended Reading

Bolton, Herbert E. *The Spanish Borderlands: A Chronicle of Old Florida and the Southwest.* Vol. XXIII: *The Chronicles of America.* New Haven: Yale University Press, 1921. A general study covering the whole of the Spanish exploration in the United States, including several excellent chapters on Florida.

Priestley, Herbert I. *Tristan de Luna, Conquistador of the Old South: A Study in Spanish Imperial Strategy.* Glendale, California: Arthur H. Clark Co., 1936. Focusing on the Luna expedition, Priestley analyzes Spanish imperial policy and Florida's place in securing the northern boundaries of the empire against other European powers.

Lowery, Woodbury. *The Spanish Settlements Within the Present Limits of the United States: Florida, 1562-1574.* New York: G. P. Putnam's Sons, 1905. The old classic in its field, Lowery's book is still one of the best detailed studies on the discovery and settlement of Spanish Florida.

Bennett, Charles E. *Laudonnière and Fort Caroline: History and Documents.* Gainesville: University of Florida Press, 1964. A fascinating short study on the French role along the Florida coast, which was critical in stimulating the founding of St. Augustine by Menéndez.

Trepaski, John J. *The Governorship of Spanish Florida, 1700-1763.* Durham: Duke University Press, 1964. Although Trepaski concentrates on a later period, he has good introductory material on the early exploration and settlement of Florida. Using Florida as an example, he also provides one of the most extensive treatments of the role of the colonial governor in a Spanish colony.

De Voto, Bernard. *The Course of Empire*. Boston: Houghton Mifflin Co., 1952. This volume, one of the most readable in American history, places the exploration and settlement of Florida in a continental perspective.

# CORONADO'S EXPEDITION AND THE FOUNDING OF SANTA FE

*Type of event:* Socioeconomic: desire by the Spaniards to exploit the riches of the New World and extend their settlements
*Time:* Sixteenth century (c.1540)
*Locale:* New Mexico

*Principal personages:*

ÁLVAR NÚÑEZ CABEZA DE VACA (1490?-?1557), shipwrecked explorer who first heard of the fabled seven cities of gold in 1528

FRAY MARCOS DE NIZA (?-d.1558), Franciscan who led the preliminary scouting force into Arizona and New Mexico for Coronado in 1539

ESTEBANICO (also known as STEPHEN) (?-1539), Negro companion of Cabeza de Vaca, who guided the Niza expedition

FRANCISCO VÁSQUEZ DE CORONADO (1510-1554), Governor of Nueva Galicia and leader of the first major exploration of the Great Southwest from 1540 to 1542

EL TURCO (fl. 1540-1541), Indian who led Coronado to Quivira in present-day Kansas

FRAY AUGUSTÍN RODRIGUEZ (?-1581), Franciscan who lost his life in 1581 while attempting to establish the first mission in New Mexico

ANTONIO ESPEJO (fl. 1581-1583), civilian whose search for details of Rodriguez's death initiated an extensive exploration of Arizona and New Mexico in 1582 and 1583

GASPAR CASTAÑO DE SOSA (fl. 1590), acting Lieutenant Governor of Nuevo Leon, who made an illegal and unsuccessful attempt to settle New Mexico in 1590.

JUAN DE OÑATE (1549?-?1624), founder of the first permanent Spanish settlement and the first governor of New Mexico 1595-1609

PEDRO DE PERALTA (fl. 1609-1610), second Governor of New Mexico and founder of Santa Fe in 1610

## Summary of Event

In April, 1530, Álvar Núñez Cabeza de Vaca arrived at the small frontier village of San Miguel de Culiacan in what is now the state of Sinaloa, Mexico. Cabeza de Vaca and his three companions were the only survivors of an expedition along the eastern Gulf Coast in 1528. Shipwrecked in Galveston Bay, the four Spaniards had passed from tribe to tribe through Texas and Northern Mexico protected by Cabeza de Vaca's ability to persuade the Indians that he was a man of "strong medicine" and supernatural powers.

40

When the Spanish authorities questioned the four explorers, they told of seven cities rich with gold located in an area to the north named Cibola. Spurred on by Cabeza de Vaca's stories, the Governor of the province of Nueva Galicia, Francisco Vásquez de Coronado, sent a scouting party into Arizona and New Mexico in 1539 to find the "Cities of Gold." The exploration was conducted by a Franciscan priest, Fray Marcos de Niza, who was guided by one of Cabeza de Vaca's companions, a Negro slave known as Estebanico.

The expedition traveled through the Gila River Valley in Arizona and then turned northwest toward the Zuni pueblos in northern New Mexico. Estebanico, who went ahead of Niza, urged the friar on with astonishing lies about the riches that reportedly lay ahead. When Niza arrived at Cibola, he found that the Indians had killed Estebanico for taking undue liberties with their women. Niza hurried back to Mexico, repeating Estebanico's unconfirmed tales of the vast quantities of gold in the Indian towns near Cibola.

Encouraged by Niza's reports, Coronado set out with a party of three hundred Spaniards and a large number of Indian allies to conquer the Cities of Gold. Bearing somewhat farther east than Niza, the hopeful conquistadors arrived in Cibola only to find nothing but a collection of mud huts and hostile Indians. Coronado overran the first pueblo, where he was wounded in the foot by an arrow. The nearby towns quickly surrendered to prevent further hostilities.

Using Cibola as his headquarters, Coronado sent out various exploration parties to find the reported gold. One of these parties, led by Captain Garcia Lopez de Gárdenas, visited the Grand Canyon region and was awed by the vast gorge which prevented further travel. None of these parties, however, found the gold it was seeking, though they did find a large city, Tiguex, near the Rio Grande, to which Coronado transferred his operations.

The Iberians were harsh in their treatment of the Indians; they turned the natives out of their houses, robbed them of their property, and seized their women. By the spring of 1541, the Indians wanted to be rid of the Spaniards and persuaded one of their band, known in Spanish as El Turco, to lead Coronado to Quivira, a city on the plains to the east. Coronado followed El Turco eastward as far as modern-day Kansas, where he strangled the guide because none of the promised gold had been found.

Upon his return to Tiguex, Coronado found that he was losing control of his large army because of his failure to find the riches promised them when they joined the expedition. He therefore returned to Mexico in 1542, with many unhappy members accusing their commander of incompetency.

Because of the disappointment of the Coronado expedition and a series of Indian revolts in northern Mexico, it was not until 1581 that another attempt was made to enter New Mexico. In that year, Fray Augustín Rodriguez of the Franciscan order left Nueva Vizcaya and journeyed into New Mexico via the Rio Grande. This was the first time the river route was used. At first the Indians were friendly, but within a year, Rodriguez was reported to have been murdered.

Seeking to substantiate Rodriguez's

41

death, the Franciscan order obtained the assistance of António Espejo, a man of wealth who agreed to lead and finance the search party. Arriving in the upper Rio Grande Valley in 1582 with a Franciscan friar and fourteen soldiers, Espejo confirmed Rodriguez's death. Since there was ample opportunity for further exploration, Espejo searched the entire region of northern New Mexico and Arizona, returning to Mexico by way of the Pecos river. It was during Espejo's journeys that the Spanish began to refer to "New Mexico," a name that denoted their hope to find a new region as rich as the land of the Aztecs.

Espejo's tales once again encouraged further journeys, and numerous men petitioned the viceroy to grant them licenses of exploration; but the viceroy refused to act. This reluctance on the part of the colonial administration led Gaspar Castaño de Sosa, acting governor of Nuevo Leon, to make an unlicensed exploration of New Mexico with a view to permanent settlement. Leaving Nuevo Leon in 1590 with a wagon train and 170 persons (including women and children), Castaño headed up the Pecos river for New Mexico. The journey, however, ended in failure which was compounded by the arrest of Castaño for an unlicensed and illegal entry into the northern territory.

In 1595, Juan de Oñate obtained permission to enter New Mexico. Oñate's contract provided that he and his descendants would be governor, captain general, and *adelantado* of New Mexico for two generations. He was to provide the expedition with two hundred men, provisions, livestock, horses, and medicines, all at his own expense. The King of Spain agreed to assist the new

governor by lending him three field pieces, powder, ammunition, armor, and six thousand pesos.

After numerous delays, Oñate received final permission to proceed late in 1597. He was again delayed in Santa Barbara in northern Mexico, while a royal *visitador* inspected his accounts, supplies, and men to insure the contract's observance. Then in February, 1598, the eighty-three wagons began the long journey northward up the Rio Grande Valley. Arriving in mid-summer, Oñate supervised the building of San Juan and San Gabriel, the first two Spanish towns in New Mexico. The latter became the capital of the province.

After establishing the first settlements, Oñate engaged in various explorations of the Southwest, including a trip to Coronado's Quivira, and an extensive journey in Arizona where he discovered the Bill Williams river and followed the Colorado river to its mouth in the Gulf of California. Interspersed between his explorations, Oñate hanged several deserters and stormed the pueblo of Acoma with his army after the Indians had killed some of his settlers. Oñate then condemned the survivors of Acoma to twenty years' servitude, and cut off the right foot of all males over twenty-five years of age. He also amputated the right hands of two Hopi Indians captured at Acoma and sent them home as a warning to other tribes in the area.

Oñate's heavy-handed methods led to trouble, especially after he forced a group of fleeing settlers to return to his colony in 1601. Appeals were made to the Viceroy of Mexico protesting Oñate's Administration and asking that the colony be abandoned because of its poverty. The viceroy recommended that Oñate be replaced as Governor until a further investigation could be made. Indignantly, Oñate resigned his post. Later, in Spain, he was tried for various actions, convicted, and fined.

At first, the King of Spain had thought of abandoning the colony of New Mexico, but the Church worried about the fate of the Christianized Indians and demanded the King's support of God's work. The crown assented and dispatched Pedro de Peralta as Oñate's replacement. The son of a Navarre nobleman, Peralta had been graduated in canon law and did have military experience. So that the settlers could "live with some order and decency," Peralta was ordered to establish a new village "before all else." Named San Francisco de la Santa Fe, the new town was built in 1610. Surrounding a plaza lined with the public buildings, the new capital of New Mexico was governed by four *regidores* elected by the people, and two *alcaldes* elected by the *regidores*. With the installation of the Peralta regime, the existence of New Mexico was assured, providing a center for the Spanish culture so important to the Great Southwest even today.

## Pertinent Literature

Bolton, Herbert E. *Coronado: Knight of Pueblos and Plains.* New York: McGraw-Hill Book Co., 1949.

Coronado's journey into the wilds of New Spain in often regarded as a wild-goose chase by historians, but Bolton disagrees. He finds Coronado's motivation, the desire for gold, no more absurd than the forces that drew the forty-niners to California seeking the same thing. While Coronado did not find the riches he sought, his search was one of the significant expeditions of the day. The conquistador opened North America to further exploration and ultimate settlement.

So revolutionary were Coronado's discoveries that European mapmakers failed to comprehend them correctly, says Bolton. Instead, they showed the Rio Grande flowing into the Pacific and placed Quivira on the Pacific coast instead of eastward in the middle of the plains. But many of these mistakes were also due to inadequate information dispensed to the world by the secretive King of Spain who jealously guarded the secrets of the New World.

The observations and compass readings made by Coronado have also been helpful to modern science. Coronado traveled on the plains by using a compass for direction. Scientists had assumed from scanty data that the magnetic declination in the 1500's was two degrees east of true north. Historians, however, using Coronado's reports on the location of Palo Duro Canyon in Texas have enabled scientists to correct this false notion. It is now agreed that the magnetic declination in 1540 as revealed by Coronado's observations was eleven degrees east of true north, about the same as it is today.

Bolton also challenges the traditional idea that the wild herds of mustangs found in the West descended from those horses left behind by Coronado. The expedition had few mares, and later Spanish explorers fail to mention horse-mounted Indians until the late seventeenth century. Bolton believes that the wild horses used by the American plains Indians were descended from animals brought by colonists into New Mexico much later than Coronado's time. Bolton believes that the delay in settling New Mexico after Coronado was caused by Spanish concern with Florida and a desire to prevent French settlement in South Carolina as much as anything else.

As to Coronado himself, Bolton finds him to be a responsible leader with important humane qualities. Coronado was a strict yet just disciplinarian, says Bolton, who became unpopular because he refused to allow his

men to commit outrages on the Indian villages. He was especially kind in his concern for his Indian allies, which was unusual during this period of history. Bolton also finds Coronado to have been a brave and fearless leader in combat, one who inspired his men with his recklessness. Bolton concludes that the failure of his men to desert when they first realized Cibola was a collection of mud huts was due to their faith in Coronado's leadership. These qualities helped to exonerate him of the charge of incompetence brought against him by his enemies after the expedition returned from Mexico.

Hammond, George P. *Don Juan de Oñate and the Founding of New Mexico*. Santa Fe, New Mexico: El Palacio Press, 1927.

George P. Hammond, a Bolton student at the University of California at Berkeley, first wrote his study of Oñate as a doctoral dissertation. Hammond made an extensive search through the original documents located in the Archives of the Indies at Seville, Spain, hoping to clarify many points about early New Mexico history including the founding of Santa Fe. The closest Hammond could come to determining the date when Santa Fe was established was 1610, by Don Pedro de Peralta, who succeeded Oñate as governor.

Details about Oñate's early life are obscure. He married Doña Isabel de Tolosa, who was distantly related to Cortes and the Aztec chieftain Montezuma. Oñate had some experience fighting Indians on the frontier and owned several mines of great wealth. He was also a friend of Don Luis de Velasco II, Viceroy of Mexico. This influence helped him secure the original contract to settle New Mexico in 1595,

which was modified several times before Oñate departed in 1598.

Oñate's frequent absences from the colony he set up in New Mexico and the disappointment of the settlers who fled back to Mexico resulted in his ultimate dismissal and trial on various charges. Oñate was convicted for spreading false stories about New Mexico's wealth, and for excessive cruelty in suppressing an Indian revolt and in forcing the fleeing settlers to return to New Mexico.

Hammond's work on Oñate has led to his editing a series of volumes collectively entitled the *Coronado Historical* series. Of special interest to students of sixteenth century New Mexico are three volumes coedited with Agapito Rey: *Narratives of the Coronado Expedition, 1540-1542; Don Juan Oñate: Colonizer of New Mexico, 1595-1628;* and *The Rediscovery of New Mexico, 1580-1594* (Albuquerque: University of New Mexico Press, 1940, 1953, and

1966 respectively). Each of these volumes is a collection of primary source materials, original accounts, letters, and documents relating to Spanish exploration in the Southwest. Although the general reader may not wish to examine the numerous documents, they are of value to the student. The brief introduction to each volume, moreover, provides an excellent synopsis of the events and personages instrumental in establishing the first settlements in New Mexico. — *W.L.R.*

## Additional Recommended Reading

Day, A. Grove. *Coronado's Quest: The Discovery of the Southwestern States.* Berkeley: University of California Press, 1940. This first substantial biography of Coronado written in English is also available in a paperback edition.

Bishop, Morris. *The Odyssey of Cabeza de Vaca.* New York: The Appleton-Century Co., 1933. Bishop relates the story of the first Spaniard to hear of the fabulous Seven Cities of Gold which stimulated Coronado's exploits.

Bancroft, Hubert H. *History of Arizona and New Mexico, 1530-1888.* Vol. XVII: *The Works of Hubert Howe Bancroft.* New York: McGraw-Hill Book Co., 1967. 39 vols. Originally published in 1889, Bancroft's massive history of the Far West is still of immense value and interest.

Bolton, Herbert E. *The Spanish Borderlands: A Chronicle of Old Florida and the Southwest.* Vol. XXIII: *The Chronicles of America.* Edited by Allen Johnson and Allan Nevins. New Haven: Yale University Press, 1918-1951. 56 vols. Originally published in 1921, Bolton's work has chapters on Cabeza de Vaca, Coronado, and the founding of New Mexico.

Wellman, Paul I. *Glory, God, and Gold: A Narrative History.* Garden City: Doubleday and Co., 1954. Depicting in his title the objectives of the conquistadors, Wellman has produced a readable volume on Spanish exploration in the New World.

Forrest, Earle R. *Missions and Pueblos of the Old Southwest.* Glendale, Calif.: Arthur H. Clark Co., 1929; republished, Chicago: Rio Grande Press, Inc., 1962 and 1964. Concentrating on the *padres* and their missions, Forrest's book goes beyond the initial explorations and colonization period in New Mexico, but it offers the reader much interesting material on Church activities in the Southwest.

# RALEIGH'S ATTEMPTS AT COLONIZATION IN THE NEW WORLD

*Type of event:* Political: desire to establish English colonies in the New World
*Time:* 1584-1591
*Locale:* England and Roanoke Island (part of present-day North Carolina)

*Principal personages:*

ELIZABETH I (1533-1603), Queen of England 1558-1603, after whom Virginia was named

SIR WALTER RALEIGH (1552?-1618), favorite of Elizabeth who sponsored several attempts at colonization in the New World

SIR HUMPHREY GILBERT (1539?-1583), Raleigh's half-brother, whose failure to colonize Newfoundland led to Raleigh's attempts to settle Roanoke Island

RICHARD HAKLUYT (1552?-1616), who advocated colonizing America

ARTHUR BARLOWE (1550?-?1620), commander of Raleigh's first exploratory expedition

SIR RICHARD GRENVILLE (1541?-1591), naval commander of Raleigh's second colonial venture

SIR RALPH LANE (1530?-1603), Governor of Raleigh's 1585 settlement at Roanoke

JOHN WHITE (fl. 1585-1593), Governor of the "Lost Colony"

## Summary of Event

Sir Walter Raleigh's place in history is difficult to assess. His many accomplishments ought to have won for him rank among the greats of the golden age of Elizabeth I, but they have not, perhaps because Raleigh's versatility made him a dilettante. The tragic circumstances surrounding his execution for treason in 1616 have cloaked him in the martyr's guise. Yet Raleigh demands historians' attention because of his association with England's first halting steps toward the creation of a vast empire and with the fabled "Lost Colony."

Raleigh sprang from gentle but impoverished West Country stock whose sons would have a long and intimate connection with England's colonizing activities in the sixteenth century. In addition to Walter, his brother Carew and his half-brothers Sir John, Sir Humphrey, and Adrian Gilbert became active participants in the efforts to build an overseas empire. The precise point at which Sir Walter Raleigh began to take part in these activities is uncertain, but it is clear that when in 1578 Sir Humphrey Gilbert received a patent to settle lands "not actually possessed of any Christian prince or people," Raleigh's curiosity and interest had been aroused, for he commanded one of the ships which carried Gilbert's first group of colonists to Newfoundland. There followed a hiatus in Raleigh's colonizing endeavors during which his position at Elizabeth's court

46

steadily improved. Thus strengthened, he helped to finance his half-brother's ill-fated second colonizing venture in the spring of 1583. The failure of the expedition and Sir Humphrey's death put the onus of establishing an English settlement in America on Raleigh's shoulders.

Raleigh profited from Gilbert's experience. By the time he secured a renewal of Gilbert's patent in 1584, he had decided to pick a colonizing site farther south on the North American continent, where the climate would be more temperate. To ensure a successful planting, Sir Walter resolved to send a small survey party to explore the new site, and in April, 1584, two small ships under the command of Arthur Barlowe left England for America.

The vessels sailed south to the Canaries and then to the Caribbean Islands, where they took on water and supplies before sailing north, arriving off the North Carolina coast in early July. Several days were passed in reconnoitering the vicinity for a good harbor and a place to erect a plantation and initiate trading with the Indians. Barlowe and his men returned to England in September, bringing a glowing account of the voyage, which Richard Hakluyt would print in his *Principall Navigations, Voiages, and Discoveries of the English Nation* in 1589. Raleigh named the new land Virginia after the Virgin Queen who elevated him to knighthood.

For all the glowing accounts brought by Barlowe and his men, Raleigh still lacked the information necessary for starting a colony. Encouraged by Elizabeth's generosity, he persuaded Hakluyt to write a memorial to the Queen in the hope that she would lend financial support to a new venture. Hakluyt drafted the memorial, known as *A Discourse on Western Planting,* which raised nearly every argument for planting colonies—from the promotion of trade to the advancement of religion—which would be advanced over the next two centuries. The arguments were to no avail; Elizabeth offered no more than her encouragement.

Undaunted, Raleigh put together a second expedition. In seeking advice he turned to Hakluyt's older cousin, also named Richard. The elder Hakluyt suggested that a temporary colony of specialists in map making, botany, exploring, and similar accomplishments be sent over to prepare the way for more permanent settlers. Following this advice, Raleigh in 1585 dispatched an expedition under Sir Richard Grenville and Sir Ralph Lane, who was to govern the colony. Among the experts were a young Oxford scholar, Thomas Hariot, and an artist, John White, both of whom were to supply the English with their first accurate descriptions of the New World. The colonists made a slow crossing and arrived at Roanoke Island too late to plant crops. Damage to their supplies in unloading, coupled with Indian problems, made for a difficult winter. Furthermore, Lane proved to be an inept governor and when Sir Francis Drake arrived off Roanoke Island in the spring of 1586, Lane and his men were inclined to leave. A spring storm, which destroyed the few supplies Drake had brought, stiffened Lane's determination to depart, and he persuaded Drake to take the colonists back to England. Two weeks later, Grenville arrived with a major supply, but finding no colonists, he put the supplies ashore in the care of fifteen men and sailed off to raid Spanish shipping. Raleigh's second attempt to erect a colony had failed. In 1587 Raleigh mounted a more elaborate effort. Raising a body of men, women, and children, he placed them under the jurisdiction of John White, whom he named as deputy governor. The presence of women and children and Raleigh's orders to erect a borough form of government in the new colony, suggest that he intended this venture to be a permanent settlement. Acting on a suggestion made by Lane, Raleigh ordered White to choose a more felicitous site than Roanoke Island on which to settle, but he was to take off the men whom Grenville had left there the year before. When White's colonists arrived at Roanoke Island, the pilot apparently refused to go farther, so White and his people unloaded and began to establish their position. For reasons which are not altogether clear, White returned to England with the ships. Unfortunately, he arrived just as war with Spain was breaking out, and it was four years before the English could resupply the Roanoke Island colony. When White finally returned to Roanoke Island in 1591, the colonists had vanished. What happened to them is probably best explained by the eighteenth century Virginia historian Robert Beverly. "It is supposed," he wrote, "that the Indians seeing them forsaken by their country and unfurnished of their expected supplies, cut them off. For to this day they were never more heard of."

After the loss of the Roanoke Island colonists, Raleigh turned his attentions elsewhere. The chief importance of his endeavors was the whetting of English interests in an overseas empire. Others would follow and succeed where Raleigh had failed.

## Pertinent Literature

Quinn, David B. *Raleigh and the British Empire.* Chs. I-IV. London: Hodder & Stoughton, Ltd., 1947.

The European quest for empire in the sixteenth century was not so much an expression of the desires of individual men as of social forces. Beginning with this premise, David B. Quinn has chosen Sir Walter Raleigh as a representative figure on England's maiden voyage into imperialism, and he has concentrated upon aspects of Raleigh's life which illustrate the social movement of the time.

In order to explain England's imperialistic motivations, Quinn inquires into the history of the early Tudor period. The Tudor monarchy, he observes, aimed to establish a strong middle class based largely on commercial prosperity. Merchant capital developed rapidly between 1480 and 1550 because of the boom in the export of unfinished cloth. Then a serious slump in the export trade necessitated experimentation with new products for new markets. Thus England entered her first industrial revolution. As the developing industries raised demands for overseas markets, their profits provided the capital to finance overseas explorations. At the same time, the growing centralization of the state led to the creation of administrative machinery for collecting taxes, thus enabling the government to sponsor voyages of exploration. Other developments seemed to converge to make such voyages feasible: technology made possible the building of seaworthy ships, and intellectual progress unshackled minds from some of their superstitions about the unknown world. By the 1570's, England's overseas objectives were threefold: to continue piratical attacks on the Spanish treasure fleets and colonies; to extend commerce into Eastern Europe, Asia, and Africa; and to seek a northwest passage to Asia.

Raleigh entered the world of overseas adventure as a sort of junior partner in the ill-fated enterprise of his half-brother Sir Humphrey Gilbert. From the time when Sir Humphrey's disappearance at sea thrust him into the forefront of the exploration movement, Raleigh was, as portrayed by Quinn, very much the entrepreneur. He left the actual exploring to other men while he concentrated on raising capital and organizing men and materials.

The purely exploratory voyage to Roanoke Island in 1584 served mainly to raise the hopes of Raleigh and prospective investors concerning the commercial potential of North American resources. Raleigh, in Quinn's estimation, expected too much of the initial colonial enterprise in return for the small amount of planning, effort, and money that had gone into it. The first American colonists who journeyed to Roanoke with Sir Ralph Lane as their leader in 1585 were merely the paid servants of the investors and had no personal stake in the venture. Lane was knowledgeable in military matters but he had no experience in organizing agricultural or commercial activities. Failing to devote themselves to the growing of food, the colonists depended far too much upon the Indians

for corn and fish and thereby alienated the initially friendly natives. Lane soon realized that "Mediterranean fruits" and lumber would not prove sufficiently profitable commodities to make the colony worthwhile. He considered investigation of the mainland of paramount importance. Although he soon concluded that the colony must move to a more favorable site with a suitable harbor if it were to survive, he expended his energies seeking gold in order to meet the enterprise's short-term objective of profit.

After the entire colony returned to England in 1586 without waiting for additional supplies to arrive, Raleigh understood that he must alter his ideas about colonization. His 1587 expedition, that of the Lost Colony, expressed the realization that colonists must be given an incentive to make their colony prosper. Each colonist was granted five hundred acres of land, each was encouraged to take his family so that a stable society might be developed, and a limited form of local government was established. Even during the four-year period when no communication with the Roanoke colony existed, sponsors in England were making plans to ensure its support by a continuing corporation of wealthy men.

Quinn's final assessment of Raleigh is that he was too much concerned with short-term profits to establish a permanent colony. Although Raleigh was more deeply involved in overseas exploration than any other of his English contemporaries, he was limited by his belief that colonization must pay its own way. Colonization was only one of his many activities, and he was unwilling to invest a major portion of his own fortune to bring about its success.

Quinn nevertheless acknowledges that Raleigh's efforts were important first steps toward the establishment of permanent settlements in the New World.

Wallace, Willard M. *Sir Walter Raleigh.* Princeton: Princeton University Press, 1959.

Raleigh's colonizing attempts in Virginia occupy only two chapters of Willard M. Wallace's full-length biography, which emphasizes the fact that these attempts were a small part of Raleigh's diversified life. The epitome of the Renaissance man, Raleigh was at various stages of his career a "soldier, sailor, courtier, Captain of the Queen's Guard, businessman, explorer, colonizer, Member of Parliament, devotee of science, ship designer, military engineer, musician, literary patron, historian, and poet." Raleigh's ambition to attain political power by becoming a member of the Privy Council was never realized, mainly because of his disinclination to concentrate on a single phase of human activity. Had he been willing to risk his entire fortune on his colonizing efforts, and had he been able to break away from his role as one of the Queen's favorites in order to command a Virginia expedition himself, Raleigh might not only have won enduring fame as the founder of the first permanent English settlement in America, but he might also have taken his seat on the Privy Council.

Wallace's biography, though not uncritical of its subject, is unquestionably pro-Raleigh. Consequently, the author is more inclined than some historians concerned with the colonization attempts at Roanoke Island to attribute failure to factors which Raleigh could not completely control. Much has been written, for instance, about the lack of wisdom in giving the 1585 attempt a military flavor, with the colonists serving merely as the paid servants of the investors. Wallace points out that the House of Commons in confirming Raleigh's title to Virginia in 1585 prohibited not only the sending of imprisoned debtors as colonists but also the taking of wives and indentured servants. Such prohibitions prevented the establishment of a permanent settlement by disallowing domestic activity.

Like other historians of colonization efforts, Wallace criticizes Raleigh's original concept of how such enterprises should be financed. By encouraging the commanders of the voyages to Virginia to attack Spanish bullion-carrying galleons, Raleigh diverted them from the primary task of proceeding to Virginia as quickly as possible in order to conserve supplies and to plant crops in time to reap the best possible harvest.

By 1587 Raleigh had altered much of his faulty thinking on the nature of colonization. The limited size of his ill-fated expedition of that year, Wallace conjectures, was perhaps caused by Raleigh's inability to find adequate financing. His enemies, jealous of the Queen's favor, ridiculed his enterprise, and an apathetic attitude prevailed among potential investors. Charles M. Andrews, in *Our Earliest Colonial Settlements,* accuses Raleigh of losing interest in the Roanoke Island colonists after 1587. Andrews implies that, the war with Spain notwithstanding, Raleigh and his representatives simply did not try as hard as they might have to reach America, or to find the colonists when the crossing was again possible. Wallace is more charitable, however,

50

# Raleigh's Attempts at Colonization in the New World

contending that Raleigh had lost a great deal of money in the colonizing effort, and that he felt that future endeavors must be supported either by the government or by commercial corporations. Raleigh's interest in colonization continued, nevertheless, after his withdrawal from active participation.

The remainder of Wallace's biography is primarily a detailed account of Raleigh's military and naval adventures and of the court intrigues which buffeted him about from the position of Queen's favorite to that of a convicted traitor, imprisoned in the Tower for thirteen years. Although Raleigh was opportunistic and perhaps indiscreet in some of his diplomatic dealings, he was by no means a traitor, and his trial, even when judged by seventeenth century standards, represents one of the grossest miscarriages of justice in English legal history. The Raleigh who emerges from this ordeal to take on yet another expedition to the New World, this time to Guiana in search of gold, is a figure of exceptional resiliency and optimism. Wallace's portrait of the mature Raleigh is that of a man who, despite never attaining eminence in any single endeavor, stands above many of his more powerful contemporaries because of his character. — *W.M.B.*

## Additional Recommended Reading

Williamson, James A. "England and the Opening of the Atlantic," in *The Cambridge History of the British Empire*. Vol. I, ch. 2. Cambridge: The University Press, 1929-1930. This article offers an excellent brief introduction to England's interest in the New World.

Parks, George B. *Richard Hakluyt and the English Voyages*. Edited, with an introduction, by James A. Williamson. 2nd ed. New York: Frederick Ungar Publishing Co., 1961. No examination of Raleigh's activities is complete without some reference to the important work of the younger Hakluyt.

Rowse, A. L. *The Elizabethans and America*. London: Macmillan & Company, 1959. The early chapters of this book provide a valuable background for understanding the role of England in the age of exploration.

Thompson, Edward. *Sir Walter Ralegh: Last of the Elizabethans*. New Haven: Yale University Press, 1935. A standard biography of Sir Walter which is highly laudatory and apologetic.

Craven, Wesley F. *The Southern Colonies in the Seventeenth Century, 1607-1689*. Ch. 2. Baton Rouge: Louisiana State University Press, 1949. The brief account of Raleigh's activities contained in this volume emphasizes the importance of Hakluyt's writings.

Andrews, Charles M. *Our Earliest Colonial Settlements: Their Diversities of Origin and Later Characteristics*. Ch. I. Ithaca: Cornell University Press, 1964. While not uncritical of Raleigh, this appraisal of his attempts at colonization acknowledges the importance of experience to later successful efforts.

# FOUNDING OF QUEBEC AND FRENCH EXPLORATION OF THE GREAT LAKES

*Type of event:* Politico-economic: establishment of French empire in New World
*Time:* 1603-1682
*Locale:* St. Lawrence Valley and the Great Lakes

*Principal personages:*
SAMUEL DE CHAMPLAIN (1567?-1635), father of New France
HENRY IV (1553-1610), King of France
CARDINAL RICHELIEU, ARMAND-JEAN DU PLESSIS (1585-1642), Chief Minister of France
JEAN NICOLET (1598-1642), trader and explorer
JEAN BAPTISTE COLBERT (1619-1683), French controller general of finances
JEAN BAPTISTE TALON (THE "GREAT INTENDANT") (1625?-1694), Intendant of New France
LOUIS JOLLIET (1645-1700), trader and explorer
DOLLIER DE CASSON (fl. seventeenth century), Sulpician missionary
JACQUES MARQUETTE (1637-1675), Jesuit missionary
RENÉ ROBERT CAVELIER, SIEUR DE LA SALLE (1643-1687), explorer and colonizer

## Summary of Event

By 1600, France was in a condition to undertake the serious business of establishing settlements in Canada. Verrazano and Cartier had done the preliminary work of staking French claims in the New World, and although the early attempts at colonization had failed in the North as well as in Florida in 1562-1567, these experiments had taught the French lessons that were to prove valuable. Furthermore, by 1600 the long agony of the wars of religion in France was over, and France now had a strong king, Henry IV, who was vitally interested in colonization. The death of Philip II of Spain in 1598 also helped open the colonial field to France as well as to England as never before.

Henry IV found a superb agent in Samuel de Champlain, who well deserves the title of "father of New France." He was born about 1570 at Brouage, a port near La Rochelle. From childhood, Champlain came to know the sea, and in 1598-1599 he visited both Spain and her colonies, where he remained for more than two years learning important lessons in the art of colonization. Returning to France, he reported to the King and by his careful observations roused the monarch's enthusiasm for following the fishermen who for at least a century had been sailing to Newfoundland and the Gulf of St. Lawrence for both fish and furs. In March, 1603, Champlain first set out with royal approval for the North American coast. Ascending the St. Lawrence, at Tadoussac, at the mouth of the Saguenay where fur traders had been going to barter since the days of Cartier, he made his first contact with

52

the natives. After going up river to Stadaconé, now deserted by its Indian inhabitants, he returned to France in September and reported to Henry IV. From this time forth, he was perpetually shifting back and forth across the Atlantic. In March, 1604, acting as geographer for the Sieur de Monts, to whom the king had granted semi-feudal rights in North America, he made his second voyage to Canada, with three ships. In 1605 under his direction a settlement was first made at St. Croix and finally at Port Royal, Acadia, on the Bay of Fundy. This was the first permanent French settlement in New France. A much delayed relief party from France barely saved Port Royal from abandonment in July, 1606. For three seasons thereafter Champlain explored North American waters.

In 1608 Champlain, with two ships, again ascended the St. Lawrence, while a third ship reinforced the Port Royal colony. This time he was prepared to make a permanent settlement on the banks of that river. On July 2, he landed at Stadaconé and erected buildings there, and the city of Quebec was born. At this point Indian politics entered the picture. In spite of their common origin, the Hurons and the Iroquois had become deadly enemies, and the Hurons were anxious to enlist Champlain as their ally against the recently formed confederacy of the Five Nations. In an evil moment for New France Champlain did so, thinking that his act was the means of securing Quebec from Iroquois attack. In June, 1609, escorted by a fleet of Huron canoes, Champlain went farther up the St. Lawrence. Arriving at the mouth of the Richelieu river, the expedition turned south into Iroquois country.

Champlain was now treading what was for the next two centuries to become the great warpath between Canada and the English provinces. On July 29, probably in the vicinity of Crown Point on the lake now bearing his name, Champlain encountered an Iroquois party. The two groups prepared for battle, and the next day Champlain fired the three musket shots which brought down three Iroquois chiefs. Thus began the eternal warfare between the Five Nations and the French —a warfare which was to affect profoundly the life of New France.

Although he had permanent residence at Quebec, Champlain continued his work of exploration. In 1609 he visited France, and in 1610 he turned again to the North American interior, but briefly. He went back to France and remained until 1611. Growing numbers of Indian traders troubled the natives, and in 1612 Champlain endeavored to secure aid from the French court in governing the new colony. In 1613 he returned to it as "Lieutenant-General for the King in New France," but again in 1614 the Viceroy found himself in the Mother Country, attending the States-General and pressing for a renewal of merchant support and of missionary effort among the Indians, whose savagery amazed and saddened him. Upon his return to Canada, Champlain made his farthest trip west in 1615, and reached Lake Huron. On the way back, he saw Lake Ontario and wintered with the Hurons. This was the last of his explorations. Fortunately, he carefully recorded his experiences, and eventually published four invaluable volumes (the last in 1632) containing full and accurate maps.

Meanwhile, since Henry IV's murder in 1610, France was plunged into turmoil. The new monarch, Louis XIII, was a child, and under the regency of Marie de Medicis religious factionalism resumed, and the French colonizing effort was placed in jeopardy. The advent of the Thirty Years' War (1618-1648) brought strong leadership to the fore in the person of Armand-Jean du Plessis, Cardinal Richelieu, who exalted the crown power and forced everyone to yield to the royal prerogative. By 1624 Richelieu had secured his position as chief minister of France, and, like Henry IV, he became deeply interested in New France. Unlike a predecessor, the Duc de Sully, who believed that colonization was folly, Richelieu backed overseas planting, which had now become a reality. The French, however, never sought the new world in such numbers as their English rivals. Not displacement of the Indian but trade with him for furs had become the French method, for Richelieu promoted commerce through a variety of trading companies which were also colonizing ventures under royal direction.

In 1629, however, English forces carried Anglo-French warfare to Quebec, where they forced Champlain to surrender. Charles I returned Canada and Acadia to France in 1632 after Champlain persuaded Richelieu that the seizure had followed Anglo-French peace agreements and that the territory was too valuable to be left in English hands. In 1633 Richelieu sent Champlain back to New France with the title of governor, an office he held only two years until his death on Christmas Day, 1635. He was buried in the city he had founded, but now no one knows where the remains of the founder of

New France lie. A noble character, devout, patient, and a thoroughgoing seaman, Champlain made New France a reality, inaugurated the continuing French policy of friendly relations with the Indians, and with surprising accuracy, mapped and described the lands he had visited.

Meanwhile, a new force had entered the life of New France. The seventeenth century in Europe witnessed a revival of the Roman Catholic Church, and revival meant missionary spirit and activity. The powerful order of Jesuits, untiring missionaries who were always looking for new worlds to conquer, began to take an interest in New France and its Indian allies. In 1613 two Jesuits, the forerunners of a devoted army of martyrs, sailed for Port Royal. Two years later the Récollets, a branch of the Franciscans, followed suit. Four Récollet friars, including Father Joseph Le Caron, set out with Champlain from France; Le Caron preceded him on the western trip of that year, and spent a winter with the Hurons. Pressing on to the lake that bears the Huron name, he and his men were the first Europeans on record to see any of the Great Lakes.

The French proved to be better at exploration and trade with the Indians than at colonization. In contrast with their English rivals to the south, they were slow at filling up the settlements on the seacoast and along the St. Lawrence. But they continued to move westward. The first to follow in the steps of Champlain appears to have been Jean Nicolet, who in 1634-1635 served as a Huron emissary to negotiate peace with the Winnebagoes on the shores of Lake Michigan. Nicolet explored as far west as the Fox and Wis-

54

consin rivers. He was in all probability followed by fur traders and missionaries, but their names are lost to history.

The next great thrust to the west came several decades later as renewed French expansion followed the revival of the fur trade under the leadership of entrepreneurs, such as Médard Chouart, Sieur des Grosseilliers, and Pierre-Esprit Radisson. In 1665 Louis XIV and his minister Colbert, both greatly interested in New France, sent out as intendant Jean Talon, who became the strong man of the colony. Talon had a real vision of empire to match the one for which his royal master became famous, and he encouraged exploration, built forts on Lake Champlain and the Richelieu river to guard the Iroquois route to the St. Lawrence, and renewed war against the Iroquois enemies of Indian allies. In 1669 Talon sent out Louis Jolliet, a native-born Canadian, who in his search for the source of copper traveled only as far as Lake Erie. He was followed by Dollier de Casson, a courtly soldier whose physique matched the wilderness life of hardship which he embraced in his monastic order's missionary rivalry with the Jesuits. In 1671 he became superior of the Sulpicians at Montreal, and there he stayed until he died in 1701.

Under the governorship of the Comte de Frontenac (1672-1682) expansion in New France reached beyond the Great Lakes into the Missis-

sippi Valley. In 1673 Louis Jolliet and Père Marquette, of the Jesuit order, set out on a notable voyage. Traversing the Great Lakes, they went down the Mississippi as far as the Arkansas. Their work was continued by Robert Cavelier, Sieur de La Salle, who in 1669, accompanied by a party of Sulpicians led by Dollier de Casson, had roamed through New York, crossed from Lake Erie to the headwaters of the Ohio, and paddled down that river toward the Mississippi. But his men deserted him, and he turned back. In 1678-1680 La Salle crossed the Great Lakes to the Illinois river, bent upon extending the borders of New France to Spanish Mexico. Not until 1682 did he lead his famous party from the Great Lakes, via the Illinois river, down the Mississippi to the Gulf of Mexico; there, on April 9, he claimed the vast interior for Louis XIV. Although the colony that La Salle proceded to establish did not last, and the great explorer himself was murdered by his own men in 1687, others such as Lemoyne d'Iberville, took up the challenge of making good the French claims to Louisiana by planting settlements. These are only the most notable of the French explorers, but the net result of their activities and those of many unsung adventurers was that by 1682 Frenchmen had roamed from the Gulf of St. Lawrence to the site of the city of New Orleans, laying claim to a far-flung empire and challenging English and Spanish rivals in America.

## Pertinent Literature

Bourne, Edward G. and A. N. Bourne, eds. *The Voyages and Explorations of Samuel De Champlain, 1604-1616; Narrated by Himself.* 2 vols. New York: A. S. Barnes, 1906.

The student of the history of early French Canada is fortunate in having at his disposal an excellent narrative written by the man who is universally called "the father of New France." In 1604 Champlain published the narrative of his first voyage; this was followed by other accounts as his experience increased, and in 1632, three years before Champlain's death, a final and corrected version appeared. This material was not available in English until 1859, when the Hakluyt Society brought out an edition of the *Brief Discours*. Other versions followed, and the one under review was done with the purpose of making Champlain's works accessible in a fairly popular form.

The editing is well done. Parts of the earlier narrative are included in the translation of the 1632 version in order to produce a complete and full story. The footnotes are good. Champlain's occasional errors in dating are corrected, and all the place names are translated into modern place nomenclature so that the reader may follow Champlain's course on a modern map.

The writing is as good as the editing. One is inclined to compare this work with two other contemporary accounts of North American colonization, Bradford's *Of Plymouth Plantation* and John Smith's account of colonial Virginia. Champlain shows up well in the comparison. Bradford's charming narrative is confined to a small and less important colony, and Smith's is marred by doubts of his veracity.

Champlain gives us facts, straight and unadorned. He begins his narrative by a summary account of previous attempts at French settlement. This is done not merely to tell a complete story of French colonization efforts, but more importantly, to attempt to account for the failure of Champlain's predecessors, such as Ribaut, Laudonniere, and Roberval, and partly to arrive at a proper method of successful colonization. Thus, when Champlain himself founded a colony, a lasting one, he had what might be called a plan of colonization. As he explored, he was careful to note the nature of the country, its fitness for agriculture, its fauna and flora, its harbors—all that would help a would-be settler. As a result of spending a winter among the Hurons, Champlain provided a long chapter on Indian life done with a considerable sympathy for the natives and their customs. This contrasts sharply with the usual approach of the English settler, to whom the native was ordinarily a savage enemy to be despised, pushed out, or exterminated.

Beyond all this, the pages of this work give us a portrait of a man, "perhaps the ablest of the earlier makers of America," who was energetic, hopeful, devout, careful, tolerant of strange ways—a true humanitarian.

Wrong, George M. *The Rise and Fall of New France*. New York: The Macmillan Company, 1928.

George M. Wrong was trained for the ministry of the Anglican Church in Canada, but he never functioned as a parish priest. Devoting his life to teaching and writing, he taught first at Wycliffe College, then at the University of Toronto. Eventually he earned a reputation as the most notable of modern Canadian historians, and the volumes under review constitute his major work.

Anyone who writes about the rise and fall of New France inevitably invites comparison with Francis Parkman. It is interesting to see how Wrong eludes this comparison. Parkman was opening up new territory in historical writing. Basing his work solidly on the sources, his footnotes are long and copious, and in them he carefully discusses the sources and carries on a debate with previous writers who had covered parts of the field. Wrong has no footnotes whatsoever. This does not mean that his work is superficial. At the end of each volume there is an extensive and critical bibliography which the reader can take or leave as he pleases. Parkman was, of course, a master of historical narrative whose writing is graphic and eloquent. Wrong writes in a simple, straightforward style completely without purple passages.

The scope of Wrong's narrative is wide. He begins his account with Marco Polo, has a chapter on the Norse discoveries and Spanish explorers, then one on the English claim to North America, and another about the English on the Pacific coast. Until the middle of the eighteenth century, the English colonies were largely ignored by the English government. New France, on the contrary, was always rather rigidly controlled by Old France. A knowledge of the French history of the period is, therefore, essential to an understanding of the fate of New France. It is one of the merits of Wrong that he carefully tied Canadian and French history together. Henry IV, Cardinal Richelieu, Louis XIV, Colbert, all played their part in the drama, and all are admirably sketched into this narrative. But, argues Wrong, it was Champlain who was "the man destined to make New France a reality," and Wrong makes a good case for this thesis.

The chapter entitled "Champlain Among the Hurons" is much more than its title would indicate. It is a thorough sketch of the Indians of that name, and it is better than Parkman's description, for it is in part based on material not available to the earlier historian. Wrong, having a full comprehension of the great part played by the Roman Catholic Church in the founding of New France, discusses the Catholic revival in France in the seventeenth century, the work of the missionary orders in the founding of the colony, and the place occupied by Bishop Laval in the life of the colony. Parkman manages fairly well to escape from the Protestant bias characteristic of the New England historians of his age, but occasionally traces of it do crop up. From this fault Wrong is completely free. He has produced one of the best introductions to the history of New France that has been written. — *D.R.G.*

## Additional Recommended Reading

Biggar, H. P., ed. *Works of Samuel de Champlain.* Toronto: University of Toronto Press, 1971. Contains the French text and English translation, and is probably the definitive edition.

Parkman, Francis. *La Salle and the Discovery of the Great West.* Boston: Little, Brown, and Company, 1897. This volume of Parkman's great work on New France is marked by good scholarship and sound composition.

De Champlain, Samuel. *Voyages of Samuel De Champlain.* Translated by Charles P. Otis.

New York: Ben Franklin Press, 1964. 13 vols. An excellent translation, similar in form and purpose to that by the Bournes though the Bourne notes are better.

Winsor, Justin. *From Cartier to Frontenac: Geographical Discovery in the Interior of North America in Its Historical Relations, 1534-1700.* Boston: Houghton, Mifflin Co., 1894. Like all of Winsor's works, a competent book with many good maps and illustrations, but with no notes or bibliography.

Eccles, William J. *France in America. New American Nation* series. New York: Harper & Row Publishers, 1972. This volume contains a good account of early French exploration of the St. Lawrence and Great Lakes area.

Morison, Samuel Eliot. *Samuel de Champlain: Father of New France.* Boston: Little, Brown, and Company, 1972. Based readily on Champlain's writings, this biography is written in informal style to honor one of the greatest pioneers, explorers, and colonists of all times.

# SETTLEMENT OF JAMESTOWN

*Type of event:* Politico-economic: establishment of a British colony as a commercial enterprise
*Time:* May 24, 1607
*Locale:* Jamestown, Virginia

*Principal personages:*

SIR FERDINANDO GORGES (1566?-1647), leader in the English mercantile community and coauthor of the petition for chartering the Virginia Company

SIR JOHN POPHAM (1531?-1607), Lord Chief Justice of England and coauthor of the petition for chartering the Virginia Company

SIR THOMAS SMYTHE (1558?-1625), active commercial promoter in early seventeenth century England who became head of the Virginia Company in 1609

CHRISTOPHER NEWPORT (?-1617), sea captain who commanded the first voyage to Jamestown

EDWARD MARIA WINGFIELD (1560?-?1613), first president of the council in Jamestown

CAPTAIN JOHN SMITH (1580-1631), second president of the council in Jamestown

POWHATAN (1550?-1618), chieftain of the confederation of Indian tribes in the Jamestown region

SIR GEORGE SOMERS (1554-1610), veteran sea adventurer who commanded the ill-fated fleet of 1609 to Jamestown

THOMAS WEST (LORD DE LA WARR) (1577-1618), first Governor of Virginia after the reorganization of government in 1609

## Summary of Event

In 1605 peace with Spain had finally been won, and in England capital was accumulating and commerce was flourishing. Captain George Weymouth had just returned from a voyage to Nantucket and Maine to explore the possibilities of a refuge for Catholics. The five Indians whom Weymouth had brought back with him and the glowing account of the expedition in James Rosier's *Relation* had attracted much attention.

Their interest having been aroused, Sir John Popham, Lord Chief Justice of England, and Sir Ferdinando Gorges, both powerful members of the mercantile community, petitioned the crown in the name of a group of adventurers for a charter incorporating two companies, one of London and one of Plymouth. The patent issued on April 10, 1606, granted them the territory known as Virginia, located between latitude 34° and 41° North. The London Company was authorized to settle between latitude 34° and 41° North, and the Plymouth Company, between latitude 45° and 38° North, but neither was to settle within one hundred miles of the other. Because of Sir Walter Raleigh's explorations in the Chesapeake Bay area and Weymouth's investigations in Maine, the adventurers knew exactly what to request.

The absence, before 1618, of the official minutes of the Virginia Company, as the two companies were jointly called, has forced historians to turn to fragmentary, and usually biased sources. It seems clear, however, that the central theme of Virginia's early history was the pursuit of England's national interest. The instructions concerning the manner in which the enterprise was to be carried out indicate that it was strictly a commercial undertaking.

On December 20, 1606, the Virginia Company of London dispatched for America three ships, the *Goodspeed,* the *Discovery,* and the *Sarah Constant,* carrying 144 men and boys. Captain Christopher Newport, a well-known sailor of fortune, was to be in charge until the expedition reached land. Entering Chesapeake Bay on April 26, 1607, the 105 survivors searched for a favorable site to settle. On May 24, they disembarked and called the place "Jamestown." Although the area was low and marshy, it was beautiful, defensible, and provided anchorage for deepwater vessels. The great James river offered the possibility of penetration into the interior for exploring and trading with natives.

Only when the settlers had landed and opened the sealed box containing their instructions, did they learn the names of their council, or local governing body, which had been appointed by the company. This council was inferior to a royal council in England appointed by the king. Unfortunately, a considerable number of the settlers were headstrong adventurers, and the lack of a concentrated authority in Virginia, combined with a plethora of would-be leaders, resulted in bickering and the formation of factions. Only the strong leadership of Captain John Smith, the second president of the council, held the settlement together after fear and suspicion led to the ousting of the council's first president, Edward Maria Wingfield.

More pressing than matters of government was the necessity of providing for the settlers' physical needs. Upon their arrival in America, they had divided themselves into three groups: the first was to concentrate on construction and fortifications; the second was to plant crops and keep watch downriver; and the third was to explore the surrounding area. Although the company hoped to find a water route through the continent to the South Sea and encouraged search for minerals, there was little time for such adventurous activity. Establishment of a settlement and development of trade were more urgent matters to be considered.

The successful accomplishment of both these aims depended upon the establishment of amicable relations with the Indians. Such good relations were not achieved easily because the settlers not only insisted upon their right to share the plentiful resources of the country with the Indians, but also tried to convert the red men to Christianity and the European way of life.

Although the strict discipline of John Smith's council presidency and the addition of more immigrants improved conditions at the settlement, the first two years must be judged as disappointing. The adventurers in London therefore embarked upon a more ambitious program to be financed on a joint-stock basis. Having negotiated a new charter, the Virginia Company, under the leadership of Sir Thomas Smythe (originally Smith), launched a vigorous campaign for financial support. Sixteen hundred persons were to emigrate to Virginia on two great expeditions in the summer of 1609. The joint-stock arrangement would allow a pooling of labor with common stock, since each person's migration to America was counted as equal to one share of stock. By this means a community of interest was developed between the adventurer in England and the colonist.

The new charter of 1609 abolished the royal council and placed control in the hands of the council of the company. A governor with absolute authority was to replace the local council in the colony.

The first great contingent of settlers, carrying with them so many hopes, set out on May 15, 1609, with Sir George Somers in command. Ironically, the ship carrying the leaders was blown away from the others in a hurricane and foundered in Bermuda, its passengers not arriving in Jamestown until nearly a year after they had set out. To make matters worse, when the other ships arrived in Virginia, Captain John Smith refused to give up his post as council president, though eventually he yielded leadership to Captain George Percy.

The arrival of almost four hundred new settlers in weakened condition placed considerable strain upon the economy of the colony and set in motion a cruel set of circumstances. When the leaders of the expedition arrived the following summer, they found only sixty settlers still living, with the settlement in ruins about them. Famine, disease, and attacks by Indians had left even the few survivors on the brink of death. Since the new arrivals were without sufficient provisions, the settlers abandoned hope of maintaining the colony and prepared to leave for England by way of Newfoundland. But as the disheartened colonists were sailing down the James river, miraculously they met Thomas West (Lord De La Warr), their new Governor, coming up. Lord De La Warr ordered the colonists to return and reëstablish the settlement. The new leadership, with additional supplies and manpower, gave the colonists courage to continue. Many difficult days lay ahead, but the Virginia Company was determined to keep the colony alive.

## Pertinent Literature

Craven, Wesley F. *The Southern Colonies in the Seventeenth Century, 1607-1689.* Baton Rouge: Louisiana State University Press, 1949.

In his account of the settlement of Jamestown, Craven exhibits a rare talent for conveying genuine feeling for the event which he is describing. Craven pictures Jamestown Island as the colonists must have seen it for the first time from the James river. He describes the entire Chesapeake Bay area as John Smith probably explored it in his expedition of 1608. Yet it is not only through his descriptions of the setting and the colonists' experiences that

Craven helps the reader to understand them. He also analyzes the factors which probably prompted particular policies and activities concerning the colony within the seventeenth century setting.

Craven points out that the paucity of unbiased source materials relating to Jamestown has allowed historians to give a number of different interpretations of the reasons for the establishment of the colony. There can be no question, he states, that the pursuit of the national interest was the central theme in Virginia's early history. While he acknowledges the importance of the English mercantile community, he sees it as "an instrument for the achievement of national ends" within "a chronicle of epic proportions." Keeping this theme in mind, Craven offers new insight into the matter of the unfortunate division of authority in the original government of Jamestown. The decision to place a royal council in control was logical in the light of the stability which royal authority would give the colony. One of the most difficult tasks facing the colonists was the transplanting of forms of authority to the wilderness environment.

Despite the temptation to look upon the settlers' early exploration in search of a passage to the South Sea and of gold and mineral deposits as naïve and foolish, these projects appear logical within the context of the pursuit of the national interest. Was it not natural, asks Craven, for the settlers to explore and experiment in the hope of producing an early return to be reinvested in future endeavors?

By present-day standards the settlers' attitude toward the Indians appears as hypocritical and unfeeling, yet it was no more hypocritical than that of any other people, Craven contends. The land and resources seemed to be unlimited, and the English believed in their natural right to trade. They would simply share the rich resources with the Indians. If they did not claim the land, the Indians would be left to the Catholic missionary efforts of France and Spain. The slowness of English missionary efforts was not the result of any lack of sincerity, Craven argues. The godly intentions so loudly advertised during the campaigns for subscribers simply had to take second place to the more pressing physical needs of the colonists. The settlers were confident that the Indians would soon be converted both to Christianity and to European attitudes of economy and landholding. Powhatan was chieftain of the confederation of Indian tribes in the Jamestown region, and when he refused to coöperate, the settlers were forced to demand tribute of the Indians, but the English remained convinced that the red men would profit from exposure to European values and techniques.

Craven's description of the great campaign of 1609 to recruit subscribers to the company and emigrants to the colony is particularly vivid. Probably spurred on by appeals to their patriotic and religious sentiments, many laborers decided to go "on adventure" in hopes of gaining some land and a return from the joint stock. Others contracted with the company for wages or entered the service of particular colonists or subscribers. The great pooling of labor with common stock created a community of interest and a sense of equality between the colonists and subscribers in England. In the colony itself the pooling of resources and community effort was essential. Craven's ability to convey the hopes, the confusion, and the sufferings of the infant settlement in the wilderness enables the reader to understand the Jamestown experience more fully.

Morton, Richard L. *Colonial Virginia. The Tidewater Period, 1607-1710.* Chapel Hill: University of North Carolina Press, 1960. 2 vols.

This volume is a recent general history of Virginia's colonial period. It does not, however, present any startling new thesis about colonial Virginia, a fact much in evidence in the two chapters on the settlement of Jamestown. These chapters are, in essence, a narration of the principal events after Sir Walter Raleigh's unsuccessful colonizing activities in the 1500's until the "starving time" in the winter of 1609-1610.

Raleigh's efforts at colonizing were a consequence of English interest in the New World. Sir Walter hoped to succeed where his half-brother Sir Humphrey Gilbert had failed, but three attempts to plant a colony in the area called "Virginia" left Raleigh a broken man. Morton sees in Raleigh's failure a valuable lesson which other Englishmen quickly learned: colonization was beyond one man's means. For this reason, those persons interested in colonies turned to the chartered trading company as a device for marshaling the necessary human, material, and capital resources. By 1606, a group of men secured a charter for the company which successfully planted a colony in North America.

In analyzing the motives of the London Company's organizers, Morton does not present the detailed examination offered by Wesley Frank Craven. Instead, he catalogues the traditional reasons: trade with the natives, the desire to find a Northwest Passage to the Orient, the hope of duplicating Spain's discovery of gold and silver. Morton does, however, give a passing reference to colonization as an instrument of national policy which Craven emphasizes.

Morton's account of the landing and the colonists' first years is fairly traditional. He imputes the initial difficulties to poor choices of colonists and leaders. Wingfield, first president of the council in Jamestown, emerges as an inept leader who was hampered by his gentle background and poor health, but Morton is less condemnatory of Wingfield and the council than he is of scholars, such as Thomas Jefferson Wertenbaker and Alexander Brown.

It is John Smith who emerges as the colony's savior during the first critical year and a half. Smith's temperament and background suited him to the ordeal, and as long as the wily adventurer remained in the colony it had a chance of survival. When Smith was wounded in a gunpowder explosion, the lack of his steadying influence brought the colony close to disaster during the winter of 1609-1610.

While Smith and the other colonists struggled to make the Virginia venture succeed, Jamestown's backers in London realized that the organization of the colony's government and the lack of adequate funds were hampering the colonists' efforts. Armed with this realization, the London Company sought, and obtained from the Crown, a new charter which reorganized and refinanced the entire operation. This reorganization led to the sending of the "third supply" of men and material. The arrival of new colonists late in the summer of 1609, however, was followed by nearly total disaster the following winter. Morton argues that had these new arrivals and the other colonists been directed by a "strong and forceful leader," the winter of 1609-1610 would not have become the 'starving time." Responsibility for the widespread suffering and death lay with the leaders who replaced Smith after his accident. Only the timely arrival of Thomas West (Lord De La Warr) in the spring of 1610 prevented the colony's demise.

Although Morton's treatment of the settlement of Jamestown is not as detailed as that of Craven, it does provide a clear account of the establishment of the first permanent English settlement in North America. — *W.M.B.*

## Additional Recommended Reading

McCary, Ben C. *Indians in Seventeenth-Century Virginia.* Williamsburg: Virginia 350th Anniversary Celebration Corporation, 1957. Concentrating on the Powhatans, this booklet by the foremost authority on the subject describes the culture of seventeenth century Virginia Indians.

Barbour, Philip L. *The Three Worlds of Captain John Smith.* Boston: Houghton Mifflin Co., 1964. The most recent biography of John Smith, which explodes many of the myths which have grown up around him.

Smith, Bradford. *Captain John Smith, His Life and Legend.* Philadelphia: J. B. Lippincott Company, 1953. This laudatory biography presents evidence that the adventures described by John Smith in his writings, long considered of questionable veracity, are indeed true.

Andrews, Charles M. *The Colonial Period of American History.* Vols. I-III: *The Settlements;* Vol. IV: *England's Commercial and Colonial Policy.* New Haven: Yale University Press, 1934-1938. In the first volume Andrews details events in London to provide background in understanding the founding of Virginia.

Wertenbaker, Thomas J. *Virginia Under the Stuarts, 1607-1688.* Princeton: Princeton University Press, 1914. Highly sympathetic toward the colonists and critical of the London Company, this account begins with the 1607 landing and details the early struggle for survival.

Notestein, Wallace. *The English People on the Eve of Colonization, 1603-1630.* New York: Harper & Row Publishers, 1954. A brief but penetrating analysis of the English people at the beginning of the colonizing activities.

# CALLING OF THE FIRST GENERAL ASSEMBLY IN VIRGINIA

*Type of event:* Political: beginning of representative government in British North America
*Time:* July, 1619
*Locale:* Virginia

*Principal personages:*

SIR EDWIN SANDYS (1561-1629), Treasurer of the London Company, who instructed the governor of Virginia to call the first General Assembly

SIR GEORGE YEARDLEY (1587?-1627), Governor of Virginia, who presided over the first session of the General Assembly

SIR SAMUEL ARGALL (fl. 1609-1624), Deputy Governor of Virginia 1617-1619

JOHN PORY (1572-1635), Secretary of the colony and Speaker of the House of Burgesses in its first session

## Summary of Event

By 1618 Virginia had been in existence for a decade, but the colony had neither prospered nor realized the expectations of the London Company which had been responsible for founding it. Twice before 1618, the London Company had been reorganized in unsuccessful efforts to make the Virginia venture turn a profit, and it was again on the verge of bankruptcy. As inducements to settlement, the company had sanctioned the introduction of private land tenure and the creation of particular plantations which had resulted in widely scattered settlements and confusion over land titles. Even so, the colony's economic base was insecure, and the colonists grew more restive, especially after 1617 when Sir Samuel Argall became governor and returned the colony to stricter discipline by rigorously enforcing the *Lawes, Divine, Morall, and Martiall.*

Against this background, the London Company in 1618 resolved anew to revitalize its Virginia venture. Led by Sir Edwin Sandys, the company embarked upon an ambitious course of action which aimed at a comprehensive reorganization of the entire colonial operation. The company embodied its plans in a series of instructions and commissions, the so-called "Great Charter," which was designed to reform land tenure, to improve local administration, and to supplant the *Lawes, Divine, Morall, and Martiall* with English common law and a more representative resident government.

Accordingly, the London Company instructed its newly appointed Governor, Sir George Yeardley, to call an assembly consisting of himself, a Council of State appointed by the company, and burgesses elected by the freemen of the colony. The assembly would meet not more than once a year, except upon "very extraordinary and important occasions." It would serve as a court of justice, and it was to have the power to enact such general laws and ordinances for the colony's welfare as

65

should seem necessary. These laws were to be subject to a gubernatorial veto and review by the London Company.

Following his arrival in Jamestown, Yeardley issued a call for the assembly, and on July 30, 1619, the first meeting of a representative legislative body in the New World convened in the church at Jamestown. It was composed of the Governor, six councilors, and twenty-two burgesses—two from each of eleven settlements ("plantations," "hundreds," and towns). The burgesses had been elected by the votes of all who were seventeen years old or older. After selecting John Pory (secretary of the colony and a member of the council) as Speaker, and taking the oaths of allegiance and supremacy, the general assembly proceeded to its business.

After deliberating on the qualifications of its members (two of whom were rejected pending clarification of their patents from the London Company), the assembly moved on to its legislative work. It adopted several revisions of the Great Charter which the company had suggested, and enacted a series of laws dealing with such matters as Indian relations, the dress and conduct of the settlers, church attendance, and measures to promote certain industries, including the manufacture of flax, hemp, silk, and wine. After resolving some criminal cases, "the intemperature of the weather and the falling sick of divers of the Burgesses" forced Yeardley to terminate the assembly after a session of only six days.

Despite the brevity of the meeting, the General Assembly of Virginia had made an important beginning. It had ushered in a new departure in colonial government, and had transformed Virginia "from a mere plantation colony, supported and governed by a trading company largely for profit, into a political community, self-supporting and partially self-governing." While the assembly would undergo modifications in its functions, and its right to exist would be challenged after the London Company lost its charter in 1625, that first meeting in July, 1619, established the precedent for the development of representative political institutions in English North America. And, except for a few interruptions, the General Assembly of Virginia has continued to this day.

## Pertinent Literature

Wertenbaker, Thomas J. *Virginia Under the Stuarts, 1607-1688.* Reprint ed. New York: Russell and Russell, 1958.

Thomas Jefferson Wertenbaker was a pioneer in the study of seventeenth century Virginia history. Writing *Virginia Under the Stuarts* at a time when history had only begun to emerge as an academic discipline, his work left a profound impression on subsequent scholars. Nowhere is this fact more in evidence than in Wertenbaker's treatment of the origins of the first General Assembly.

Reaching intellectual maturity when Charles A. Beard, Carl Becker, and other historians were developing what is now known as the "progressive school of historiography," Wertenbaker shared the prevailing assumptions about the processes of history. Consequently, in his analysis of the origins of the General Assembly, Wertenbaker posited a fundamental conflict between James I, King of Great Britain, and his people over what forms of government should exist in Virginia. James, he argued, "had no desire to see the liberal institutions of the Mother Country transplanted to Virginia." Instead, the King wished to keep the colony dependent upon himself, thus augmenting the power of the Crown and making it less dependent upon Parliament.

But the London Company resisted such encroachments. Led by Sir Edwin Sandys, a liberal faction within the company attempted, through successive revisions of the company's charter, to put the government of the colony more in the people's hands. A conservative faction of the company tried to thwart these aims, but that effort was frustrated when Sandys became company treasurer in 1619 and drafted a set of instructions which gave the Virginia colonists broad jurisdiction over their affairs and allowed them to establish democratic institutions in the New World.

These instructions, or the "Virginia Magna Charta" as Wertenbaker termed them, were the cornerstones of liberty in the New World. The establishment of the first representative assembly provided a bulwark against tyranny and the royal prerogative until 1776.

Wertenbaker evinced an abiding fascination with the growth of the General Assembly, for it was through that institution that one could examine the people's struggle for political power. Viewed in these terms, Wertenbaker assumed that the General Assembly, from its inception, acquired all the characteristics of a fully grown, modern legislative assembly. From the start, he maintained, the people's representatives, the members of the House of Burgesses, began to check any encroachment on the people's rights. The entire colonial history of Virginia could be explained in terms of this ongoing struggle.

Unfortunately, few scholars have challenged Wertenbaker's assumptions; present knowledge regarding the origin and the development of the General Assembly has not yet progressed much beyond the pioneering work of Thomas Jefferson Wertenbaker.

Craven, Wesley F. *The Dissolution of the Virginia Company: The Failure of a Colonial Experiment.* Reprint ed. Gloucester, Massachusetts: Peter Smith Publisher, Inc., 1964.

One scholar who has not accepted the Wertenbaker assumptions about the origins of the General Assembly of Virginia is Wesley Frank Craven. Commencing with the premise that "the most common error in writing the history of the Virginia Company has been a failure to understand the fundamental character of that corporation," Craven constructed a thesis which de-

nies most of the arguments advanced by Wertenbaker.

Craven argues that the "true *motif* of the company's history is economic rather than political." The company's reorganization and the issuance of new instructions to Sir George Yeardley in 1618, were not prompted by the liberal political theories of Sir Edwin Sandys, but by a hard-headed desire to make

67

the Virginia venture turn a profit. The so-called "Great Charter" represented the culmination of a two-year debate on the colony's future and the adoption of a new course of action which, it was hoped, would put Virginia on a firm economic footing. Major alterations were required in the colony's structural organization, including the creation of a general assembly.

As Craven interprets the birth of the assembly, the company envisioned that body as one of two resident councils charged with the management of local affairs. A newly created Council of State would handle daily administrative and judicial matters. The Council of State, together with the Governor and representatives from the colony's local jurisdictions, would meet annually to ratify company instructions and to enact local laws. The new government would, in short, act in a manner similar to that of the parent company.

To buttress his thesis concerning the company's purpose in altering the government of Virginia, Craven under-takes a comprehensive examination of Sir George Yeardley's instructions. He demonstrates that the portion which provided for the establishment of the assembly was only a small part of a larger plan. Most of the instructions dealt with such matters as the provision of adequate supplies, the maintenance of good morals, and most importantly, the settlement of land tenure and internal organization. Their objective was the establishment of a uniform system of management with limited local control.

Viewed in these terms, the creation of the General Assembly was not the signal event which Wertenbaker saw. In Craven's opinion, the calling of the first assembly in 1619 was "merely one of many improvements made in the colony's life" before the company's dissolution. The convening of the assembly did provide a precedent for the future, but the assembly's growth into a representative legislative body would be a slow, evolutionary process. — *W.M.B.*

### Additional Recommended Reading

Morton, Richard L. *Colonial Virginia*. Vol. I: *The Tidewater Period, 1607-1710.* Ch. 4. Chapel Hill: University of North Carolina Press, 1960. This summary statement on the House of Burgesses leans toward the Wertenbaker analysis but recognizes some of Craven's revisions.

Craven, Wesley F. " '. . . And so the Form of Government Became Perfect,' " in *Virginia Magazine of History and Biography*. LXXVII (April, 1969), 131-146. Craven's most recent analysis of the origins and growth of Virginia's General Assembly.

Bruce, Philip A. *Institutional History of Virginia in the Seventeenth Century*. Vol. II, part v, chs. XIX-XXII. New York: Charles Scribner's Sons, 1910. The classic institutional study of the House of Burgesses.

Van Schreeven, William J. and George H. Reese, eds. *Proceedings of the General Assembly of Virginia, July 30-August 4, 1619, Written and Sent from Virginia to England by Mr. John Pory*. Jamestown, Virginia: The Jamestown Foundation, 1969. The newest and best edition of Pory's account of the first proceedings of the first General Assembly.

# ARRIVAL OF THE FIRST NEGROES AND THE ORIGINS OF SLAVERY IN BRITISH NORTH AMERICA

*Type of event:* Sociological: slavery arising from the need for a labor force
*Time:* August, 1619
*Locale:* Jamestown, Virginia

## Summary of Event

In 1619 a Dutch warship carrying twenty African Negroes landed at Jamestown, Virginia. These Negroes, the first to arrive in the British colonies, were put to work not as slaves but as servants. Neither the laws of the Mother Country nor the charter of the colony established the institution of slavery, though the system was developing in the British Sugar Islands at this time, and was almost one hundred years old in the Spanish and Portuguese colonies. To be sure, Negro servants were early discriminated against—their terms of service were usually longer than those of white servants, and they were the object of certain prohibitions which were not imposed on white servants—but in the early seventeenth century at least some Negro servants, like their white counterparts, gained their freedom and even acquired some property. Anthony Johnson, who was freed about a year after coming to Virginia in 1621, imported five servants thirty years later, receiving 250 acres on their head rights. Another former servant, a carpenter named Richard Johnson, obtained one hundred acres for importing two white servants in 1654. These two men were part of the small class of free Negroes that existed in Virginia throughout the colonial period.

Such cases as the two Johnsons were rare by mid-century. As early as the 1640's some Negroes were already serving for life, and their numbers increased throughout the decade. In 1640, for example, in a court decision involving three runaway servants, two of them, who were white, were sentenced to an additional four years of service, while the other, a Negro named John Punch, was ordered to serve his master "for the time of his natural Life." In the 1650's some Negro servants were being sold for life, and the bills of sale indicated that their offspring would inherit slave status. Thus slavery developed according to custom before it was legally established in Virginia.

Not until 1661 was chattel slavery recognized by statute in Virginia, and then only indirectly. The following year, the House of Burgesses passed a law declaring that children followed the status of their mothers, thereby rendering the system of slavery self-perpetuating. In 1667 the Virginia Assembly further strengthened the system by declaring that in the case of "children that are slaves by birth . . . the conferring of baptisme doth not alter the condition of a person as to his bondage or freedome; that divers masters, freed from this doubt, may more carefully endeavour the propagation of christianity." Until this time, Americans had justified enslavement of Africans on the ground that they were heathen, and had recognized conversion as a way to freedom. This act closed

69

the last avenue to freedom, apart from manumission, available to Negro slaves. By the beginning of the eighteenth century, Virginia had established a slave code which completed the gradual process by which most Negroes were reduced to the status of chattels. Slaves could not bear arms or own property, nor could they leave the plantation without written permission from the master. Capital punishment was provided for murder and rape; lesser crimes were punished by maiming, whipping, or branding. Special courts were established for the trials of slaves, and Negroes were barred from serving as witnesses, except in cases where slaves were being tried for capital offenses.

In the other British colonies the pattern was similar to that of Virginia. Negro slavery existed early in both Maryland and the Carolinas. Georgia attempted to exclude slavery at the time of settlement, but the trustees eventually yielded to the protests of the colonists and repealed the prohibition in 1750. The Dutch brought slavery to the Middle colonies early in the seventeenth century. The advent of British rule in 1664 proved to be a stimulus to the system in New York and New Jersey; but in Pennsylvania and Delaware the religious objections of the Quakers delayed its growth somewhat and postponed legal recognition of slavery until the early eighteenth century. In seventeenth century New England the status of Negroes was ambig-

uous, as it was in Virginia. There were slaves in Massachusetts as early as 1638, possibly before, though slavery was not recognized by statute until 1641. New England became heavily involved in the slave trade, particularly after the monopoly of the Royal African Company was revoked in 1698. Like Virginia, all the colonies enacted slave codes in the late seventeenth or early eighteenth century, although the New England codes were less harsh than those of the Middle or Southern colonies. In all the colonies a small class of free Negroes developed alongside the institution of slavery, despite the fact that manumission was restricted.

Slavery grew slowly in the seventeenth century. In 1625 there were twenty-three Negroes in Virginia, and most of them were probably servants, not slaves. By mid-century, a decade before statutory recognition of slavery, the Negro population was only three hundred. But in 1700 there were twelve thousand Negroes and eighteen thousand whites. In the Carolinas the Negro population was about equal to the white population, whereas in New England Negroes numbered only about one thousand out of a total population of ninety thousand. The eighteenth century would see the rapid development of the system of Negro slavery, particularly in the Southern colonies where it became an integral part of the emerging plantation economy.

## Pertinent Literature

Jordan, Winthrop D. *White Over Black: American Attitudes Toward the Negro, 1550-1812.* Chapel Hill: University of North Carolina Press, 1968.

Winthrop Jordan's monumental study of American attitudes toward the Negro sheds new light on the origins of slavery in the British colonies, long a controversial issue among American historians. The contemporary debate goes back to 1950 when Oscar and Mary Handlin published an article in the *William and Mary Quarterly* entitled "Origins of the Southern Labor System." They argued that enslavement of Negroes in the Southern colonies was a relatively late and gradual process. Originally, Negroes were servants, but whereas the condition of white servants improved throughout the seventeenth century, the status of Negroes gradually deteriorated until, in the 1660's, they had been reduced to the status of chattels. In addition, economic conditions, particularly the growth of the plantation system, conspired to degrade the condition of the Negro. In the Handlins' view, American Negro slavery did not develop in imitation of other systems, nor was it "a response to any unique qualities in the Negro himself." Rather, it was a product of the adjustment of "traditional European conceptions of servitude" to the peculiar conditions of the American environment.

In 1959, Carl Degler challenged the Handlins' thesis in an article in *Comparative Studies in Society and History* (later incorporated into his survey of American history, *Out of Our Past: The Forces That Shaped Modern America*). Against the Handlins' view that enslavement of the Negro was a consequence of factors other than racism,

Degler argued "that the status of the Negro in the English colonies was worked out within a framework of discrimination." Degler demonstrated that prejudice against the Negro existed before slavery was legally established. "As a result, slavery, when it developed in the English colonies, could not help but be infused with the social attitude which had prevailed from the beginning, namely, that Negroes were inferior."

Writing in 1968, Winthrop Jordan suggested a new way of looking at an old problem. He argued that slavery and prejudice were two sides of the same coin, "twin aspects of a general debasement of the Negro." A "mutual relationship" developed between slavery and prejudice. "Rather than slavery causing 'prejudice,' or vice versa, they seem rather to have generated each other. . . . Slavery and 'prejudice' may have been equally cause and effect, continuously reacting upon each other, dynamically joining hands to hustle the Negro down the road to complete degradation."

One source of both slavery and prejudice in the colonies was the image of the Negro which the British took with them to the New World. Sixteenth and seventeenth century Britons emphasized the distinctive appearance and condition of Africans and saw them as essentially "a separate category of men." The Negro's color had long been a "symbol of baseness and evil"; the fact that he was a heathen also set him apart from the British, as did his condition of savagery, which

Britons tended to associate with beastliness and lecherousness. Transplanted to the New World, seventeenth century British colonists retained the attitude of their forefathers toward Negroes. Though British institutions provided no model for the system of chattel slavery which ultimately developed, Britons both at home and in the New World did possess a concept of slavery "formed by the clustering of several rough but not illogical equations. The slave was treated like a beast. Slavery was inseparable from the evil in men; it was God's punishment upon Ham's prurient disobedience. Enslavement was captivity, the loser's lot in a contest of power. Slaves were infidels or heathens." It is not difficult to see the implications of this concept of slavery, however vague, for the recently discovered "new men" of Africa. As Jordan observes, "On every count, Negroes qualified."

Thus the very qualities which made the Negro distinctive in the minds of sixteenth and seventeenth century British colonists also identified him as a slave, even before the system of slavery had been legally established. The practices of other nations in setting up systems of involuntary servitude rein-forced the equation between Negroes and slavery. Economic necessities, especially the universal need for labor in the colonies, also played upon the settlers' ideas about Negroes and slavery. Above all, Jordan emphasizes the sense of difference which British colonists experienced between themselves and the Negro, a sense of difference in which the African's heathenism and color played the crucial role. The religious distinction was probably more significant in the early years of settlement, according to Jordan, but during the seventeenth century a shift of emphasis occurred which made the Negro's color seem the more important distinguishing characteristic.

Thus a whole range of factors—foreign models, traditional concepts of slavery and servitude, the environment of the New World, the British reaction to Negroes, and above all the "sense of difference" between the two races—led to the "unthinking decision" by which slavery was established in the British colonies. In describing the complex of rational and irrational impulses underlying that decision, Jordan has made a considerable contribution to our understanding of such a momentous event.

Greene, Lorenzo J. *The Negro in Colonial New England.* New York: Columbia University Press, 1942; reprinted, Atheneum Press, 1968.

This early work, now reprinted, studies the condition of free and slave Negroes in colonial New England. As portrayed by Greene, slavery in New England contrasts sharply with the system that existed in the rest of the colonies; the system of involuntary servitude which developed in that region was milder than that of the Middle or Southern colonies. One reason was the comparatively small number of Negroes, which in turn dictated less severe restrictions. Significantly, where the proportion of Negroes to whites was high, as in Boston and South Kingston, Rhode Island, local regulations were harsh.

Another reason for the comparative mildness of New England slavery was the religious and social philosophy of

72

Puritanism. New Englanders offered religious as well as legal and economic justifications for slavery, but their religion also introduced an element of ambiguity into the system. New England slavery was "a curious blending of servitude and bondage"; the slave occupied "a more or less indeterminate status, varying between that of person and that of property." As property, slaves could be bought, sold, and taxed. As persons, they had some of the legal rights enjoyed by freemen: the right to life, to own property and make contracts, to serve in the armed forces, and to testify and bring suit in the courts. A number of slaves actually sued their masters for freedom and some of them won their liberty by such means. The influence of Puritanism is also seen in the fact that masters were encouraged to provide religious and secular instruction for their slaves, and in the shaping of the family life of the slaves.

Paradoxically, although the Puritan religious and social philosophy shaped a milder system of slavery in New England than existed in the other British colonies, the condition of free Negroes in that region "was probably no more favorable than elsewhere in colonial America." Free Negroes occupied a legal status inferior to that of whites, could not vote, were excluded from the militia, and suffered economic discrimination as well. Despite these proscriptions, a number of free Negroes gained prominence in New England, including the poet Phillis Wheatley and Captain Paul Cuffee, a famous Quaker merchant, philanthropist, and colonizer of Liberia.

Greene wrote before the present debate regarding the relation between slavery and prejudice, but his contrast between the lot of slaves and that of free Negroes raises some interesting questions which, when answered, may shed further light on the complicated process which led to the general debasement of the Negro in seventeenth century America. — *A.C.L.*

## Additional Recommended Reading

Herskovits, Melville J. *The Myth of the Negro Past.* Boston: Beacon Press, 1941. This pioneer work studies the African cultural heritage which the Negro brought to the New World and which survives in the United States in various forms.

Craven, Wesley F. *The Southern Colonies in the Seventeenth Century, 1607-1689.* Baton Rouge: Louisiana State University Press, 1949. In this general survey of the Southern colonies, Craven argues that prejudice on the part of white settlers led to early enslavement of the Negro.

Russell, John H. *The Free Negro in Virginia, 1619-1865.* Baltimore: The Johns Hopkins University Press, 1913. Russell was one of the first historians to argue that the early status of Negroes in Virginia approximated servitude rather than slavery. The subject of this study is the class of free Negroes which existed prior to the development of slavery in Virginia and persisted even after it was legally established in 1662.

Mannix, Daniel P. and Malcolm Cowley. *Black Cargoes: A History of the Atlantic Slave Trade, 1518-1865.* New York: Viking Press, 1962. Unique in its broad coverage, this book offers a general picture of the Atlantic slave trade from its beginnings, through its abolition in the early nineteenth century and the rise of an illegal trade, to its downfall in the 1860's when slavery was abolished in the United States.

# LANDING OF THE PILGRIMS AT PLYMOUTH

*Type of event:* Sociological: early stages of European migration to America
*Time:* December 25, 1620 (1620-1626)
*Locale:* Plymouth, Massachusetts

### Principal personages:

WILLIAM BRADFORD (1590-1657), second Governor of Plymouth and the Pilgrims' principal leader during his lifetime

WILLIAM BREWSTER (1567-1644), leader in the Scrooby congregation and elder of the Pilgrim church at Plymouth

JOHN CARVER (1576?-1621), first Governor of Plymouth

THOMAS WESTON (1575?-?1644), leader of a group of London merchant adventurers who obtained the patent and provided the financial backing for the Plymouth venture

SAMOSET (fl. early seventeenth century), Wampanoag Indian chief who first befriended the Pilgrims

SQUANTO (?-1622), Patuxent Indian who came to live at Plymouth as adviser and interpreter

## Summary of Event

Meeting at the home of William Brewster, the postmaster, a small group of yeomen farmers in the village of Scrooby, England, decided in 1606 to form a congregation separate from the Church of England. Called Brownists, after Robert Browne, the founder of the Separatist movement—and considered to be radicals by their neighbors—the group was concerned more with the politics than the theology of their religion. The Church, they believed, should be essentially democratic, consisting of equal members joined together in a covenant. In 1608, the Scrooby congregation, determined to escape the scoffs of their neighbors and the harassment of the authorities, emigrated to Holland. After a brief sojourn in Amsterdam, they moved to Leyden and soon settled into the life of the city. Although they could worship freely in Holland, the "Pilgrims," as they called themselves, were disturbed by their children's loss of contact with English culture, by the difficulty of gaining entrance to the Dutch guilds, and by the threat of war with Spain.

The Pilgrims were in all likelihood familiar with stories of the explorations in the New World and with the settlement in Virginia. Although they possessed neither adequate resources, nor patrons, nor a patent, they decided to go to America. Fortunately for them, the Virginia Company was at this time attempting to cure its financial ills by offering privileges and plantations to "undertakers" who would set up private plantations. With the help of Sir Edwin Sandys, they secured a patent on June 19, 1619, and an unofficial assurance that the King would not molest them. Although the patent provided that they should settle within Anglican Virginia, they were to be allowed to live as a distinct body with their own government, subject only to

74

the laws of the colony as a whole. They expected to obtain a grant of religious toleration. During the delay that ensued while the Pilgrims awaited royal approval of their grant, Thomas Weston, the leader of a group of London merchant adventurers, obtained a patent from the Virginia Company in the name of John Pierce, one of his associates. Approaching the Pilgrims in Leyden, he persuaded them to abandon their patent and join his group with the promise that the adventurers would supply the funds and handle the business end of the undertaking.

According to the agreement reached by the two parties, those persons going to the colony were to stand as equal partners with the London adventurers in the company. Three groups shared in the investment: seventy London adventurers who paid ten pounds sterling per share; planters who received one share each for their labor; and adventurer planters who were reckoned as having two shares each, one by purchase and a second by going to America. The adventurers in London were to exercise no civil authority over the planters.

In addition to the forty-eight officers and crew, 101 passengers departed from Plymouth, England, on September 16, 1620. The Pilgrims comprised less than half the group. There were thirty-five Pilgrims from Leyden, but of the sixty-six passengers recruited by the adventurers from London and Southampton, most were "strangers." Because the *Speedwell,* in which the Pilgrims had come from Leyden, proved unseaworthy, all had to crowd aboard the *Mayflower* at Plymouth.

On November 9, Cape Cod was sighted. Although they were outside the bounds of their patent and at first planned to continue southward to Virginia, treacherous seas convinced the immigrants that they should remain in New England. In order to avoid future difficulties with some of the "strangers" who seemed inclined toward mutiny, the Pilgrims drafted an agreement called the "Mayflower Compact," which was in the form of a Separatist Church covenant. By its terms, the forty-one signatories (nearly all the adult male passengers) formed a "civill body politick" giving them the power to enact laws for the common good and obligating all to obey such laws.

After several parties had explored the area, one group landed on December 11 at Plymouth, as it had already been named by Captain John Smith during his earlier exploration of the region. The *Mayflower* then entered the bay, and by December 25 a site had been chosen and work had begun on a common house. The Pilgrims' choice of a site for settlement was extremely fortunate. Because an epidemic had decimated the Patuxent Indians who inhabited the area around Plymouth, there was no threat of hostile neighbors, and there was cleared land ready for planting.

Although the winter of 1620-1621 was a mild one, over half the settlers, weakened by hardships experienced during the voyage, died of pneumonia, tuberculosis, or scurvy. Upon the death of Governor John Carver in the spring, William Bradford, who would be the Pilgrims' outstanding leader for thirty-five years, succeeded him in office. When members of the Wampanoag Indian tribe, most notably Samoset, appeared, they proved to be friendly and helpful. Squanto, the last of the Patuxents, became a permanent resident of Plymouth and Bradford's closest friend and agricultural adviser.

The residents of Plymouth were simple farmers and artisans almost totally lacking in formal education. None of the Pilgrim leaders had experience in government, but with the Scriptures as their guide, they sought to establish a Christian commonwealth in which civil and religious functions would be kept separate. Often disturbed by what they considered the improper and immoral activities of the "strangers" among them, the Pilgrims were concerned with maintaining the purity of their way of life. They accused the merchant adventurers of trying to undermine the religious exclusiveness of the colony. Because their original patent was useless outside Virginia, the merchant adventurers obtained from the Council of New England in June, 1621, a new patent which granted the lands to the Pilgrims and merchants jointly.

During the first year at Plymouth, the Pilgrims experienced hunger and great hardship. Their plight was complicated by the arrival of new settlers whom Thomas Weston had directed to be housed and fed until a new settlement could be established. William Bradford saw that the communal system of agriculture was not producing satisfactory results, and in 1624, he assigned to each family its own parcel of land. The final break with the London merchants came late in 1626 when the Pilgrims bought out their shares in the company.

## Pertinent Literature

Smith, Bradford. *Bradford of Plymouth.* Philadelphia: J. B. Lippincott Company, 1951

Although the Pilgrims who landed at Plymouth in 1620 would have been appalled at the thought of being called democrats, their unabashed admirer Bradford Smith, credits their movement with the founding of American democracy. To the Separatist Church's emphasis upon the voluntary association of equal members bound by a covenant, and upon separation of the Church and the state, Smith attributes the principles embodied in the federal Constitution.

Smith's hero, William Bradford, epitomizes the desires and principles which motivated the Pilgrims. The story of their leader's life is the story of their flight from England and their struggle to maintain their chosen way of life at Plymouth. With convincing verisimilitude Smith conveys the atmosphere of Elizabethan England and of the life which William Bradford probably knew in the village of Scrooby. The orphaned child of a yeoman wool raiser, Bradford took an early interest in religion and joined a Separatist church in which he was influenced by William Brewster. Displaying a decided bias in favor of the Separatists, the author summarizes the events of the Reformation in England and the founding of the Puritan and Separatist movements. Unlike some other historians who contend that the Separatists were merely heckled by their neighbors, Smith relates a tale of harassment and imprisonment by the government, which forced the religious revolutionaries to flee the country.

Smith claims that the Pilgrims formed many of their democratic ideas and institutional concepts during their stay in Holland. He pictures the Dutch as thrifty, wholesome, and resourceful—generally superior to the "be-ribboned dandies" of England. Despite the advantages of the city of Leyden, the Pilgrims wished not only to escape the threat of war with Spain, but also to find a pastoral "Promised Land." Although most historians, including William Bradford, state (and the patent certainly implies) that the *Mayflower* passengers were headed for a settlement in Virginia, Smith insists that the Pilgrims had decided before setting out to avoid living under the laws of Anglican Virginia by landing in New England.

The London adventurers who financed the Plymouth enterprise are the villains of the piece. The eminent colonial historian, Charles M. Andrews, writes that it was simply consistent with good contemporary business practice for the merchants to insist that the lands and buildings in the settlement be divided among the shareholders at the end of seven years and that until then all the settlers' labor be for the common interest. But Smith pictures the adventurers as sinister charlatans bent on making bond servants of the Pilgrims. While it is true that the leader of the adventurers, Thomas Weston, later dealt unfairly with the settlers, Smith's view is colored by his sympathy for the Pilgrims' desire for independence.

One of the strongest points of this book, and the feature that makes it pleasant reading, is the author's feeling for the times. He vividly describes the discomforts aboard the incredibly crowded *Mayflower,* the construction of the houses at Plymouth, the methods of cultivation, the food served at Bradford's table, and many other facets of daily life in the colony. Though he has a tendency to become sentimental while attempting to invest Bradford with emotion, his use of dramatic technique does make the historical personages appear as real people having tempers, prejudices, and a sense of humor. Smith's Bradford barely escapes being too virtuous to be likable. The author admits that his hero was intolerant of lesser men, yet he manages to convey the Pilgrim governor's simple faith and basic practicality.

Bradford, William. *Of Plymouth Plantation, 1620-1647.* Edited by Samuel Eliot Morison. New York: Alfred A. Knopf, Inc., 1952

No portrait or description of William Bradford, the greatest of the Pilgrim leaders, has come down to us from the seventeenth century. But, in the words of Samuel Eliot Morison, Bradford himself created "as fair a permanent monument as any man could wish" in his history *Of Plymouth Plantation.*

The book was employed as a source by several colonial historians before 1730, and was deposited by one of them in a treasury of Americana in Boston's Old South Church. Apparently spirited away by the British during the Revolution, it disappeared until 1855, when it suddenly turned up in the library of the Bishop of London. Complicated negotiations finally succeeded in returning the volume to Massachusetts in 1897. It has come to be recognized not only as a priceless historical source, but also as a literary classic.

*Of Plymouth Plantation* is not a

spiritual autobiography. In fact, its author is extremely reticent about his personal feelings. Yet in relating the hopes, fears, and determination of his people, William Bradford reveals his own character and spirit. Bradford's religion was unquestionably the guiding force in his life. He had no doubt that God had chosen the Separatists as divine instruments for "propagating and advancing the gospel of the kingdom of Christ in those remote parts of the world." In a sense, he—as did another great religious rebel, John Milton—sought in his book to justify the ways of God to man. Satan had wrought the confusion and corruption which held sway over the Church of England during the reigns of Elizabeth and James I. But the Lord himself would assist his "free people" who joined themselves in a covenant "to walk in all His ways made known" though it might cause them hardship.

While the faith of Bradford and the Pilgrims is evident throughout the history, the work is in no way theological. The frequent allusions to God's purpose and to the Pilgrims' assurance of their role in it are those of a man whose religion was a natural part of his existence. Thus the allusions fall naturally within the relation of everyday events. Bradford's style is plain and forceful. Although we may wish that he had done so, he seldom stops to describe the appearance or condition of things, preferring to proceed with the narration of events. Yet this very sparseness of style manages to convey the sparseness of the settlement on the harsh New England coast and of the Pilgrims' plain way of life. With touching sympathy Bradford confides his concern for the apprehensions of his people and for their feelings of desolation and loneliness in the wilderness.

Bradford's business sense and practicality also come to light in his explanations of relations with the merchant adventurers in London and the other settlements in Massachusetts. He cannot hide his indignation over the unfair treatment of the Pilgrims by Thomas Weston, the leader of the adventurers. In his dealings with the adventurers, the Indians, the neighboring settlers, and the unruly members of his own settlement, he merges as a tough-minded, hard-bargaining leader. His intolerance of those outside the Separatist faith, and his harsh treatment of what he considered to be immoral behavior too easily conjure up the picture of the stern, unsmiling Pilgrim in the black cloak and tall black hat. Within the context of his religious convictions, however, these qualities are but further evidence of his belief that he was an instrument of God. — *W.M.B.*

**Additional Recommended Reading**

Adams, James Truslow. *The Founding of New England.* Ch. 5. Magnolia, Massachusetts: Peter Smith Publisher, Inc., 1921. And in paperback by Little, Brown, and Company. In contrast to the "democratic" tradition in historiography, Adams views the persecutions of the Pilgrims with skepticism and also presents the merchant adventurers' side of the economic question.

Andrews, Charles M. *The Colonial Period of American History.* Vol. I: *The Settlements.* Chs. 13 and 14. New Haven: Yale University Press, 1964. An excellent and detailed narrative which is particularly useful in explaining the preliminary arrangements with the London Company and the merchant adventurers.

Morison, Samuel Eliot. "The Pilgrim Fathers: Their Significance in History," in *By Land and By Sea.* New York: Alfred A. Knopf, Inc., 1953. Morison contends that the Pilgrims were of little significance in the development of American political and economic institutions, but their unflagging faith in the face of hardship contributed significantly to our spiritual tradition.

Rutman, Darrett B. *Husbandmen of Plymouth.* Boston: Beacon Press, 1967. Provides details, through extensive statistical information, of the agricultural life which was central to life at Plymouth in the early days.

Willison, George F. *Saints and Strangers.* New York: Reynal and Hitchcock, 1945. Spanning the period from William Brewster's youth to the end of the existence of Plymouth as a separate colony, this detailed account attempts to humanize the Pilgrims by emphasizing their goals and accomplishments.

Langdon, George D., Jr. *The Pilgrim Colony: A History of New Plymouth, 1620-1691.* New Haven: Yale University Press, 1966. An account which emphasizes the advantages of the early settlers over their successors in attaining political and economic power.

# ALGONQUIN INDIANS SELL MANHATTAN ISLAND FOR TWENTY-FOUR DOLLARS

*Type of event:* Economic: desire of the Dutch to legalize their settlement at New Amsterdam and maintain good relations with the Indians
*Time:* May 6, 1626
*Locale:* Manhattan Island, New Netherland

*Principal personages:*

HENRY HUDSON (?-1611), English navigator who explored the Hudson river for the Dutch East India Company and thereby provided the basis for its claim to the area

CORNELIUS MAY (fl. 1624), first Governor of New Netherland, who brought settlers to the area

PETER MINUIT (1580-1638), third Governor and first Director-General of New Netherland, who purchased Manhattan Island and developed New Amsterdam

WILLEM KIEFT (1597-1647), fifth Governor of New Netherland whose efforts to levy taxes on the Indians caused a cruel Indian war

PETER STUYVESANT (1592-1672), last Dutch Governor of New Netherland, who surrendered the colony to the British

## Summary of Event

In the early seventeenth century, the Netherlands, like other nations of northern Europe, sent out explorers to search for a sea route around North America to the riches of the Far East. The principal explorer for the Dutch was Henry Hudson, an Englishman, who, in 1609, explored the river which bears his name. When Hudson and other navigators failed to find the Northwest Passage, the Dutch, like other Europeans, decided to occupy the lands which they claimed in the New World and exploit their resources. While hoping to discover gold and silver as the Spanish had done in the south, the Dutch soon found that the most readily exploitable resource of the middle Atlantic coastal region which they claimed was the furs which they could obtain by trading with the na-

tives. The demand for furs and pelts was so great in Europe that one shipload could make its owners wealthy.

In the interests of further discovery and to stimulate trade, the Dutch parliament, the States-General, granted to its traders and explorers the exclusive right to make four voyages to any new lands which they might explore. Under this grant, in 1614 five ships visited the Hudson river, which the Dutch called the Mauritius. Later that same year, these traders combined as the United New Netherland Company and received a monopoly of the trade of the Hudson Valley from the States-General. Ignoring Manhattan Island, these early traders sailed up the Hudson to the site of present-day Albany, where they erected Fort Nassau on Castle Island as a base of operations and exchanged their goods for the furs of the Mohican Indians. Following the expiration of the charter of the United New Netherland Company in 1618, a succession of different companies exploited the Hudson river fur trade.

In 1621, a number of influential merchants obtained from the States-General a charter for the Dutch West India Company with the sole right to trade on the Atlantic coasts of Africa, and North and South America for twenty-four years. Although the new company was organized primarily to challenge Spanish control of Latin America, it was also interested in the Hudson river area. In 1624, the company dispatched Captain Cornelius May with a shipload of thirty families to settle in North America. Opposite Castle Island they established a trading post named Fort Orange, and formed a settlement on the Delaware river. They may also have established a trading house on Governor's Island in New York Harbor.

The first two governors, Cornelius May and William Verhulst, lived and administered the colony from the Delaware river site, but Peter Minuit, the third governor and first director-general of New Netherland, shifted his base of operations to Manhattan Island. A native of Wesel, then in the Duchy of Cleves, he was probably of French or Walloon descent. Minuit was described as a shrewd and somewhat unscrupulous man. One of his first acts upon arriving on Manhattan Island early in 1626 was to buy the land rights to the island from the Canarsee Indians for sixty guilders, or about twenty-four dollars, in trinkets. Since the Manhattan tribe, for whom it was named, had a better claim to the island

than did the Canarsee, Minuit later also bought the island from them. Through this, their first major land purchase from the Indians, the Dutch secured a semblance of a legal title to Manhattan. At the time of the purchase, it was a beautiful island, being covered with a great forest and abounding with game and wild fruits.

Minuit made New Amsterdam, at the southern tip of Manhattan, the center of Dutch activity in the area. A large fort, pentagonal in shape, surrounded on three sides by a great moat and fronting on the bay, was one of the first structures to be built. When it was finished, Minuit brought several families from Fort Orange to settle in the town, and ordered Fort Nassau on the South river, near present Gloucester, New Jersey, evacuated and the garrison transferred to New Amsterdam. Despite his vigorous administration of the colony, Minuit was recalled to Holland for examination in 1632, and was dismissed from the West India Company's service.

In the meantime, in 1629, the directorate of the company, with the approval of the States-General, issued a Charter of Freedoms and Exemptions which provided for the grant of large estates, called patroonships, to those members of the company who would settle at least fifty persons above the age of fifteen on their lands within four years. Ostensibly designed to promote farming in New Netherland, these grants were intended primarily to encourage settlers to go up the Hudson to settle and make further contacts with the Indians and thereby extend the fur trade. The furs, it was expected, would be sent down the river to New Amsterdam from where the West India

81

Company had the sole right to export them. With one exception, Rensselaerswyck, these patroonships were unsuccessful.

Relations with the Indians remained good, and the fur trade continued to prosper until 1641, when hostilities with the natives broke out. Called Governor Kieft's War, the fighting was caused by the Governor's attempt to collect taxes from the Algonquin tribes for Dutch "protection." The conflict was terminated by a treaty of August 29, 1645. It produced some disruption of the fur trade of the Hudson river and forced Governor Kieft to surrender some of his arbitrary power to advisory bodies in order to obtain popular support for the prosecution of the war. In 1647, Kieft was succeeded by Peter Stuyvesant, the last Dutch Governor or Director-General of New Netherland. It was he who surrendered the colony to the British in 1664.

## Pertinent Literature

Trelease, Allen W. *Indian Affairs in Colonial New York: The Seventeenth Century.* Ithaca: Cornell University Press, 1960.

The purchase of Manhattan is by itself of little significance and should be viewed in the light of Dutch-Indian relations in the seventeenth century. The Dutch initially came to the New World to exploit its rich storehouse of furs. As traders, the Dutch provided the Indians with new or better articles of life. Mirrors, beads, cooking utensils, guns, ammunition, and liquor were traded for the precious pelts. These trading goods were prized by the Indians, for they improved the standard of living in the tribes.

In the early 1620's, however, Dutch policy in New Netherland changed. Although furs were still sought by the Dutch West India Company, permanent settlers were introduced. Their arrival posed a new problem for the Dutch in their relations with the Algonquin tribes: how could the Indians be induced to give up their land? It was a delicate matter. Farmers competed with the Indians for a dwindling supply of available land, while the fur traders had posed no threat to the tribal lands at all.

The Dutch solved the problem by determining that all lands had to be obtained from the tribes by purchase. Above all, land cessions were to be voluntary, not forced, nor obtained by "craft or fraud" according to the West India Company charter. There are few records extant before 1630, so it is hard to determine if the colonists followed official Dutch policy. But the first great purchase of note is the one by Peter Minuit of Manhattan Island in 1626. Four years later, the Dutch bought Fort Orange (Albany) from the Mohicans, legalizing the fort's presence although it had been built some years before.

After 1630, land purchases from the Indians were commonplace. The patroons were required to obtain title to their large land grants by purchase from the nearest tribe. Dutch insistence on the Indians' selling their lands for a mutually satisfactory price contributed much to the friendly relations between the two peoples. Only when Willem Kieft became governor in 1638 was there any major Dutch-Indian fighting, and that was caused in large part by Kieft's insistence that the tribes pay a tax for Dutch "protection." The arrival of Stuyvesant led to a strict reassertion of earlier governmental policy, and the end of most of the fighting.

Trelease's volume is a good study, not only of the Dutch era, but of Indian relations during the British era that followed. He devotes fully half of his book to Dutch policy, the early attempts at settlement, land purchases (of which Manhattan Island was the first), and the ensuing wars. Most interesting is his preliminary chapter which discusses the various Algonquin tribes and their neighbors, the powerful Iroquois, who determined much of the history of colonial New York.

Davies, D. W. *A Primer of Dutch Seventeenth Century Overseas Trade.* The Hague: Martinus Nijhoff, 1961.

One of the major faults of American history is that it is too often seen in isolation from the rest of the world. The purchase of Manhattan Island occurred because the Dutch were interested in world trade of which New Netherland provided a small, but important, part.

In this slim volume, D. W. Davies discusses the origin of Dutch sea interests, stemming from their ability to preserve fish which they traded to the interior countries of Europe. In the twentieth century, it is difficult to imagine that one of the mightiest powers of seventeenth century Europe was the Dutch Republic. Hardly anything moved by sea unless it was carried on a Dutch ship. The Dutch empire stretched around the world, and Dutch traders visited China, Africa, Australia, the Levant, the Baltic States of Europe, and North and South America. The Dutch West India Company was an important carrier for the slave trade, stimulating settlement on the Brazilian coast and also conducting the trade along the coasts of the regions now known as Delaware, New Jersey, and New York.

With regard to the company's activities in North America, Davies points out that contradictory policies were carried out in New Netherland: efforts to promote the establishment of permanent settlements and a farming economy ran counter to trading interests because settlers drove out the fur-bearing animals and ruined the fur trade. The company also showed that it was incapable of governing New Netherland when quarrels arose between the civilian population and Governors Kieft and Stuyvesant. In fact, the colony proved to be a liability to the West India Company, costing the directors over half a million guilders between 1626 and 1644 alone. — *W.L.R.*

## Additional Recommended Reading

Wilson, Charles. *Profit and Power: A Study of England and the Dutch Wars.* London: Longmans, Green, and Co., 1957. A detailed study of the strategic, political, dynastic, and economic rivalries between Great Britain and the Netherlands during the seventeenth century which resulted in the Dutch loss of New Netherland.

Geyl, Pieter. *The Netherlands in the Seventeenth Century.* 2 vols. London: Ernest Benn Ltd., 1964. This work discusses the rise of the Netherlands as a European power, but contains good short sections on the Dutch colonies, including New Netherland.

Boxer, Charles R. *The Dutch Seaborne Empire, 1600-1800.* London: Hutchinson and Co., Ltd., 1965. This work includes little on New Netherland, but it is a good study of the Dutch empires and is useful for background.

Riemersma, Jelle C. *Religious Factors in Early Dutch Capitalism, 1550-1650.* The Hague: Mouton and Co., 1967. A short study in which the author analyzes the importance of Protestantism in stimulating the Dutch to set up one of the first really successful world trade empires.

Kessler, Henry H. and Eugene Rachlis. *Peter Stuyvesant and His New York.* New York: Random House, 1959. An account of the work of the controversial last Dutch governor of New Netherland.

Flick, Alexander C., ed. *History of the State of New York.* 10 vols. New York: Columbia University Press, 1933-1937. The first volume gives an excellent account of the founding of New York and includes a bibliography.

# THE GREAT PURITAN MIGRATION

*Type of event:* Cultural: desire to establish a Puritan Commonwealth
*Time:* 1630-1643
*Locale:* Massachusetts Bay

*Principal personages:*

JOHN WINTHROP (1588-1649), Governor of Massachusetts and its leading citizen

JOHN COTTON (1584-1652), teacher at the First Church in Boston and an eminent divine

ANNE HUTCHINSON (1591-1643), an enthusiastic disciple of John Cotton

ROGER WILLIAMS (1603?-1683), one of the founders of Rhode Island

## Summary of Event

Credit for the successful establishment of a Puritan Commonwealth in North America belongs as much to Charles I, King of England and Puritan antagonist, as to any other single individual. On March 2, 1629, he dissolved Parliament, thereby denying the Puritans a public forum from which to continue their agitation for reforming the Church of England; a few days later he granted a royal charter to the Puritan-controlled Massachusetts Bay Company which provided the framework for establishing a colony in the New World. By thus harassing the Puritans in old England even as he allowed them to procure a beachhead in New England, Charles virtually guaranteed the success of their colonizing venture.

The charter granted to the Massachusetts Bay Company contained, contrary to established custom, no clause stipulating that the company should hold its meetings in England. This omission enabled several leading Puritan stockholders to carry the charter with them to the New World and so transfer control of both company and colony to North America. Massachusetts thus became an autonomous Commonwealth, the government of which evolved out of a transplanted joint-stock company. The stockholders who emigrated to Massachusetts became the voting citizens of the state, the board of directors, known as assistants, developed into a legislative assembly, and the company president served as governor of the colony.

The first contingent of settlers came to America in 1630. In the Great Migration which lasted until 1643, some twenty thousand people came to Massachusetts to make the greatest colonizing exodus that England has ever known.

John Winthrop, first Governor of Massachusetts Bay, realized soon after his arrival in the colony that too few members of the company had emigrated to provide a secure basis for government. In 1631, therefore, Winthrop arranged for the admission of more than a hundred settlers to the status of "freemen," as stockholders were then

85

called in England, and this number was gradually increased as the colony grew. Although the original stockholders had hoped to contain the rights of these newly-created citizens within definite limits, such restrictions proved to be increasingly difficult to enforce. By 1644, the freemen had broadened their participation in the legislative process through the establishment of a lower house in the legislature consisting of two deputies from each town who shared, along with the governor and assistants, in the enactment of laws for the affected territory.

Despite these changes in the structure of government and the remarkable growth of the colony, Massachusetts remained safely under the control of a Puritan oligarchy. A law of 1636 helped to maintain this alliance of the Church and the state by providing that only members of an approved congregation could apply for the status of freemen. Moreover, Puritan political theory held that although the people had a right to elect their leaders, once magistrates were installed in office they held a commission from God and were responsible to Him rather than to the electorate. Therefore, as Boston's influential minister John Cotton repeatedly pointed out, the freemen had no right to deprive a man of elective office unless they found him guilty of some grave offense. The remarkable durability of Puritan magistrates attests to the effectiveness of this advice.

The difficulty of maintaining orthodoxy in a congregational system of church government presented the Puritan commonwealth with its greatest challenge during the early years of settlement. Despite John Winthrop's efforts to maintain unity within the col-

ony, zealots, such as Roger Williams, one of the founders of Rhode Island, and Anne Hutchinson, an enthusiastic disciple of John Cotton, threatened to divide the province into warring factions by convincing their respective congregations that the Church stood in need of further purification. Since each congregation was presumably independent of outside authority, it was difficult to discipline any heretic who succeeded in winning support from his or her local church.

Williams arrived in Massachusetts in 1631 and almost immediately began to challenge the purity of the New England churches, as well as the basis on which the Puritans had erected their civil government. He contended that the Massachusetts congregations retained too many contacts with the Church of England, that the civil government had no right to enforce religious uniformity, and that the King had acted illegally in granting a charter to the colony. These arguments threatened established authority and yet, because Williams enjoyed the confidence of his congregation at Salem, both the magistrates and the ministers found it difficult to deal with him.

Hutchinson presented an even greater problem. She argued that personal revelation might supplant the teachings of the ministers, and that each individual must obey the voice of God rather than the commands of either church or state. Although holding no official church position, she enjoyed the support of a majority in the Boston congregation and, like Williams, proved a thorny problem for the ministers and magistrates.

The ultimate expulsion of both Williams and Anne Hutchinson demonstrated the means by which orthodoxy would continue to protect itself in Massachusetts. The Puritans continued to insist upon the autonomy of each congregation but they managed to maintain uniformity through their control of the government. In theory the ministers of the colony exercised no authority over a particular congregation except through persuasion. They could, however, declare an individual a heretic and it then became the duty of the civil government to see that he was punished. Through this partnership of the Church and the state, formalized by the Cambridge Platform of 1649, the Puritans maintained a virtually unchallenged control of Massachusetts throughout the first half of the seventeenth century.

## Pertinent Literature

Morgan, Edmund S. *The Puritan Dilemma: The Story of John Winthrop.* Boston: Little, Brown, and Company, 1958.

Professor Morgan's interesting and informative biography of Winthrop is one of the best short introductions to the early development of Massachusetts. Although Morgan's focus is on the life of the colony's first governor, he presents a well-rounded account of events in the Puritan settlement during the first two decades. He deals with the causes of the Puritan migration from England, the organization of the Church and the civil government, the internal threats precipitated by both Williams and Anne Hutchinson, and the problems faced by Massachusetts in its dealings with England and other parts of the Atlantic community.

Generally sympathetic to Winthrop, Morgan credits the Massachusetts leader with having guided the colony on a middle path between excessive zeal on one side and corruption on the other. As a young man Winthrop had come to believe that the Puritan, though he had to avoid compromising with the evils of the world, must do more than learn to discipline himself. He discerned, as Morgan explains it, that the Puritan could not withdraw from the world but must learn to live in it and work to improve it. This lesson was applied to the government of Massachusetts. Winthrop insisted that the colonists maintain the purity of their ideals, but he opposed the fanaticism of those who wanted to achieve that end through isolation and withdrawal. In so doing, Winthrop enabled Massachusetts to solve, temporarily, the problem which Morgan has labelled "the Puritan dilemma."

In discussing the government of Massachusetts, which he describes as "absolute authority resting on a consent that was renewed every year," Morgan makes a case for justifying the despotism of Puritan leadership. He admits that the "belligerent precisionism" of Thomas Dudley, the deputy governor of Massachusetts, or the "hasty temper" of John Endecott might have made such a government intolerable, but believes that under Winthrop it was efficient, just, and intelligent.

Morgan is most critical of Winthrop in his discussion of the trial of Hutchinson, a member of the Boston congregation who threatened the authority of civil and ecclesiastical leaders by her insistence that divine inspiration took precedence over the Scriptures. The author describes her as Winthrop's intellectual superior and insists that the Governor resorted to "blind dogmatism" in order to defeat her. The trial, which resulted in her banishment, is described as such a farce that "it might have been better for the reputation of her judges if they had simply banished her unheard."

Like Perry Miller in his essay "Errand into the Wilderness," Morgan regards the Civil War in England as a turning point for American Puritanism. Bewildered and outraged by the decision of the English Puritans to endorse toleration, the people of New England "found themselves suddenly alone in the wilderness." Once again Winthrop was confronted with the problem of separatism, although this time it was the danger of "a whole people lost in satisfaction with their own collective holiness." Winthrop's com-

mon sense told him that Massachusetts must not isolate itself from the world, and he used his influence to prevent self-righteousness from playing a decisive part in Massachusetts' foreign policy. He argued that the colony must display charity toward its sister settlements in North America and insisted that the Puritans must engage in business dealings with other people, regardless of religious differences.

The value of Morgan's work is less in the originality of his conclusions than in the clarity and detail of his synthesis. *The Puritan Dilemma* generally follows prevailing interpretations of the settlement of Massachusetts Bay, but it brings the story together in a succinct and comprehensive account which is otherwise unavailable. At the same time it is an outstanding biography of Winthrop which gives a personal and political picture of one of the most important figures in American colonial history.

Rutman, Darrett B. *Winthrop's Boston: A Portrait of a Puritan Town, 1630-1649.* Chapel Hill: University of North Carolina Press, 1965.

Whereas most accounts of the early Puritan settlements in North America have dealt with the principal leaders of the Massachusetts Bay colony, Professor Rutman approaches his task somewhat differently. His focus is on the city of Boston rather than the entire colony, and he repeatedly reminds his readers that it was "only the great who wrote" and that the mind of any given period is not simply a "compilation of assumptions" gleaned from the writings of leading figures. In attempting to convey a sense of what Boston was like in its early decades, Rutman has produced a volume which is remarkable

for its vigorous narrative style and careful scholarship.

In describing the settlement of, and early developments in, Boston, the author presents a variety of material not readily available in other sources. He describes in detail such problems as the limited amount of land available to the inhabitants of the city, the process by which such land was distributed, the lack of adequate supplies of wood, and the duties of various town officials. Rutman is particularly interested in the early tendency of the town to assume authority over itself, and suggests that leaders, such as Winthrop, were willing

88

to grant such local authority because of the overwhelming demands of "commonwealth duties." This interpretation places more importance on town government than most narrators have done, and demonstrates Rutman's effort to assess the influence of the "incoherent many as well as the vociferous few."

Although *Winthrop's Boston* is primarily concerned with events in the city itself, it also deals with other areas of the colony. The controversy with Anne Hutchinson, since it directly concerned the First Church in Boston, receives considerably more attention than the problems caused by Williams. Yet both are adequately covered and the narrative presents a broad general picture of the early years of Massachusetts.

In general outline Rutman's narrative does not differ significantly from other historical accounts. He presents a sympathetic picture of Puritan Massachusetts and emphasizes the importance of common-sense solutions to the problems facing the colony.

Most of the author's historical revisions stem from his determination to free himself from dependence on the writings of major figures and his at-tempt to deal with the total community. He is particularly concerned with denying the validity of the term "Puritan mind" when applied to the city of Boston. Rutman attempts to redress the stress on intellectual processes which has resulted from the remarkable work of Perry Miller, by demonstrating that the people who lived and worked in Boston were "ordinary people, neither wholeheartedly humanistic nor frigidly glacial, neither entirely emotional nor entirely rational."

Like many recent narratives, *Winthrop's Boston* describes a utopian scheme which began to crumble during the first decade of settlement. Outwardly, the Puritan oligarchy maintained its domination of the colony throughout the seventeenth century, but the forces of decay had long since decreed its fall. The dispersal of population, the availability of land, and the creation of a church establishment were incompatible with Winthropian ideals. Most destructive of all was Boston, with its commercial prosperity, its internal fragmentation, and the "preoccupation of the Bostonians with their own town rather than the community."
— *D.L.A.*

## Additional Recommended Reading

Miller, Perry. *The New England Mind:* Vol. I: *The Seventeenth Century.* Cambridge: Harvard University Press, 1939. A brilliant study of Puritan theology by the author who has done much to explain the intellectual history of New England.

Miller, Perry. *Orthodoxy in Massachusetts, 1630-1650.* Cambridge: Harvard University Press, 1933. A brief but detailed account of Miller's theories of the establishment of congregationalism in Massachusetts Bay.

Miller, Perry. *Errand into the Wilderness.* Cambridge: Harvard University Press, 1956. Paperback edition in Harper Torchbooks. Sees the Civil War in England as a turning point for American Puritanism.

Battis, Emery. *Saints and Sectaries: Anne Hutchinson and the Antinomian Controversy in the Massachusetts Bay Colony.* Chapel Hill: University of North Carolina Press for the

Institute of Early American History and Culture, 1962. The author gives a detailed study of the Antinomian controversy with suggestions about the psychological, sociological, and physiological undercurrents of the event.

Bailyn, Bernard. *The New England Merchants in the Seventeenth Century.* Cambridge: Harvard University Press, 1955. This work is a study of the development of a mercantile community in the New England colonies and the effect which that development had on the decline of Puritan control.

Pettit, Norman. *The Heart Prepared: Grace and Conversion in Puritan Spiritual Life.* New Haven: Yale University Press, 1966. An excellent study which revises and enlarges our understanding of the process by which the Puritans prepared for and achieved conversion.

Simpson, Alan. *Puritanism in Old and New England.* Chicago: The University of Chicago Press, 1955. A lucid account of the impact of Puritanism in both England and America which provides some provocative suggestions about the relationship between them.

# SETTLEMENT OF CONNECTICUT

*Type of event:* Sociopolitical: settlement of a new colony by migrants from another colony
*Time:* 1635-1662
*Locale:* Connecticut River Valley and coast of Long Island Sound

*Principal personages:*

EDWARD WINSLOW (1595-1655), Plymouth colonist who explored the Connecticut River Valley in 1632

ROBERT RICH, SECOND EARL OF WARWICK (1587-1658), President of the Council for New England, who solicited a patent for Connecticut from the council in 1632

JOHN WINTHROP, JR. (1638-1707), Founder of the settlements at Saybrook and New London, and Governor of Connecticut

THOMAS HOOKER (1586?-1647), Massachusetts Bay divine who headed the Hartford settlement and who was instrumental in framing the "Fundamental Orders"

ROGER LUDLOW (1590-1664?), Leader of Massachusetts Bay colonists who settled at Windsor in 1635, and co-founder of Stratford and Fairfield

JOHN DAVENPORT (1597-1670), Founder and co-leader of the New Haven colony

WOUTER VAN TWILLER (c.1580-c.1656), Governor-General of New Netherland who protested on behalf of the Dutch government the English settlement of Connecticut

THEOPHILUS EATON (1590-1658), English merchant and co-founder along with John Davenport of the New Haven colony

## Summary of Event

As more and more immigrants arrived in the Massachusetts coastal towns, land prices rose dramatically. News of the Connecticut River Valley with its fertile bottom land and easy access to the sea attracted English settlers in large numbers. The lure of the West, so prominent in American history, was already making its appeal to the adventurous spirit of the New Englanders. Edward Winslow of New Plymouth had explored the region in 1632 choosing as a site for a trading post the present-day location of Windsor. The trading post, originally established for the purpose of tapping the valuable fur trade, symbolized the intention of English settlers to possess the entire Connecticut River Valley. The Dutch, however, also claimed the region as part of the West India Company's holdings in New Netherland. These rival claims, intensified by the increasing influx of land-hungry New Englanders, signaled a race for empire.

In 1635, a group of settlers from Massachusetts Bay colony ignored New Plymouth's claim to the region and settled around Windsor. Van Twiller, the Dutch Governor of New Netherland, protested this intrusion asserting that the question of the ownership of the disputed territory was a matter to be settled by the Dutch and British home authorities. The Dutch protest went unheeded. New Plymouth sold their claims to the Bay colony settlers and the process of settlement went on. In the fall of 1635 Hartford became the seat of fifty farmer residents of New Towne (Cambridge). English claims were now effectively supported by occupation. The Dutch authorities could only watch with growing concern the piecemeal erosion of their territorial rights.

Robert Rich, the Earl of Warwick and President of the Council for New England, had meanwhile obtained a patent for the region and had issued the deed to a group of Puritan gentlemen. On July 7, 1635, this group authorized John Winthrop, Jr. to erect a fort and dwellings at the mouth of the Connecticut river. The strategic importance of such a settlement was well recognized by the English lords. By establishing a fort at the mouth of the river, the English settlers could take advantage of both the river and coastal trade, cut off the Dutch contact with the interior, and guard Long Island Sound. When Winthrop declared that settlement must be by consent of the grantees, the Reverend Thomas Hooker and his flock at New Towne were preparing to move in. Hooker and his congregation agreed to Winthrop's terms and accepted him as the Governor of the territory. Winthrop, having no authority to permit the setting up of colonial government, agreed to a plan whereby the Massachusetts General Court served as a broker in giving the agreement legal validity. On March 3, 1636, the General Court issued a plan for government. The commission envisioned by the court was to have governmental authority for one year. Although this governmental body was temporary, it provided for a remarkable degree of popular participation, indicative perhaps of a native American proclivity for democratic institutions.

Hooker's band of thirty-five men and their families were only partially motivated by land hunger. Dissatisfaction with the church at Massachusetts Bay and the patrician oligarchy of Bay colony divines inspired these pilgrims to seek a "christian refuge in the wilderness." Hooker's politics were quite advanced and the democratic principle, long submerged in the Bay colony, expressed itself in a popular belief that authority should reside in the hands of as many as were competent to exercise it. All Christian freeholders were allowed a voice in the government, although, once elected, leaders had an unbounded right to govern as they wished.

At the General Court called at Hartford in 1637, committees representing the three towns of Hartford, Windsor, and Wethersfield elected their magistrates and made preparations for war with the Pequot Indians. In a three-week campaign the Pequots were nearly destroyed, resulting in relative peace for forty years.

Soon after the Pequot War the second colony within the present limits of Connecticut was established. English Puritans under John Davenport, a minister, and Theophilus Eaton, a wealthy merchant, founded a "plantation" at New Haven. These emigrants had come to America to establish a new Puritan Canaan which they hoped would provide spiritual leadership and economic success. By the spring of

1638 the town limits had been set out and the infant colony was on a sound footing.

The New Haven colony adopted a republican government similar to its neighbors, and the inhabitants looked to Davenport and Eaton for leadership. Eaton, always more practical than spiritual, was the right man for the job. His sound leadership and astute financial policies enabled the colony to prosper. Eaton played a role in New Haven similar to that of John Winthrop in Massachusetts. Other settlements were soon established, and by 1644 these had attached themselves to New Haven to form the colony of New Haven.

Meanwhile, the other English settlements had adopted a number of laws, known as the "Fundamental Orders." The document, issued on January 14, 1639, included a preamble declaring a covenant among the inhabitants and enacted eleven laws which provided for a government consisting of a General Court, or legislature, meeting bi-annually, and a Governor. The franchise, following English practice, was restricted to qualified householders. Office-holding, however, was limited to "freemen" or those who could demonstrate to the General Court that they possessed substantial property. As a result, the ensuing years witnessed the growing prestige of the magistrates, and the "democratic principle," so fondly cherished in earlier times, was lost.

By the middle of the seventeenth century there were two autonomous governments in Connecticut. Expansion continued both eastward and westward along the coast and rivers. Winthrop organized the plantation of New London in 1646, and Stratford and Fairfield grew out of Roger Ludlow's plantation at Peguannack. The economy of the region was basically agricultural, with trade and industry having only secondary importance.

The governments in Connecticut, however, rested on no legal basis. Having never acquired a charter from the Commonwealth government in England, the Connecticut settlements and their governments lacked the legal status of Massachusetts Bay and Virginia. Late in 1661, Winthrop departed for England as agent for the Connecticut government, exclusive of New Haven. His mission was to seek confirmation of the old Warwick patent and then to obtain a royal patent from the newly restored Charles II. Influential backers in England helped persuade the Puritan-hating monarchy to grant the desired patent. The colony obtained a charter on May 10, 1662. This grant, based essentially upon the Fundamental Orders, was issued in utter disregard of the claims of New Netherland and New Haven. Connecticut became a corporate legal government with authority vested in the Governor and freemen.

The government of Connecticut, now resting on firm legal grounds, was determined to annex New Haven. Without a patent, New Haven could afford no agency in London. Hence, despite attempts to remain independent, New Haven formally submitted to annexation in 1664. Dutch claims were settled in the same year when an English fleet sailed up Long Island Sound and forced the surrender of the Dutch fort at New Amsterdam. By 1664 the entire Eastern Coast of North America was effectively under English dominion.

## Pertinent Literature

Andrews, Charles M. *The Colonial Period of American History.* Vol. II: *The Settlements.* Chs. 3-5. New Haven: Yale University Press, 1964.

Connecticut may be said to be the first of the colonies to typify the American frontier spirit—the desire to find new lands for expansion. Charles M. Andrews attributes the settlement of Connecticut not to the search for religious freedom but to the search for land. Unlike the sites of Jamestown and Plymouth, whose inhabitants had chosen hastily, the Connecticut River Valley had been highly recommended by the Indians and first explorers for its fertility. Despite many ventures into trade and industry in the early decades of settlement, life in seventeenth century Connecticut, Andrews states, was essentially agrarian.

Andrews' treatment of the settlement of Connecticut is extremely thorough. Each settlement and each leader are fitted into the complex total picture. In less certain hands the picture could easily have become confused because of the many localities and personalities which must be dealt with simultaneously. Several of Connecticut's leaders, most notably Winthrop, changed their habitations regularly, so that one has difficulty in associating a particular leader with a particular town. Without losing sight of these diverse activities, Andrews manages to focus upon the broader institutions and policies of the colony as a whole.

Theology never played a dominant role in Connecticut's early history, for its leaders adhered almost without exception to the Puritanism of Massachusetts Bay. Andrews contends, however, that Thomas Hooker, Roger Ludlow, and the other framers of the "Fundamental Orders" were dissatisfied with the authoritarianism of the Massachusetts magistrates and sought to place authority in the hands of as many as were competent to exercise it. In practice, the rights of the inhabitants were far removed from the twentieth century concept of democracy.

It is discussion of the Puritan concept of government compared with the modern idea of democracy that underlies Andrews' chapters on Connecticut. The Puritan government, Andrews emphasizes, sought to promote the welfare of the community rather than that of the individual. In the distribution of lands, the maintenance of the towns and resources, and the obligation to labor for the common benefit, one sees that the interest of the community came first. On the commonwealth level, the magistrates, once elected, retained control of affairs with little concern for the opinions of the inhabitants. The limiting of the franchise by the General Court is indicative of the government's willingness to subordinate individual rights to what it considered the need to exclude undesirable elements from influence in the community. In order to become even an "admitted inhabitant" a settler had to be a householder of "honest conversation," that is, deemed suitable by the authorities. Admission to the more prestigious status of freemanship required selection by the General Court. The court records of the period attest to the concern of the magistrates for the individual morality and behavior of the inhabitants, and to the harsh punishments meted out to those who fell short.

Yet the Connecticut leaders apparently carried with them out of the Massachusetts experience a suspicion of the all-powerful magistrate. Among the Fundamental Orders are safeguards for maintaining ultimate control in the hands of the freemen should the magistrates and governor fail to summon the General Court as prescribed.

Andrews' account of the Connecticut experience is extremely well-balanced. He acknowledges the colony's commitment to wider participation in government without confusing its progressive tendencies with democracy.

Black, Robert C., III. *The Younger John Winthrop.* New York: Columbia University Press, 1966.

In this well-written and frequently witty biography of the sometime Governor of Connecticut, Robert C. Black exhibits a tendency common to nearly all who are acquainted with his subject—to be utterly charmed by the man. Part of an age and environment which immediately evoke thoughts of sober-sided magistrates and tortuous theological controversies, Winthrop emerges unblemished by any of the Puritan stereotypes. Black succeeds admirably in investing Winthrop with human qualities and in depicting the spirit of the times in which he lived.

Chapters seven through seventeen are concerned with Winthrop's activities from the authorization by the Warwick grantees of the establishment of Saybrook in 1635 to the securing of Connecticut's charter in 1662. Yet this is by no means a simple story of life in a Connecticut settlement. Winthrop was too restless a man to remain with one project for long. Black characterizes him as one who enjoyed arranging enterprises, but who left the administration for someone else. "Bi-colonial," he remained an assistant (magistrate) in the Massachusetts government until his father's death in 1649, although he was living and holding office in Connecticut during much of the time.

Black suggests that Winthrop probably regarded politics "as less a matter of principle than of possibility." Supremely practical, he wasted no time on democratic ideas of equality when he established New London in 1646, preferring to run the government in the manner which he believed to be efficient. Although he reveled in political controversy, theological controversy did not interest him. Routinely orthodox, but more tolerant than many Puritans, he neglected to attend the Massachusetts General Court, of which he was a member during the Antinomian crisis concerning Anne Hutchinson.

Always ready to try a new business venture, Winthrop at various points in his career involved himself in the production of iron, salt, indigo, glass, and goats. Winthrop's interest in metals was more than a matter of business. The sciences, and particularly alchemy, fascinated him. Although his inability to remain interested in a single project for long precluded his engaging in serious scholarship, he owned perhaps the finest library in the colonies, enjoyed the friendship of numerous European scholars, and was the first North American to be elected to the Royal Society. In the absence of a physician, he often ministered to the medical needs of his neighbors.

Winthrop was so popular a political figure that New Haven and Connecticut vied with each other for his residence, each proffering him economic and political advantages. "Winthrop was never so naïve as to confuse public service with unintelligent self-sacrifice," writes Black. While he lived in New London, he enjoyed "one of the most generous assortments of rights and privileges ever seen in New England." Yet New Haven lured him away with her iron bogs, only to be outdone eventually by Connecticut's offer of the governorship. That Winthrop was an opportunist cannot be denied, but that he possessed a certain

irresistible charm is also certain. It is too easy to place Winthrop in the mold of the slick modern politician, long on affability but short on principle. Black has not done so, but neither has he explained why Winthrop was Connecticut's most sought-after political figure. We do know that through his diplomatic talents he obtained royal approval for Connecticut's charter. Perhaps it is too much to expect to know completely what made the man attractive to his contemporaries. In trying to find out, Black has nonetheless written a thoroughly readable and revealing study of early Connecticut politics. — *W. W. B.*

## Additional Recommended Reading

Adams, James Truslow. *The Founding of New England.* Magnolia, Massachusetts: Peter Smith Publishers, Inc., 1921. Paperback edition by Little, Brown, and Company. Displaying his dislike for the Massachusetts Bay Puritans, Adams contends that the Connecticut settlers opened up the frontier to establish a more democratic way of life.

Archibald, Warren S. *Thomas Hooker.* New Haven: Yale University Press for the Tercentenary Commission of the State of Connecticut, 1933. This laudatory pamphlet traces Hooker's early years and his leadership, particularly as a preacher, in Connecticut.

Deming, Dorothy. *The Settlement of the Connecticut Towns.* New Haven: Yale University Press for the Tercentenary Commission of the State of Connecticut, 1933. Both the Connecticut and New Haven colony settlements are covered concisely in this booklet which extends the history beyond the seventeenth century.

Deming, Dorothy. *The Fundamental Orders of Connecticut.* New Haven: Yale University Press for the Tercentenary Commission of the State of Connecticut, 1934. A brief introduction by George M. Dutcher precedes the text of the Fundamental Orders with seventeenth century spelling and symbols intact.

Jones, Mary J. *Congregational Commonwealth: Connecticut, 1636-1662.* Middletown, Connecticut: Wesleyan University Press, 1968. A full-length work on Connecticut's early years which focuses on the Fundamental Orders as an expression of Puritan life and government rather than attempting to provide a much needed general study of the period.

# FOUNDING OF RHODE ISLAND

*Type of event:* Politico-religious: establishment of Rhode Island by dissatisfied members of Massachusetts Bay colony
*Time:* 1636-1663
*Locale:* Narragansett Bay region of Rhode Island

*Principal personages:*

ROGER WILLIAMS (1603?-1683), founder of Providence in 1636, who remained Rhode Island's most important leader

WILLIAM CODDINGTON (1601-1678), founder of the Aquidneck Island settlements of Portsmouth and Newport

SAMUEL GORTON (1592?-1677), controversial supporter of Anne Hutchinson, who established Warwick

DR. JOHN CLARKE (1609-1676), physician and minister who helped to found Rhode Island and who as Rhode Island's agent in England secured confirmation of its charter in 1663

ANNE HUTCHINSON (1591-1643), who was banished from Massachusetts Bay colony for advocating Antinomianism, and who helped to found Portsmouth

## Summary of Event

The founding of Rhode Island was more complicated than the founding of most of the other American colonies because it involved five separate settlements and unusual leaders bent on expressing their individualistic beliefs. The earliest settlers in Rhode Island represented those who were forced out of Massachusetts Bay colony for their "dangerous" opinions or who left of their own accord because they were dissatisfied with certain aspects of the Puritan oligarchy.

The first of these, with the exception of the recluse William Blakston, was Roger Williams, who was ordered to leave the Bay colony on October 9, 1635. Escaping deportation to England, he set out for the Narragansett region in January, 1636, and took refuge among the Indians for several months. Soon after purchasing land near the Seekonk river from Mas-

sasoit, he was joined by five other men. The warning from the Governor of Plymouth that they were trespassing forced them to establish a new settlement, which they called Providence, on the Great Salt river. It is not known whether Williams had an actual plantation in mind or whether he simply envisioned a trading post or Indian mission. But other outcasts were soon welcomed, and each settler was given a home lot and a farm from the land which Williams had purchased from the Indians. Providence was strictly an agricultural community. Though the colony was built without capital or outside assistance, its population and economy grew slowly. The heads of families participated in a "town meeting" type of government, and signed a compact agreeing to obey the laws passed by the will of all. The compact contained the phrase "only in civil

97

things," signifying a commitment to the separation of the Church and the state.

In April, 1638, another band of exiles led by William Coddington left Boston in search of religious freedom. They were preceded in March by Anne Hutchinson and her family. Arriving at Providence, they all arranged to purchase the island of Aquidneck from the Indians and by the following spring they had laid out the new settlement of Pocasset (Portsmouth). By seventeenth century standards the settlement had a democratic form of government with Coddington serving as judge.

Two such dominant personalities as Coddington and Anne Hutchinson could not exist in harmony for long. When their two factions split over Hutchinson's eccentric supporter, Samuel Gorton, Coddington was ousted and with his followers began the new plantation of Newport. In March, 1640, he succeeded in uniting the two settlements on Aquidneck so that they could manage their own affairs apart from Providence. The union, the most orderly civil organization in the Narragansett region, was to endure for seven years. By twentieth century standards the democracy which they proclaimed in 1641 was limited because it excluded half the adult males from participating in government. Probably because Coddington was unsuccessful in obtaining a patent for Aquidneck, the people of Portsmouth became disillusioned and broke away from Newport in 1648.

Meanwhile, the controversial Gorton, driven from both Portsmouth and Providence for defying the authority of the government, purchased Indian lands to establish Warwick. After enduring harassment and imprisonment

by Massachusetts officials, he obtained an order compelling Massachusetts to cease molesting him and lived in peace as an honored citizen of Warwick.

Of all the Rhode Island leaders, Williams emerged as the dominant figure. His efforts to maintain peace among the Indians were of inestimable service to the whole of New England. Yet the ambitions of other political leaders in the British settlements both in and around Rhode Island were to remain his chief problem. Convinced that the settlements of Rhode Island had to coöperate in order to remain intact, he worked selflessly for a federation of the four main towns. When the formation of the New England Confederation in 1643 threatened Rhode Island's integrity, Williams sailed for England to obtain a charter from the Long Parliament. The patent which he brought back in September, 1644, authorized the union of Providence, Portsmouth, and Newport as "The Incorporation of Providence Plantations." Warwick was included later.

The uncertainty of the Civil War in England delayed putting the newly authorized government into effect, but in May, 1647, an assembly of freemen met at Portsmouth to organize the government and draft laws. A federal system whereby the towns maintained their individual rights as parts of the larger community, was created. Their code of laws was one of the earliest made by a body of men in America and the first to embody in all its parts the precedents set by the laws and statutes of England. By 1650 a representative assembly composed of six delegates from each town was operating. The assembly at first also served as a judicial body until a separate court for trials was established in 1655. Town courts preserved the local peace.

Coddington continued to deal underhandedly in an attempt to separate Aquidneck from the union. In 1651 he succeeded in obtaining a lifetime appointment as Governor of Aquidneck and Conanicut Islands from the Council of State. The residents of the islands supported Williams' successful mission to England which resulted in the annulment of Coddington's patent in 1652. Distrust of central government and antagonism between the mainland and islands persisted until 1654, when Williams, with the support of Oliver Cromwell, restored the atmosphere of coöperation.

The Restoration in England imperilled the validity of Rhode Island's charter of 1644. Dr. John Clarke, its agent in London, petitioned the crown for confirmation. Confirmation of Connecticut's grant to include half of Rhode Island's territory necessitated submitting the matter to arbitration. The decision was in favor of Rhode Island and the new charter of 1663 also confirmed the colony's policy of complete liberty of conscience, the only charter to do so.

## Pertinent Literature

Andrews, Charles M. *The Colonial Period of American History.* Vol. II: *The Settlements.* Ch. 1 and 2. New Haven: Yale University Press, 1964.

Most historians of early Rhode Island have chosen to concentrate on a particular settlement or leader, usually Roger Williams or Anne Hutchinson. This is understandable in the light of the mélange of territorial, political, and religious eccentricities peculiar to this colony. For this reason, Charles M. Andrews' detailed account is all the more remarkable. Andrews himself points out that Rhode Island can hardly be considered a colony in the early period. Lacking a patent and backers in England, it started with no more than Indian deeds and social compacts. It was actually five petty states "in embryo," each having its own political and religious atmosphere. Despite the complexity of the situation, Andrews succeeds in tracing in detail the development of the settlements, their unification, and the operation of the government after union was achieved. He also delineates the reli-

gious and political ideas which brought the settlements into being and made coöperation so difficult.

Because Andrews' account of Rhode Island's beginnings occupies only two chapters in a monumental four-volume work, it cannot really be said to propound a thesis. Yet Andrews' admiration for the establishment of freedom of conscience and democratic government permeates his writing. Choosing to deëmphasize the qualities which must have made Williams and Gorton difficult men with whom to deal—assurance of the rightness of their own opinions and a penchant for controversy—Andrews presents their efforts to find free expression for their beliefs and to live in peace in a sympathetic light.

The Williams whom he portrays bears no resemblance to the smug preacher who denounced the churches of Massachusetts Bay for not separating from the Church of England. According to Andrews, Williams espoused absolute liberty of conscience and respected religions with which he disagreed. Williams viewed the Church as but "one of the civil corporations that the state was bound to protect" and declared that the Church should regulate its own affairs without interference from the civil authorities. Well aware of the disorder which unbridled freedom had wrought in the early years of settlement, he came to advocate the need for responsibility with freedom.

Although Williams naturally remains the dominant figure of Andrews' narrative, Gorton emerges as a fascinating figure worthy of further study.

A pariah to the Massachusetts authorities and most of the Rhode Island leaders, he possessed a strong instinct for justice and the sanctity of English common law. Only the treacherous Coddington fails to elicit a sympathetic biography. Although his wealth and education made Newport the most prosperous of the settlements, his thirst for power nearly destroyed the colony.

It would be difficult to conceive of a better summary of Rhode Island's early years than the one in this work. Without confusing the reader, Andrews manages to weave together many diverse elements of the story and to create a feeling for the drama of the events.

Winslow, Ola E. *Master Roger Williams.* New York: The Macmillan Company, 1957.

In the prologue to her biography of Williams, Ola Elizabeth Winslow admits to making only a beginning in the process of understanding an extremely complex and controversial man. Cutting through the romantic myths which have often over-simplified Williams' ideas or have mistakenly placed them in a twentieth century context, Winslow acknowledges her subject's contributions without losing sight of his shortcomings.

That Winslow possesses an uncommon knowledge of seventeenth century life and thought is evident from the first chapter. Although only the barest details of Williams' youth and education are known, the author succeeds in reconstructing the milieu in which he matured and in which his ideas were shaped.

Separatist sympathies apparently prompted him to set out for Massachusetts Bay in 1630. But Governor Winthrop had no sooner welcomed

him than he affronted the magistrates by refusing the post of teacher in the First Church of Boston. Not only did he protest that the church was not completely separated from the Church of England, but he also denied the magistrates' authority in matters of conscience. His strange opinions were to arouse further discontent when he moved on to the pulpits of Salem and Plymouth. Because the New World actually belonged to the Indians, he declared, the King's patent for Massachusetts Bay was invalid. He could not have chosen a worse time to attack the patent, for the King was threatening to withdraw it and impose royal government. Williams' opinions were not only devoid of courtesy and common sense, but they were also dangerous to the colony. Finally, when he claimed that the magistrates had no right to administer oaths to unregenerate men, the General Court had no choice but to banish Williams from the colony. In the light of seventeenth century practice, their decision was logical, and, contrary to romantic myth, he was given six weeks to depart. Many historians have read their history backwards at this point and have seen in Williams' protests the beginnings of religious freedom and the idea of separation of church and state. While Winslow acknowledges a foreshadowing of Williams' later convictions, she contends that his ideas were far from mature and that he had in no way come to respect the convictions of others.

The early Providence settlement which Williams founded with a handful of companions was by no means an immediate democracy. Williams apparently regarded himself as a proprietor and considered banning settlers of whom he did not approve. But he soon changed his mind, and Providence offered religious freedom from the start.

Because Williams was a puzzling and inconsistent person, Winslow speculates upon the reasons for his liberalization. Perhaps because the wilderness allowed him to speak freely and to be listened to, he learned to listen to others and to speak more cautiously. The reader finds the impetuous, hot-headed preacher of the Boston days evolving into the steady conciliator of Indian disputes and the selfless state-builder. As a mature leader, Williams came to understand the need for responsibility combined with freedom of conscience. During the unsettled years of factional disputes and rival claims which tormented Rhode Island, he labored selflessly for unity.

Yet Williams' appetite for controversy was never satiated. He remained the intrepid polemicist, carrying on a prolonged argument in print with John Cotton over the matter of his banishment, and advocating complete religious toleration. On his journeys to England to obtain support for the Rhode Island Charter, he became intimate with powerful Puritan politicians and entered into the religious controversy.

*Master Roger Williams* is first and foremost the story of a man and his ideas, not an account of the founding of Rhode Island. For a detailed narrative of the years of turmoil which preceded the confirmation of the charter in 1663, one should turn to a study such as that in the second volume of Charles M. Andrews' *The Colonial Period of American History.* Yet Winslow has gone a long way toward the goal of unraveling the complex mind of a man whom historians will probably never fully understand. — *W.M.B.*

## Additional Recommended Reading

Andrews, Charles M. *Our Earliest Colonial Settlements: Their Diversities of Origin and Later Characteristics.* Ch. 4. New York: New York University Press, 1933. Like Andrews' Rhode Island study in *The Colonial Period of American History,* part of this volume details the political turmoil of the early years and the lives of the colony's principal leaders.

Brockunier, Samuel H. *The Irrepressible Democrat: Roger Williams.* New York: The Ronald Press Company, 1940. Views Roger Williams as the first great American democrat, a fighter against the tyranny of the Puritan oligarchy.

Miller, Perry. *Roger Williams: His Contribution to the American Tradition.* New York:

Atheneum Publishers, 1962. Liberally interspersed with selections from Williams' writings, Miller's study contends that Williams was concerned basically with theology, not democratic political reforms.

Morgan, Edmund S. *Roger Williams: The Church and the State.* New York: Harcourt Brace & World, Inc., 1967. Concentrating upon the thought of Roger Williams as presented in his writings, Morgan seeks "to expose the symmetry of the ideas that lay behind the polemics."

Greene, Theodore P. ed. *Roger Williams and the Massachusetts Magistrates.* Boston: D. C. Heath & Co., 1964. Part of the *Problems in American Civilization* series, this collection of readings presents disparate views from the seventeenth century to the present on the question of Williams' banishment.

Rugg, Winnifred K. *Unafraid: A Life of Anne Hutchinson.* Boston: Houghton Mifflin Co., 1930. The Rhode Island experience is treated only in the final chapters of this book, which focuses on the Antinomian controversy in the Massachusetts Bay colony.

# ESTABLISHMENT OF HARVARD COLLEGE AND ENACTMENT OF THE MASSACHUSETTS SCHOOL LAW

*Type of event:* Cultural: beginnings of higher education and public education in America
*Time:* 1636-1647
*Locale:* Massachusetts Bay colony

*Principal personages:*

JOHN WINTHROP (1588-1649), Governor of Massachusetts Bay colony after 1637, and charter member of the Board of Overseers

THOMAS DUDLEY (1576-1653), Deputy Governor of Massachusetts Bay colony, and member of the Board of Overseers 1637-1653

RICHARD BELLINGHAM (1592?-1672), Treasurer of Massachusetts Bay colony, and member of the Board of Overseers 1637-1672

SIR HENRY VANE (1613-1662), Governor of Massachusetts Bay colony in 1636

NATHANIEL EATON (1609?-1674), the first professor to be appointed by the Board of Overseers but who was dismissed for cruelty and mismanagement in 1639

JOHN HARVARD (1607-1638), the first benefactor of Harvard College

HENRY DUNSTER (1609?-1659), the first president of Harvard College

## Summary of Event

In *New England's First Fruits*, the famous tract extolling the virtues of New England to possible supporters in the old country, the Puritans proclaimed that one of their first concerns had been ". . . to advance *Learning* and perpetuate it to Posterity; dreading to leave an illiterate Ministry to the Churches, when our present Ministers shall be in the Dust." Because the Puritan church tenets emphasized interpretation and discussion of the Scriptures rather than mere ritual or emotion, it required a learned clergy. Therefore on October 28, 1636, the Massachusetts General Court passed a legislative act to found "a schoale or colledge" and

voted four hundred pounds sterling for its support. The Antinomian crisis centering around Anne Hutchinson delayed action on the matter until November 15, 1637, when the Massachusetts General Court passed an order that the college be built at Newtown, soon to be renamed Cambridge. A few days later, the building of the college was committed to six magistrates and six church elders, the first Board of Overseers.

By June, 1638, Nathaniel Eaton, the professor engaged by the overseers, had moved into the house acquired for him in the midst of a cow pasture, and the Massachusetts General Court had

103

granted three lots to him for the college. Within a few months, the first classes were being taught, the building was being constructed, and a library was being assembled.

Thus the college was already operating when, on September 14, 1638, a young clergyman named John Harvard died and left his library and half of his estate, amounting to about eight hundred pounds sterling, to the new institution. Although John Harvard was certainly not responsible for the founding of the college, nor did his legacy make its establishment possible, his gift was a remarkable one for the times, and the Massachusetts General Court voted on March 13, 1639, to name the college after him.

Unfortunately, Professor Eaton's most praiseworthy accomplishment was the planting and fencing of the yard to keep the cows out and the students in. His tyrannical tenure was marred by beatings and dismal living conditions for the students who boarded at his home. Mistress Eaton's "loathsome catering," featuring such items as "goat's dung in their hasty pudding," provided an inauspicious beginning for that much-maligned institution, the college dining hall. When Eaton's cruelty finally came to the attention of the Massachusetts General Court, he was fined and dismissed, and the college closed its doors.

In 1645, Henry Dunster, a graduate of Magdalene College, Cambridge, accepted the presidency of Harvard College and soon infused life into it, providing a firm foundation for its growth. The Class of 1642 returned, a new freshman class entered, and a three-year course in the arts was established. A thorough knowledge of Greek and Latin was required for admission. Dunster personally instructed the three classes in the arts, philosophies, and Oriental languages, and he also moderated the students' disputations. Although the Puritans believed that knowledge without Christ was vain, Harvard College was less ecclesiastical than the universities at Oxford or Cambridge, for it strove to provide a course in philosophy and the liberal arts which would be suitable either for a general education or as a basis for entering one of the professions.

Determined to establish in America the collegiate system as it was practiced in England, under which the students lived, studied, ate, and disputed together with their tutors, Dunster and the Overseers were anxious to complete the first building despite the economic depression. Donations made possible the occupation of the "Old College" in September, 1642, in time for the commencement of the first nine graduates. Within this building the students attended classes, studied, ate, and slept.

During its early years, Harvard College had serious financial problems. Lacking any sort of endowment or income-producing lands, it struggled along on tuition fees, and the ferry rents and town levies which it was granted. A fund-raising mission to England met with moderate success, and in 1644 representatives at the meeting of the United Colonies of New England agreed that all the Puritan colonies should share in supporting the college. Each family was obligated to give a peck of wheat or one shilling annually. Unquestionably, the establishment and support of a college was an ambitious undertaking for such a new, economically insecure community. Only the strong religious faith of the Puritans in the purpose of their endeavor carried it through.

Contrary to the claims of various educational historians, the Puritans took a greater interest in intellectual pursuits than other Englishmen of their day. Their concentrated system of settlement in towns rendered the accomplishment of popular education easier than in Virginia, where the population was dispersed. Even before the law required it, a number of towns established schools: Boston hired a master in 1635, and Charlestown, in 1636. The first New England school legislation, the Massachusetts Act of 1642, required the heads of families to teach their children and servants "to read and understand the principles of religion and the capital laws of the country" and to see that they were employed in useful occupations. Thus the Puritans envisioned education as serving social and economic needs: it provided training for citizenship and serv-

ice in the community.

But the laissez-faire system apparently proved to be unsatisfactory, for in 1647 the Massachusetts General Court passed a law requiring every town of fifty families to appoint a schoolmaster "to teach all such children as shall resort to him to write and read." His wages were to be paid by the parents or the town, as the town should choose. Towns of one hundred families were to establish grammar schools to instruct youth "so far as they may be fitted for the Universitie." The cost of supporting the schools was a hardship on some of the smaller communities, and the uneducated complained of the ruling class trying to force its high standards upon the poor. Thus interest in public education did not work its way up from the bottom but down from the top. Only because the Puritan leaders possessed such high standards and determination was it possible for them to lay the foundations for public education in a hostile environment.

## Pertinent Literature

Morison, Samuel Eliot. *The Founding of Harvard College.* Cambridge: Harvard University Press, 1935.

In his preface to this work, Samuel Eliot Morison jokes about his failure to heed the warning of an eighteenth century historian who began his "Chronological History of New-England" with the Creation and died before he reached the year 1631. Although Morison begins his history of Harvard in the Middle Ages, happily he has lived well beyond the completion of the monumental, definitive four-volume work. The first ten chapters of this first volume are concerned with the origin, history, and description of some of the

great Western European universities, particularly Oxford and Cambridge, and with the colleges of Harvard's founders. They are followed by an account of the founding of Harvard College itself.

This story is related in great detail. Morison has assembled a vast amount of information, and he quotes liberally from a staggering array of sources. Not satisfied with limiting his attention to the institutional and curricular organization of the university, he delves deeply into such matters as the selec-

105

tion of the site, the backgrounds of the founders, the books in the library, and the architecture of the original building. The daily lives of the students, down to their diet and sleeping arrangements, as well as the rules of behavior which governed them, are the objects of careful scrutiny.

Because the beliefs and practices of the Puritan church are inextricably bound up with the reasons for the founding of Harvard College, Morison's overriding concern is the explanation of the purposes of the founders. Since the Puritans' emphasis on scriptural study and exegesis presupposed a learned clergy, the founders' immediate objective was the education of ministers. For this reason the suppression of Anne Hutchinson and the Antinomians was necessary to the establishment of the college, Morison contends, since Antinomianism was basically anti-intellectual, relying on divine revelation.

While the founders had as their long-range purpose the perpetuation of learning, it was only natural that religion should be deeply impregnated in the Harvard curriculum as it was in the Puritan way of life. The word *"Veritas"* on the Harvard coat of arms refers to divine truth, Morison explains, for the goal of each student was to be "to know God and Jesus Christ. . . ." But the curriculum was designed not only for students who planned to enter the ministry. The founders intended the course in philosophy and arts as either a general education or as preparation for the professions of divinity, law, or medicine.

The story of Harvard's quest for revenue demonstrates how great was the determination of the founders to maintain their ambitious undertaking. Morison reports in detail the sources and disposition of all known income received by the college from the original gift of four hundred pounds sterling by the General Court and John Harvard's legacy, to the six thousand pecks of wheat collected from all the families of the United Colonies of New England. He discusses at some length tuition, scholarships, and faculty salaries.

That Morison manages to present such a profusion of facts on a relatively narrow historical subject and still write an extremely witty and enjoyable book is no mean feat. Perhaps because he has been intimately associated with Harvard for so many years, he can write of its successes and failures in very familiar terms and in so doing strip it of the image of the sacred cow.

Morison, Samuel Eliot. *The Intellectual Life of Colonial New England.* New York: New York University Press, 1956.

Historians of education have tended to debunk Puritan efforts in the establishment of public education in America as attempts to enforce conformity to their religious beliefs. Samuel Eliot Morison here champions the Puritans, insisting that they did not prevent, but actually stimulated, intellectual pursuits and took a greater interest in education than other Englishmen of their time.

Morison's purpose in this volume is to describe the institutions and facilities that fostered intellectual life and what native-born or American-educated New Englanders made of these opportunities. Seeking to explain why New England alone among the

106

English colonies succeeded so quickly in encouraging intellectual life, Morison argues that only a rigidly controlled society possessed with great emotional drive could have accomplished this end amid the need for so much physical work. Paradoxically, the humanistic tradition fared better among the Puritans than elsewhere, nurtured by leaders who had been educated in the classics at Oxford and Cambridge.

Because the founding of Harvard in Morison's opinion is the best indication of the Puritans' high intellectual ambitions, he provides a detailed summary of the material found in his definitive work on the college's early years. He describes the first awkward attempts at administering and financing the fledgling institution, as well as the curriculum and living accommodations for the students. Yet Morison admits that New England could claim only about six hundred college students in the entire seventeenth century, since few boys could master the Latin required for entrance or could afford the cost of an advanced education.

Accurate information on colonial elementary and grammar schools is difficult to find, Morison explains, and so it is not surprising that much inaccurate history has been written about them. Early historians tended to be too lavish in their praise of colonial education. The contention of Professor Edgar W. Knight that the Massachusetts School Act of 1647 "seems rather to have been an effort to restrict the influence of Catholics and adherents to the English Church and to impose the Puritan creed upon the first generation of native-born New Englanders" typifies more recent judgments. Although the preamble to the act begins, "It being one chief project of that old deluder, Satan, to keep men from knowledge of the scriptures, . . ." the motive behind the law was by no means solely religious. The preamble merely added religious sanction to an obligation which many members of the community were loathe to assume. Morison argues that we should take the Puritans' stated motives—to promote education as training for citizenship and service in the community—at face value rather than view them as mere propaganda. By insisting that their teachers be laymen and by placing their schools under the control of the community and the commonwealth, the Puritans actually moved forward in the process of the secularization of education.

The New England schools were not democratic, for the Puritan colonies had never considered democracy as a proper form for governing themselves. There was no provision for educating girls, and boys who could not master Latin were not allowed to continue their schooling. But in comparison with Virginia's the system was democratic. Only children who could afford it were asked to pay tuition, and even a poor boy had an opportunity to work his way through college. Yet sentiment for public education did not come up from among the poor country people; it "percolated from the top down," being forced upon the community by its ambitious leaders.

In his chapters on the elementary and grammar schools, Morison explains the methods of setting up and financing the schools and describes the curricula and books employed. This book's importance, however, lies in

Morison's thesis that the motives of the Puritan leaders to produce a learned clergy and a lettered people were the roots of public education and of the maintenance of the tradition of learning in America. — *W.M.B.*

## Additional Recommended Reading

Adams, James Truslow. *The Founding of New England.* Boston: Atlantic Monthly Press, 1921. Disagreeing with Morison, Adams contends that the early intellectual life of New England was narrowly theological and that education was promoted only for religious ends.

Best, John H. and Robert T. Sidwell, eds. *The American Legacy of Learning: Readings in the History of Education.* Philadelphia: J. B. Lippincott Co., 1969. Included among the readings here are *New England's First Fruits,* the Harvard Regulations, and selections from the *New England Primer.*

Bailyn, Bernard. *Education in the Forming of American Society: Needs and Opportunities for Study.* Chapel Hill: University of North Carolina Press, 1960. Stresses the need for looking at elements bearing on education throughout society and allowing for changes in response to particular conditions.

Knight, Edgar W. *Education in the United States.* 2nd ed., revised. Boston: Ginn and Co., 1941. This anti-Puritan study by a professor of education argues that early New England education was neither public nor secular.

Morison, Samuel Eliot. "Harvard's Past" in *By Land and By Sea.* New York: Alfred A. Knopf, Inc., 1953. In this brief article, Morison speaks of John Harvard and the founding of Harvard College, and reasserts the importance of the institution's role in carrying the Western tradition of learning into American life.

Morison, Samuel Eliot. *Three Centuries of Harvard, 1636-1936.* Cambridge: Harvard University Press, 1963. The first few chapters of this book are a digest of the material found in the author's comprehensive *Founding of Harvard College.*

# CONFEDERATION OF THE UNITED COLONIES OF NEW ENGLAND

*Type of event:* Political: organization for intercolonial coöperation
*Time:* 1643
*Locale:* Massachusetts Bay, Plymouth, Connecticut, and New Haven colonies

*Principal personages:*

JOHN WINTHROP (1588-1649), Governor of Massachusetts Bay colony and commissioner of the United Colonies of New England

THOMAS DUDLEY (1576-1653), Deputy Governor of Massachusetts Bay colony and commissioner of the United Colonies of New England

EDWARD WINSLOW (1595-1655), commissioner from Plymouth of the United Colonies of New England

WILLIAM COLLIER (c.1612-1670), commissioner from Plymouth of the United Colonies of New England

JOHN HAYNES (1594-1654), Governor of Connecticut and commissioner of the United Colonies of New England

EDWARD HOPKINS (1600-1657), Governor and Deputy Governor of Connecticut and commissioner of the United Colonies of New England

GEORGE FENWICK (1603-1657), commissioner from Connecticut of the United Colonies of New England

THEOPHILUS EATON (1590-1658), Governor of the New Haven colony and commissioner of the United Colonies of New England

THOMAS GREGSON (?-1646), commissioner from New Haven of the United Colonies of New England

THOMAS HOOKER (1586?-1647), Puritan divine and a leader in Connecticut

## Summary of Event

As New England settlements expanded north, south, and west during the 1630's, territorial conflicts became inevitable. Not only did the Puritan colonies attempt to encroach upon one another's territory, but they also came into hostile contact with the Indians, the Dutch, and the French. Although the British had nearly destroyed the Indians in the brief Pequot War of 1637, the lack of coördinated effort had con- vinced them that some form of intercolonial coöperation was necessary for determining military policies and participation, as well as for arbitrating territorial disputes and regulating trade. Religious and political turmoil in Great Britain prevented the Mother Country from supervising colonial affairs directly, and the colonies preferred it that way. Yet in the absence of formal control from above, the Puritan colonies saw the need for defending their expanded boundaries against foreign aggression. The joint action in the Pequot War had apparently fostered a feeling of unity among the Puritan colonies. Furthermore, if the smaller, weaker colonies of Plymouth, Connecticut, and New Haven could enter into an agreement with the Massachusetts Bay colony as political equals, they should then be free from that powerful colony's attempts to encroach upon their territory. The Massachusetts Bay colony, in turn, would profit from a union by gaining legal approval from the other members in its efforts to annex territory in Maine.

In the late summer of 1637, a synod of New England church leaders meeting in Cambridge seriously broached the subject of union for the first time, but disagreements marred that and several other attempts to achieve union during the next few years. Fear of an Indian uprising in 1642, however, spurred Plymouth to send representatives to negotiate with the Massachusetts Bay colony about their mutual defense. About the same time, Connecticut also sent a proposal for mutual defense efforts to Massachusetts. The Massachusetts General Court, therefore, ordered the magistrates to meet with deputies of Connecticut, Plymouth, and New Haven on the matters of unification and defense.

Meeting in Boston on May 29, 1643, the representatives "readily yielded each to the other, in such things as tended to the common good," and drew up Articles of Confederation. When the last of the four General Courts ratified them on September 8, 1643, the articles became binding. The

United Colonies of New England, thereby established, encompassed all the settlements along the coast and rivers from Long Island to New Hampshire. Rhode Island, which the Puritans disdainfully considered anarchical, and Maine were not included.

As stated in the preamble to the articles, the purposes of the confederation were: (1) to preserve the purity of the Puritans' religion and to worship free of interference; (2) to promote cöoperation; and (3) to provide for defense. The articles themselves specified the duties and powers of the confederation's commissioners, the structure of the confederation, and the rules of procedure. Because there was no judicial authority over all the members, each colony could interpret the articles to its own liking—a situation which was to cause problems later.

The governing body of the confederation was to consist of two commissioners chosen annually from each colony. The only qualifications demanded were that they be church members and that they bring "full power" from their general courts. Meeting in each colony successively, the commissioners were to convene each September. Anyone who had advice to offer was welcome to speak before them. Three magistrates from any colony could call a special meeting if necessary. Approval of a matter required the votes of six commissioners, although only four could declare war in a state of emergency. Thus the Massachusetts Bay colony could not veto the wishes of the other three colonies.

How much actual power did the commissioners possess? The answer to this question is essential to understanding the accomplishments and defects of the confederation. It must be remembered that the United Colonies of New England did not consider themselves a nation, but rather individual governments allied by a treaty. Each commissioner actually served as one of his colony's ambassadors. In matters of military preparation, declaration of war, and arbitration, the four colonies did surrender to the commissioners their individual power to act. Yet, while the confederation in theory possessed vague executive and judicial powers, in actuality it had only advisory powers in most areas.

The articles specified that each colony's military obligation should be in proportion to its means and population. Each must send aid if one of the other three colonies should be invaded and must participate in all "just" wars. The commissioners were empowered to decide if the confederation should wage an offensive war, and no colony could do so without their approval.

Apart from military affairs, actual power rested with the general courts of the member colonies. The commissioners could not pass legislation binding on the general courts, nor were they directly responsible to the people. They could neither levy taxes nor requisition supplies. Because the commissioners had no powers of enforcement, a colony which disagreed with a particular decision could simply nullify it by refusing to comply. To avoid conflict,

the remaining colonies usually compromised.

Although lacking in power, the Board of Commissioners did perform numerous important services for the four participating colonies. It established various civil agreements of interest to all four colonies and arbitrated intercolonial disputes. Policies concerning the Indians, and regulations governing runaway slaves and the extradition of criminals were also within its domain. In the judicial realm, the Commissioners established uniform standards for probating wills, and served as an admiralty court. Their other duties included fund-raising for Harvard College, settling tariff disputes, and promoting religious orthodoxy.

Unquestionably, serious flaws were inherent in the Confederation of the United Colonies of New England. The illusion of power survived only for the first decade of its existence. Yet it was to be the longest-lived interstate confederation in American history. The leadership which the confederation provided was essential to the existence of the colonies in their early years. It concentrated the colonies' resources in military emergencies and protected the three weaker colonies from encroachment by the Massachusetts Bay colony. Most important of all, it preserved the peace in New England.

## Pertinent Literature

Ward, Harry M. *The United Colonies of New England, 1643-1690,* New York: Vantage Press, 1961.

Harry M. Ward's recent study of the United Colonies of New England represents the only full-scale attempt to deal with a long-neglected subject. Beginning with an investigation of the precedents and ideas that influenced the founders, Ward moves on to a detailed explanation of the practical reasons that prompted attempts at unification. In the first half of the book he carefully chronicles the actual process of organizing the United Colonies of New England, outlines the structure of the governing body, and analyzes the duties and powers of the Board of Commissioners.

For Ward, the Confederation of the United Colonies of New England was important not merely because of its actions in settling intercolonial disputes, but also because it "was destined to implant in the minds of the colonists the idea of federal union and to serve as a precedent for the later American Union." As an independent effort of the colonies in search of a system of common government, Ward ranks it as "one of the most noble experiments of all time."

Since Holland was the center of Puritanism in the early seventeenth century, and many of the New Englanders had lived there for a time, Ward contends that the formation of the Dutch United Provinces in 1579 had no doubt influenced them in the direction of union. In the Puritan religion he also finds seeds of federal ideas. The Puritans were accustomed to reasoning in both particular and general terms, as exemplified by the dual importance of the individual congregation and the general will of the synod, and by the compromise between grace and works. The concept of a union of believers bound by a covenant under God also contributed to federal thinking. Their victory in the Pequot War in

1637 had led the New Englanders to think of themselves as God's chosen people, Ward suggests. Thus they sought to consolidate their gains. While acknowledging the Puritans' sincere desire to promote uniformity of religion, the author sees the need to survive in the wilderness as the most important reason for unification.

The extent to which the Board of Commissioners possessed actual power is a matter of prime concern to the author. In military matters and the conduct of foreign affairs the commissioners could claim sovereignty. With them lay the responsibility for negotiating with foreign powers, preparing for war and declaring it. So active was the confederation in this realm that Ward devotes several chapters to relations and conflicts with the Indians, the French, and the Dutch. Ward claims, however, that the constant activity and success of the confederation in matters of foreign affairs during its first decade created the illusion that it possessed sovereign power in other areas. In actuality, however, power resided in the four member colonies. The founders of the United Colonies of New England had failed to work out enforcement procedures and thus had provided no means for making the commissioners' decisions binding on the individual colonies. Ward, nevertheless, credits the confederation with many important achievements, most notably, the keeping of the peace. For a basic understanding of the formation, structure, and significance of the United Colonies of New England, Ward's study is essential.

## Confederation of the United Colonies of New England

Osgood, Herbert L. *The American Colonies in the Seventeenth Century.* Gloucester, Massachusetts: Peter Smith Publisher, Inc., 1957.

Osgood was a progenitor of the "imperial school" of American colonial historiography, an interpretation of the period which stresses the English foundations and views colonial development from the vantage point of London. His three volumes on *The American Colonies in the Seventeenth Century* are an institutional history of England's mainland colonies. The work does not give much attention to the growth of social or intellectual institutions, nor, unlike Charles M. Andrews, does Osgood focus on the commercial relationship between Great Britain and America. His special preoccupation is with the transformation in English political institutions which was wrought by their transplantation to America. While Osgood may have slighted other facets of colonial developments, he is not unaware of an ever widening breach between the Mother Country and the colonies, which began to develop as royal control increased during the seventeenth century, with implications inherent in such a rift.

Osgood attributes the gap to several factors. By the end of the century the colonists were still subordinate to the larger policy designs of the British Empire. Their own personal and local concerns were, however, "as distinct from those of contemporary Europeans as time or space could well make them." Their culture, language, and traditions were European, but these had all been tempered by the New World experience, in which environmental factors had played a key role. The colonists, Osgood maintains, had by 1700 "become colonials in the full sense of the word but had not yet reached a developed American type."

Some of these ideas emerge in Osgood's discussion of Confederation of the United Colonies of New England. Osgood sees the organization of the Confederation as a response to border and trade disputes between the confederating colonies, their fear of Indian attacks, their proximity to the Dutch and French settlements, and a sense of mission which was "so strong among the New England Puritans." These were matters concerning which there was "no umpire or sovereign in Europe to whom [the New Englanders] would willingly have submitted their controversies, and none whose sympathy could have been enlisted in the furtherance of their cherished projects."

The confederation, in Osgood's view, illustrates how the colonists adapted themselves to their environment. Because unsettled conditions in Great Britain prevented the British from actively, or adequately, defending New England, the colonists created their own institution for that purpose. As Osgood notes, the United Colonies of New England remained viable until after the Restoration when the Mother Country took a more lively interest in colonial affairs.

Like later historians, Osgood devotes much of his discussion to the predominant position of the Massachusetts Bay colony within the United Colonies of New England. Because the Massachusetts Bay colony was the largest, the most populous, and the only New England colony with a royal charter at the time of the confederation's inception, it soon became the predominant member of the organization. And during the active life of the United Colonies of New England it was the commissioners from Massachusetts who made most of the important decisions.

Osgood concludes his examination of the United Colonies of New England with an account of the Confederation's missionary activity among the Indians. This work came to a ruinous end with the outbreak of King Philip's War in 1676.

Osgood does not reach any general conclusion about the importance of the Confederation of the United Colonies of New England. It may be inferred that he regards the attempt at colonial union as an important first step. And it did represent an effort to respond to unique New World problems. — *W.M.B.*

**Additional Recommended Reading**

Andrews, Charles M. *The Colonial Period of American History.* Vols. I-II: *The Settlements.* New Haven: Yale University Press, 1964. The chapters on the New England colonies contain frequent references to the affairs and problems of the Confederation of the United Colonies of New England.

Bradford, William. *Of Plymouth Plantation: The Pilgrims in America.* Edited by Harvey Wish. New York: Capricorn Books, 1962. Bradford records the Articles of Confederation and a brief account of the union in his chronicle for 1643.

Adams, James Truslow. *The Founding of New England.* Boston: Atlantic Monthly Press, 1921. Concentrates on the motives for unification and the actions of the commissioners without details of the administrative structure but with an anti-Puritan bias.

Winthrop, John. *Winthrop's Journal: History of New England, 1630-1649.* Edited by James Kendall Hosmer. New York: Barnes and Noble Inc., 1946. Winthrop's entries for the year 1643 include an account of the formation of the United Colonies of New England and the text of the Articles of Confederation. In the narrative which follows, he conveys a feeling for New England life during the years of the confederation.

# PASSAGE OF THE MARYLAND ACT OF TOLERATION

*Type of event:* Religious: formal expression of a policy of religious toleration
*Time:* April 21, 1649
*Locale:* St. Mary's, Maryland

### Principal personages:

GEORGE CALVERT (FIRST LORD BALTIMORE) (1580?-1632),
who petitioned Charles I for a charter to found a colony north
of the Potomac river
CECILIUS CALVERT (SECOND LORD BALTIMORE) (1605-1675),
son of George Calvert, and the first proprietor of Maryland
LEONARD CALVERT (1606-1647), brother of the first proprietor,
and the first Governor of Maryland

## Summary of Event

In his instructions to his brother Leonard Calvert and the commissioners leading the first settlers to Maryland in 1633, the colony's first proprietor, Cecilius Calvert, second Lord Baltimore, cautioned that "they be very carefull to preserve unity and peace amongst all the passengers on Shipp-board, and that they suffer no scandall nor offence to be given to any of the Protestants. . . ." George Calvert, the First Lord Baltimore and father of Cecilius and Leonard, had died the previous year before his goal of founding a colony free from religious animosity could be realized. While the sincerity of Lord Baltimore's position is unquestionable, it was nonetheless necessary to the recruitment of Protestant settlers for the venture. It would have been impossible to find enough British Catholics willing to emigrate; so advantages had to be offered men of humbler rank, usually loyal practicing members of the Church of England, to persuade them to participate in an undertaking led by Catholic gentlemen.

Although the inability of some Catholic settlers, particularly the Jesuits, to restrain their proselytizing zeal which frequently provoked ill will, religious toleration was practiced from the first. Maryland was indeed unique. Nowhere else had anyone experimented with the concept that Protestants and Catholics could live together amicably and enjoy political and religious equality. Anyone who dared attempt to force his beliefs upon another could expect to meet the fate of one William Lewis, a Catholic who was fined heavily in 1638 for proselytizing among the Protestants. Cecilius Calvert, loyal to his father's purpose, encouraged missionary work by all Christians among the Indians, and Catholics and Protestants used the same chapel for their services of worship. That there should be no established church in Maryland Cecilius Calvert had determined; likewise, the government should not interfere in spiritual matters.

In ensuring the first of these tenets, the first proprietor became involved in a long dispute with the Jesuit missionaries in the colony. Claiming that they were exempt from the civil authority, the Jesuits wanted to obtain land di-

115

rectly from the Indians rather than through the proprietary, as the charter specified. They also demanded special privileges, such as exemption from paying quitrents, and preferred treatment for their retainers and servants. Lord Baltimore finally prevailed when the Jesuits' father provincial ordered them to renounce their claims.

The decade between 1640 and 1650 was an inauspicious time for trying to stabilize a colony founded on the principle of religious toleration. Leonard Calvert barely managed to recover the province after having been forced to flee to Virginia in 1644 when William Claiborne, a troublemaker of long standing, captured Kent Island, and Richard Ingle took St. Mary's and plundered the colony. The combination of American discord and England's Civil War was almost fatal for Lord Baltimore's proprietorship. Only through his shrewdness was he able to ward off revocation of his charter by the triumphant Puritans, and as it was, Catholics and loyalists were threatened with imprisonment and confiscation of their property.

Amid this turmoil Lord Baltimore drafted the famous document "An Act Concerning Religion," which has come to be known as the Toleration Act. The General Assembly passed the measure on April 21, 1649. Since toleration had been practiced from the colony's founding, the act represented no change in Lord Baltimore's policy. It apparently was passed in order to refute the charge by those who had tried to annul the charter that the colony was a hotbed of popery. The act had two parts, each with its own preamble, but the second part, positive in its sentiment, was apparently framed by Cecilius Calvert. This section proclaimed that no person "professing to believe in Jesus Christ shall from henceforth be any waies troubled, molested or discountenanced, for or in respect of his or her Religion, nor in the free Exercise thereof within this Province. . . ." It further provided for the punishment of anyone failing to respect these rights. The first clause of the act was added later by the General Assembly, then controlled by a Protestant-Puritan majority, to accord with an act passed by the Long Parliament in 1648 to punish heresies and blasphemies. As punishment for blasphemy, or for denying the Holy Trinity, or that Jesus Christ was the Son of God, it prescribed the penalty of death and confiscation of property. Paradoxically, the next section again emphasized toleration, prohibiting disparagement "in a reproachful manner" of any religious group and stipulating penalties for offenders. Finally, the act forbade swearing, drunkenness, recreation, and labor on the Sabbath.

"An Act Concerning Religion," therefore, did not guarantee complete religious liberty, freedom of thought, or separation of church and state. The first part, added by the General Assembly, actually represented a regression, since it formally limited toleration to Trinitarian Christians. What the act did accomplish was the official, formal expression of the toleration of Catholics and Protestants for each other's beliefs which had been practiced since 1634.

Following an investigation into the colony by Parliamentary commissioners, the Puritan-dominated Assembly which was called on October 30, 1654, repudiated Lord Baltimore's authority, repealed the Toleration Act, and replaced it with an act denying Catholics protection. When the Calverts regained control in 1657, however, Lord Baltimore promised to stand firm for "An Act Concerning Religion."

## Pertinent Literature

Andrews, Matthew P. *The Founding of Maryland.* Baltimore: The Williams & Wilkins Co., 1933.

It is the contention of Matthew Page Andrews that historians who have based Maryland's claim to priority in the matter of liberty of conscience upon "An Act Concerning Religion" have failed to look carefully at the period of the colony's founding. Maryland's distinction, he claims, rests not on the act but on the actual practices of her founders and early colonists. The records of the early years offer no evidence of persecutions of groups or individuals either for their beliefs or the lack thereof. Such persecutions as did take place were directed against persons who interfered with the freedom of others or tried to enforce conformity to a particular creed.

Briefly tracing the history of attempts to keep religious freedom alive, Andrews admits that, while all seventeenth century churches probably had at least a few advocates of toleration, the Church in general was largely lacking in the qualities of charity and brotherly love. Thus George Calvert, perhaps reacting to his experience as a government official sent to enforce conformity in Ireland in the days before he became a Catholic, stands out as an enlightened man ahead of his time. In his earlier effort to establish the Avalon colony in Newfoundland as a haven for Catholics, he had welcomed Anglicans. Cecilius Calvert, says Andrews, adhered faithfully to his father's intentions and, in addition, evolved a princi- ple of separation of church and state. In rebutting historians who argue that the Maryland charter does not provide sufficient evidence of adoption of these principles, Andrews says that even Charles I would not have openly promulgated a plan for a government free of ecclesiastical influence. Yet Cecilius Calvert cautioned the provincial commissioners as they embarked for Maryland to permit no offense among the colonists on matters of religion. The first proprietor's dispute with the Jesuits over their claims to land and special privileges is offered as further evidence of his determination to prevent clerical influence in political matters.

In Andrew's view "An Act Concerning Religion" actually introduced limits upon the previous conditions of freedom, and laid down particular beliefs from which one could not dissent without facing persecution. Andrews attributes the act to the influence of intolerant Puritan elements who immigrated to Maryland in increasing numbers after 1642 and wielded power during the Cromwellian period. Because the first part is decidedly more restrictive than the second, explains Andrews, the act represents a compromise between the tolerant ideas practiced by the early settlers and the restrictive measures advocated by the Puritans. The use of the word "Sabbath" and the prohibition against swearing also show Puritan influence, Andrews argues, since both

117

Passage of the Maryland Act of Toleration

Catholics and Anglicans were generally less concerned about such matters. Despite its restrictive features, "An Act of Toleration," Andrews admits, represented an advance over the religious principles of most of the Christian world, since it ensured for all Christian sects the right to practice their own religion. The freedoms granted were broader than those of Rhode Island, Andrews concludes, for political privileges were not limited by religious beliefs.

Andrews, Charles M. *The Colonial Period of American History.* Vol. II: *The Settlements.* New Haven: Yale University Press, 1964.

This work represents the culmination of a lifetime of scholarship by one of the foremost historians of the colonial period and the leading member of the "imperial school" of colonialists.

In his preface, Charles M. Andrews asserts that seventeenth century American history must be approached from "the English end." Deploring the tendency of many American historians to find something sinister in England's early relationship with the colonies, he defends as natural England's desire to protect herself against competitors and to seek her own best interests. This theme runs throughout the four-volume work, which covers the settlement and early development of each of England's Atlantic colonies and "England's Commercial and Colonial Policy." Andrews' detailed explanations of the circumstances in England which motivated particular colonial enterprises and which affected British attitudes toward the new settlements gave American colonial history a dimension which it had lacked as long as scholars insisted upon studying the colonies in isolation.

Andrews' treatment of the colonization of Maryland reflects his clear understanding of the way circumstances in England influenced events in America. Andrews gives George Cal-

vert his due as an advocate of religious toleration, but he also sees the proprietor as a practical man. Because Catholic gentlemen willing to immigrate to the New World were scarce, Calvert was ready to offer religious toleration as an enticement to Anglicans to become part of his enterprise. Cecilius' instructions to the leaders of the expedition to ensure amity between the Protestants and Catholics show his loyalty to his father's purpose to establish a colony where men of different beliefs could live in peace.

Characterizing the Maryland experiment as an "act of religious knight-errantry," Andrews describes the turbulent religious and political climate both in England and the Chesapeake Bay region which rendered the existence of the colony so hazardous. Because of his involvement in family land disputes in England and because the Civil War was being fought, Cecilius Calvert was never able to travel to Maryland himself. Although Catholics controlled the positions of power in the colony, Protestants were consistently in the majority. In keeping with his convictions, Calvert had allowed numerous Puritans to immigrate to Maryland, perhaps in part to frustrate the aspirations of the Jesuit missionaries for power. In 1648 alone, between four hundred and six hundred Puritans came from Virginia to enjoy political and religious freedom in the settlement of Providence, which they established near Annapolis. Calvert's liberality worked against him, for the presence of so many settlers possessing strong religious and political convictions resulted in a period of anxiety and instability in Maryland, during which political power changed hands frequently.

To meet the charges of those who aimed to have his charter revoked on the grounds that the Catholics held sway in the colony, Calvert prepared "An Act Concerning Religion." The act represented no change in Calvert's policy, since he had advocated toleration for Trinitarians from the first. Yet he certainly realized that a formal declaration of toleration would aid his cause in England and attract colonists who had failed to find peace elsewhere. Perhaps, too, in light of the threat from the Protestant majority, he wished to ratify the original purposes of the colony and to protect the Catholic church. The more restrictive clause of the act,

Andrews agrees, was not Calvert's work but an addition by the Puritan-dominated Assembly.

Andrews concludes that "An Act Concerning Religion" guaranteed neither full religious liberty nor freedom of thought; it did not even separate the Church and the state. Although some men of the time envisioned these concepts as ideal, they were not, according to Andrews, part of the common consciousness. "The act went no farther than to give, as a matter of expedience and necessity, formal expression to that toleration [espoused by Lord Baltimore in 1633]."

Andrews' analysis of "An Act Concerning Religion" is particularly meaningful within the context of the chaotic situation in Maryland in the 1640's. The author's detailed description and explanation of the diverse religious and political elements which combined to create uncertainty and anxiety provide an indispensable background for understanding the act. — *W.M.B.*

## Additional Recommended Reading

Craven, Wesley F. *The Southern Colonies in the Seventeenth Century, 1607-1689.* Baton Rouge: Louisiana State University Press, 1949. Chapters VI and VII provide an excellent introduction to Maryland's beginnings, especially in religious matters.

Hall, Clayton C. *The Lords Baltimore and the Maryland Palatinate.* Baltimore: John Murphy Co., 1902. The first three lectures published in this volume are devoted to the founding efforts of the first Lord Baltimore and to the administration of government under his son Cecilius Calvert, including the promotion of religious toleration.

Hanley, Thomas. *Their Rights and Liberties: The Beginnings of Religious and Political Freedom in Maryland.* Westminster, Maryland: Newman Press, 1959. In an obscure ordinance initiated by the Maryland colonists in 1639, Hanley finds evidence of the principles of religious freedom well before the Act of Toleration.

Mereness, Newton D. *Maryland as a Proprietary Province.* New York: The Macmillan Company, 1901. The concluding chapters of Part III briefly trace the policy of religious toleration in Maryland.

Hall, Clayton C., ed. *Narratives of Early Maryland, 1633-1684.* New York: Barnes and Noble Inc., 1946. This collection of original documents includes Lord Baltimore's instructions to the colonists, the text of "An Act Concerning Religion," and various first-hand accounts of the early years in Maryland.

Steiner, Bernard C. *Beginnings of Maryland.* Baltimore: The Johns Hopkins University Press, 1903. Relations between Protestants and Catholics are among subjects covered in this detailed general history.

# PASSAGE OF BRITISH NAVIGATION ACTS

*Type of event:* Economic: attempt to increase British maritime activity
*Time:* 1660-1663
*Locale:* The British Empire

### Principal personages:

CHARLES II (1630-1685), King of Great Britain 1660-1685

EARL OF CLARENDON (EDWARD HYDE) (1609-1674), Lord Chancellor appointed by Charles

THOMAS POVEY (fl. seventeenth century), influential English merchant

JOHN SHAW (fl. 1660), English financier who brought the Navigation Bill of 1660 before Parliament

SIR GEORGE DOWNING (1623-1684), Member of Parliament and Commissioner of Customs

FOURTH EARL OF SOUTHAMPTON (THOMAS WRIOTHESLEY) (1607-1667), Lord High Treasurer of England 1660-1667

GEORGE MONCK (BARON MONCK, EARL OF TORRINGTON) (1608-1670), Privy Councilor

### Summary of Event

During the Elizabethan era, England, hitherto an agricultural country, began to emerge as a great nation ready to compete with the other European nations for wealth and power. The doctrine of mercantilism which the Crown adopted decreed that a nation must attain a favorable balance of trade—that is, to export more than it imported—in order to accumulate bullion for financing war efforts and maintaining national security. Because the navy was thought to be essential to the strength of the nation and because commercial maritime activity enhanced naval power, attention in the seventeenth century centered upon the promotion of English shipping. Success demanded the overthrow of the Dutch monopoly in the carrying trade.

That colonies existed for the benefit of the Mother Country and that the colonies' trade should be restricted to the Mother Country were tenets accepted by all the great commercial rivals of the seventeenth century. As England's knowledge of its colonies and of the new products to be reaped from them increased, so did its expectation of the colonies' potential contribution to its grand scheme. England lacked definite laws relating to commercial policy until 1650 when a combination of private corporate interests and the national interest motivated Parliament to enact legislation designed to attain the national goals. In an attempt to break Dutch control of commerce, Parliament in 1650 forbade foreign ships to trade with the colonies without a license. The following year, Parliament enacted a law stating, in part, that (1) only British-owned ships, of which the master and majority of the crew were British, could import goods from Asia, Africa, and America into Great Brit-

121

ain, Ireland, or the colonies; (2) only British ships or ships of the country of origin could import European goods into Great Britain, Ireland, or the colonies; and (3) foreign goods could be imported into England only from the place of production. Unfortunately, the act also prohibited British merchant ships from sailing from country to country to take on produce for import, and more seriously it provoked a two-year war with the Dutch. The entire period from 1651 to 1660 was marked by a great commercial struggle among the powers of western and northern Europe. Furthermore the last years before the Restoration in Great Britain were fraught with uncertainty and financial difficulties.

When Charles II came to the throne in 1660, he acted upon the urging of the merchants to promote British commerce. He established two councils, one for trade and one for plantations, consisting of lords, merchants, planters, and sea captains. Through the Crown's instructions to these councils, commercial policies were gradually defined. At the same time, Parliament gave the policies statutory authority. The first of such measures was the Navigation Act of 1660, sponsored by John Shaw, a prominent financier, and Sir George Downing, later Commissioner of Customs. Enacted by the Convention Parliament on September 13, 1660, and confirmed by the first regular Restoration Parliament on July 27, 1661, the act was in many respects similar to that of 1651. Certain defects and ambiguities in the earlier act had hindered enforcement and certain revisions were necessary. The act of 1660 provided that only British-built or British-owned ships of which the masters

and three-quarters of the crew were British could import or export goods or commodities, regardless of origin, to and from the British colonies. It further restricted shipment of certain enumerated articles produced in the colonies (sugar, tobacco, cotton, indigo, ginger, speckle wood, and dyewoods) to Great Britain or its colonies, and required ships sailing from the colonies to give bond that they would unload their cargoes in the realm. The enumeration clause was intended to increase England's customs revenues, to insure its access to raw materials, and to advance domestic industries by giving employment in the trades which employed the enumerated products.

In practice, the 1660 regulations created many problems, and shippers took advantage of loopholes and ambiguities to evade the law. Probably to facilitate enforcement, Parliament in 1662 passed the Act of Frauds. It restricted the privileges of the act of 1660 to ships built in England, except for ships bought before 1662.

Great Britain still had to clarify the dependent relationship of its colonies to the Mother Country. If the government were to recover from virtual bankruptcy incurred by the Puritans and royal debts, it could not allow the colonies to buy European products at cheaper prices, and it had to gain customs revenues from the colonial merchants. To make Great Britain the sole exporting center for colonial imports and thus constitute it a "staple," Parliament, on July 27, 1663, passed the "Act for the Encouragement of Trade." Henceforth, European goods could be imported to the colonies only from England and in English-built ships. The only exceptions to the rule were salt for the New England and Newfoundland fisheries, wine from Madeira and the Azores, and provisions, servants, and horses from Ireland and Scotland.

Because of the complexity of the Navigation Acts, administrative discretion was important in determining how they should be interpreted and enforced. In the colonies enforcement lay with the governors, who were required to send to England reports of all vessels trading within their jurisdiction together with copies of the bonds required of all ships' masters. Both colonial and English sea captains, however, found ways of continuing direct trade with Europe, and smuggling was common. In the period immediately following passage of the Navigation Acts, the colonists protested about the restriction on their markets. As English markets became glutted with colonial goods, the returns which the

colonists could expect decreased. The Puritans of the Massachusetts Bay colony objected to the acts on the basis that, since they were not represented in Parliament, they were not subject to the laws passed by Parliament. Gradually, however, most colonists adjusted to compliance, and the insurrections which occurred in the years following cannot be attributed in any large sense to the Navigation Acts.

As far as England was concerned, the legislation did achieve its purpose. Colonial trade with England and British overseas shipping increased more rapidly than before. There were sufficient causes for the American Revolution apart from the Navigation Acts, and the habits of trade which the acts established lasted beyond the eighteenth century. By the mid-nineteenth century Great Britain had become the world's greatest commercial and maritime power.

## Pertinent Literature

Andrews, Charles M. *The Colonial Period of American History.* Vol. IV: *England's Commercial and Colonial Policy.* New Haven: Yale University Press, 1964.

In keeping with his consistent approach to American colonial history from the "English end," Charles M. Andrews views the Navigation Acts of 1660 and 1663 as expressions of Great Britain's goal to develop a great commercial empire. He explains British efforts within the context of seventeenth century ideas about the nature of the nation state. Free trade, international coöperation, and mutual dependence were foreign to the seventeenth century concept of the national interest. Jealous of its rivals, Great Britain sought to establish a self-sufficient empire. Colonies were expected to accept the princi-

ple that their chief purpose was to contribute to the advantage of the Mother Country.

Andrews outlines England's commercial scheme as follows: (1) the colonies were to have a monopoly of the English market; (2) England was to have a monopoly on the colonial output; (3) England was to control the carrying trade; (4) the colonies were obligated to pay English customs duties; and (5) England was to enlarge its navy and merchant marine. These principles were designed not only to enhance England's position but also to destroy the monopoly of its Dutch rival. The Dutch at this point were superior in ship-building, conducting finances, and carrying trade. In Holland trade was, in Andrews' phrase, "the national sport," while the English had heretofore regarded it as an inferior activity.

When Parliament assumed control of the colonies in 1649, it sought to further the interests of the merchant class by promoting trade and colonial enterprises. Andrews criticizes the Navigation Act of 1651 as a reactionary measure provoked by narrow London interests. It had little effect on the colonies, he claims, but harmed the English merchants by prohibiting them from stopping at various ports to pick up goods destined for the home market. At a time when England needed peace to recoup the losses of the Civil War, it foolishly provoked war with Holland. Cromwell's subordination of commercial matters to Puritan politics allowed financial problems to accumulate. With the Restoration came an urgent effort on the part of those interested in trade and the colonies to define and implement England's plans for recovery.

Andrews carefully analyzes the purposes of the Navigation Acts of 1660 and 1663, as well as the problems of their enforcement. The acts were opposed in both England and the colonies. Some English critics of the legislation argued that foreign-built ships should be admitted to English registry, and others charged that the laws worked to the advantage of only a small number of merchants and not the nation as a whole. That enumeration increased the cost of carrying colonial staples to foreign markets was a justifiable complaint.

Andrews takes a restrained view of the colonial protests, maintaining that they were confined primarily to the periods immediately following the acts' passage. Because the inhabitants of the nonroyal colonies had become accustomed to a considerable measure of commercial independence, they naturally "felt the pinch of constriction" most sharply. In Virginia, also, Governor Berkeley himself complained that the laws enriched only a few, but kept tobacco prices down, thus inflicting poverty upon the colony. Yet, says Andrews, these protests represented the first recoil from the blow the acts administered. There is no evidence that either Virginia or Maryland, both of which had enjoyed freedom of trade with the Dutch during the Civil War in England, suffered seriously from the enumeration restrictions. The Puritans of the Massachusetts Bay colony, on the other hand, considered themselves outside the jurisdiction of Parliamentary legislation since they were not represented in that body. Determined to preserve their open trading system, they simply ignored the Navigation Acts while at the same time passing laws requiring obedience to them. Only the revocation of the Massachusetts charter achieved their submission.

Andrews concludes that although the Navigation Acts may have contributed to the unrest in the American colonies, they were not directly responsible for the insurrections which occurred.

Harper, Lawrence A. *The English Navigation Laws.* New York: Octagon Books, Inc., 1964.

Lawrence A. Harper considers the English Navigation Acts an "experiment in social engineering." It is fitting, then, that he treats his subject scientifically, testing the effectiveness of the English experiment on the basis of statistical evidence. Because his investigation of the ramifications of the acts and of corollary matters is almost exhaustive, the book requires close attention. While it is not an easy book to read, it stands as a superior example of historical research, particularly in the handling of statistical material. Harper's study thus deserves its position as the definitive work on the Navigation Acts.

The seventeenth century "social engineers," as Harper calls them, believed that England must achieve a favorable balance of trade if it was to accumulate sufficient bullion to wage war. Likewise, the navy and merchant marine must be strengthened. Therefore, these advocates of mercantilism, confident that the national interest was compatible with their individual advancement, called upon Parliament to place their plans in legislative form. Harper traces the history of English shipping legislation and suggests that through a process of trial and error Parliament stumbled upon the formula for protecting England's shipping. The Navigation Act of 1651, he explains, represented simplification of earlier attempts at legislation. Parliament erred in trying to make the act comprehensive. Learning from this experience, Restoration statesmen in the acts of 1660 and 1663 avoided the "nuisance features" of the earlier measure of 1651 and made enforcement possible.

Harper emphasizes the importance of self-seeking business interests in determining the provisions of the Navigation Act of 1663, calling it "a monument to the legislative capacity for combining diverse and unrelated topics. . . ." It serves as a stumbling block, he points out, to those who claim that the old colonial system was impartially designed for the good of the British Empire.

A large portion of Harper's book is devoted to dissecting the administrative machinery employed in the enforcement of the Navigation Acts. The author contends that, given the complexity of the legislation, administrative actions actually determined how it should operate. The Privy Council, the Lords of the Treasury, and the Commissioners of Customs all helped to shape the laws in response to practical considerations. Harper concerns himself in particular with the activities of customs officials at the waterside. Their job was a frustrating one, for even otherwise-respectable people made a game of trying to outwit the enforcement agencies. The role of the Vice-Admiralty and Exchequer courts in the prosecution of smugglers when apprehended was an important one and is fully treated by Harper. Dependence on private "informers" and an insufficient number of customs personnel made enforcement of the Navigation Acts especially difficult in the colonies, and before the establishment of the Admiralty Courts there, lack of uniformity in the "rough and ready" judicial system complicated the prosecution of violaters. Colonial governors were given more responsibility than actual authority in enforcing the laws, and they were denied flexibility of action in dealing with the variety of cases which they had to handle.

Harper's primary purpose is to test whether the Navigation Acts aided the growth of England's empire and power. He specifically examines the evidence concerning their influence on the development of shipping, the training of sailors, and the employment of shipwrights. The figures which he marshals for the period before enactment of the laws, while they were in force, and after their repeal, furnish a panoramic view of English maritime history. After 1660, the total tonnage of shipping and the number of seamen increased at a more rapid rate than before, and after 1662 the shipbuilding industry grew. He denies that England would have gained a natural monopoly of colonial trade without the laws. The very resistance to these measures, he holds, is proof that they constituted a burden to the colonists and directed their trade into new channels. That enforcement was reasonably effective is indicated by the small fraction of total commerce attributable to illicit trade. — *W.M.B.*

## Additional Recommended Reading

Barnes, Viola F. *The Dominion of New England: A Study in British Colonial Policy.* New York: Frederick Ungar Publishing Co., 1960. Describes the reaction of the Puritans to English commercial policy and the problems involved in enforcing the Navigation Acts.

Beer, George L. *The Old Colonial System, 1660-1754.* Part I. Gloucester, Massachusetts: Peter Smith Publishers, Inc., 1958. A study of the establishment, development, and operation of the English colonial system, this work examines the economic and political development of the colonies as affected by imperial policy.

Clark, George N. *The Later Stuarts, 1660-1714.* Oxford: University Press, 1955. Part of *The Oxford History of England,* this volume provides an excellent background for an understanding of the economic tendencies and domestic and foreign policies of the reign of Charles II.

Dickerson, Oliver M. *The Navigation Acts and the American Revolution.* Philadelphia: University of Pennsylvania Press, 1951. Although Dickerson is primarily concerned with the eighteenth century Navigation Acts, his early chapters are valuable for a study of the seventeenth century attempts at regulation.

# THE HALF-WAY COVENANT

*Type of event:* Religious: amendment of Puritan doctrine concerning church membership
*Time:* 1662
*Locale:* Boston, Massachusetts

> *Principal personages:*
> RICHARD MATHER (1596-1669), minister of the church in Dorchester, Massachusetts, and principal leader in devising the Half-Way Covenant
> INCREASE MATHER (1639-172?), son of Richard, who opposed the Half-Way Covenant but who later changed his position
> CHARLES CHAUNCY (1592-1672), president of Harvard College and leading opponent of the movement to revise membership requirements
> JOHN WOODBRIDGE, JR. (fl. 1662), minister in Killingworth, Connecticut, who led his congregation beyond the Half-Way Covenant and opened membership to all

## Summary of Event

One of the most compelling questions about the Puritan Commonwealth established in Massachusetts during the seventeenth century concerns the reasons for its decline. Historians have found it difficult to determine not only why the rule of the "saints" came to an end but also the time when the deterioration began. Some have contended that the system of the Church and the state established under the leadership of such men as John Winthrop and John Cotton was so well constructed that it remained almost unchanged for many years. Others believe that Puritan ideals began to falter from the beginning, and that too much stress has been placed on the pervasiveness of a group of attitudes defined as the "Puritan mind."

Among the controversial issues which have enlivened the debate over Puritan decline is the so-called "Half-Way Covenant" of 1662. The most important provision of this document, endorsed by a synod of more than eighty ministers and laymen meeting in Boston, was that children whose parents had not been admitted to full membership in a Puritan church might nevertheless be eligible for baptism.

The question of membership was one which had long plagued the churches of New England. On the one hand, Puritans believed that no one should be admitted to full communion in the Church who had not sufficiently demonstrated a personal experience by which he had become convinced that God had elected him to salvation. And yet if one believed that prospective church members must await a message from God, what part was the Church itself to play in recruiting new adherents? This problem became increasingly acute as the proportion of Puritans in New England declined in relation to the growing population of the area. It began to seem, as Jonathan Mitchel wrote, that the churches had been set up "onely that *a few old Christians* may keep one another warm while they live, and then carry away the Church into the cold grave with them when they dye. . . ."

The Half-Way Covenant did not concern the admission of new members from outside the Church but attempted rather to deal with the problems raised by the children and grandchildren of the "elect." Since the Puritans believed in infant baptism they had always permitted church members to have their children brought under the care of the congregation, although each had to await the conversion experience before being admitted to full membership. It was expected that a significant number of these young people would ultimately experience conversion, but until that time, they were not permitted to participate in communion or vote on Church business. Unfortunately, this arrangement did not provide for the third generation.

During the early days of the Puritan Commonwealth, the churches did not have to concern themselves about the grandchildren of the "elect" because there were none. Nor when they did begin to appear was there any difficulty about those whose parents had been received into full communion with a church. The problem arose with those members of the third generation whose parents had not yet achieved full membership: were such infants to be baptised or not? No one could say for certain that the parents of these children would not experience a conversion at some later time, since the Puritans did not believe that God necessarily informed the "saints" of their election at any certain age. Moreover, if these infants were to be denied baptism would

it not then become necessary to expel their parents from the privileged position they had held in a church since childhood?

The answer which the Half-Way Covenant provided to this question may have confirmed a practice which was already developing in New England. It stated that, in cases where children were born to parents who had not yet attained full church membership, the congregation should baptize the new infants. Such persons could not, however, become full members of a church unless they subsequently experienced conversion. Both they and their parents enjoyed a kind of "halfway" membership which enabled the Puritans to maintain their rigid standards for full communion in a church and yet to provide for the possible conversion of new members. Infants baptised into a church were obviously more likely to achieve full membership than those who were excluded from the fold.

The Half-Way Covenant provided the Puritan Commonwealth with one of its most prolonged controversies. Although the Synod of 1662 had strongly endorsed the covenant, it was opposed by a small and determined group of ministers and temporarily refused by a significant number of congregations. Most of its opponents charged that, despite claims to the contrary, the covenant would open up a church to persons who were not among God's elect. Richard Mather, one of those most responsible for the decision of the synod, found his congregation at Dorchester skeptical about the covenant, and his sons, Increase and Eleazar, among its most vocal opponents. Another influential leader of the opposition was

128

Charles Chauncy, who, as president of Harvard College, was among the most respected scholars in the province. Nevertheless, despite such pockets of resistance as that evidenced by the refusal of Boston's Second Church to accept the covenant until 1693, the Puritan churches in New England gradually came to accept the idea of "half-way" membership. Not until the great religious revivals of the 1740's swept through the colonies did the covenant again come under serious attack and by then the Puritan commonwealth, as such, had ceased to exist.

## Pertinent Literature

Miller, Perry. *The New England Mind.* Vol. I: *The Seventeenth Century.* New York: Macmillan Company, 1939.

Miller, Perry. *The New England Mind.* Vol. II: *From Colony to Province.* Cambridge: Harvard University Press, 1953.

Perry Miller's two volumes provide a magisterial account of intellectual life in early New England. Miller focuses on the Puritans of Massachusetts Bay colony. His richly complex study spans the entire seventeenth century.

In his first volume, Miller presents a topical survey of the major tenets of New England Puritanism. In a prose style that seldom comforts the reader, he carefully delineates the worldview of the Saints. His discussion ranges over Puritan notions about religion and learning, cosmology, anthropology, and sociology. He gives special emphasis to the Puritans' belief in covenant theology. The founders of the Bay colony, he argues, believed that they were parties to a covenant with God. Their contractual obligation to the Almighty required them to go to Massachusetts and to build a colony in the wilderness.

Miller chronicles the actual work of colonization in his second volume. He contends that the founders established their settlement with an eye to the wider world. They intended to build a model community, a "Bible Commonwealth," that would serve as an example for their European coreligionists. Miller pictures the builders of the Bay colony as men and women of high purpose and immense intellectual energy. They treated dissenters with a heavy hand and kept theological precepts foremost in mind. The church stood at the center of their lives.

According to Miller, New England Puritanism retained its pristine quality for only one generation. The passage of time and the challenges of a frontier environment changed the focus of Puritan life. Second generation Bay colonists lacked the sense of mission that inspired their immediate predecessors. Measures, such as the Half-Way Covenant, clearly reveal the decline of religious self-assurance. The Puritans continued to expand their settlements, but they labored in the name of a far less exalted purpose. Their concerns became increasingly secular. The task of building a "Bible Commonwealth" gave way to the chore of clearing the wilderness.

Perry Miller sketches the Puritan experience in bold strokes. At the same time, he shows keen appreciation for

129

the intricacies of seventeenth century Puritan thought. His two volume work stands as a seminal contribution to both American History and the History of Ideas.

Morgan, Edmund S. *Visible Saints: The History of a Puritan Idea.* New York: New York University Press, 1963.

One of the first historians to take issue with Perry Miller's long-standing contention that the Half-Way Covenant illustrated the decline of Puritanism is Edmund Morgan. In *Visible Saints,* Professor Morgan argues that biological necessity, rather than a decline of faith, forced the Puritans to modify their membership requirements. It was inevitable that children would be born to members who had not yet achieved the status of full communicants in the Church and that some provision would have to be made for them. Morgan believes that the Half-Way Covenant is not a symptom of Puritan decline but evidence of their determination to maintain rigid standards of membership.

In pursuing this argument, the author of *Visible Saints* goes back to the founding of the colony in order to demonstrate a significant difference between the churches of Massachusetts and Puritan congregations elsewhere. Morgan contends that, until the 1630s, Puritan churches neither in Europe nor America required prospective members to recount the experience which convinced them of their election. In doing this, he again suggests revisions in the conclusions of Perry Miller, insisting that this unique requirement for membership developed in Massachusetts after the settlement rather than being imported from Europe or Plymouth.

The importance of Professor Morgan's contention about the peculiarity of membership requirements in Massachusetts churches is evident in his conclusion. If Puritan churches in Massachusetts were the first to insist that members demonstrate their "election," it is easier to understand why the colony experienced difficulties such as those which resulted in the Half-Way Covenant. Since earlier churches expected nothing more than a thorough knowledge of doctrine, it was relatively easy to prepare children for full membership in the congregation. In such churches the problem of baptized but unconverted parents did not arise. By the time children of church members had reached the age at which they might themselves become parents, they had been trained for and admitted into full communion with the Church. Not so for the congregations in Massachusetts which had come to expect something more than just an understanding of church doctrine.

By the middle of the seventeenth century, Professor Morgan believes the Massachusetts churches faced an unprecedented crisis over membership, which admitted only three possible solutions. The Puritans could have ignored the problem raised by the third generation and, by making no provision for the baptism of such persons, condemned the Church to a decline of membership which would have robbed it of its influence and perhaps its existence. They could have made it easier to obtain full membership in the Church, a solution which would have provided genuine evidence of declining zeal. Instead of choosing either of these extremes, the Puritans of Massachusetts, by adopting the Half-Way Covenant, protected their rigid criteria for full Church membership without isolating themselves from the rest of the colony.

In publishing *Visible Saints,* Professor Morgan continues an interpretative slant which he expounded in his earlier study of John Winthrop, entitled *The Puritan Dilemma.* In both studies, as the author himself explains it, the attempt has been to show that the Puritan, "while trying to live as God re-

quired, learned that he must live *in* the world, face its temptations, and share its guilt; . . ." The strength of the Massachusetts Puritans was that, like Winthrop himself, they managed to maintain much of their idealism without becoming fanatics. If Professor Morgan is correct, this golden mean is evident in the Half-Way Covenant of 1662; it permitted Massachusetts to solve the problem of Church membership and yet to avoid the dual pitfalls of compromise with the world on the one hand and withdrawal from it on the other. — *D.L.A.*

## Additional Recommended Reading

Pope, Robert G. *The Half-Way Covenant: Church Membership in Puritan New England.* Princeton: Princeton University Press, 1969. The most detailed discussion of the Half-Way Covenant by an author who accepts, in general, the thesis advanced by Edmund Morgan.

Miller, Perry. *Errand into the Wilderness.* Cambridge: Harvard University Press, 1956. This collection of essays by Miller is a good introduction to Puritan theology and is especially useful for those who find his larger studies too formidable.

Murdock, Kenneth B. *Increase Mather: The Foremost American Puritan.* Cambridge: Harvard University Press, 1925. Although an older study, this is a good biography of a major Puritan divine who played an important part in the Puritan churches during their years of decline.

Morison, Samuel Eliot. *Builders of the Bay Colony.* Boston: Houghton Mifflin Co., 1930. Biographical essays on various figures in Massachusetts of the seventeenth century providing an extraordinarily readable introduction to the history of New England.

Adams, Brooks Henry. *The Emancipation of Massachusetts: The Dream and the Reality.* Cambridge: Harvard University Press, 1919. Although now outdated, this work is representative of an earlier group of historians who were hostile to Puritanism, and especially to the New England clergy.

# SETTLEMENT OF THE CAROLINAS

*Type of event:* Sociological: takeover of the Carolinas by the British Crown in place of proprietorships aimed at personal profit
*Time:* 1663-1729
*Locale:* The eastern part of the Carolinas

*Principal personages:*

EARL OF SHAFTESBURY (ANTHONY ASHLEY COOPER) (1621-1683), proprietor and architect of the Carolina proprietary system

SIR JOHN COLLETON (fl.1660), wealthy Barbadian planter who took the initiative in acquiring the proprietary charter for the Carolinas

SIR WILLIAM BERKELEY (1606-1677), Governor of Virginia (1642-1676) and an original Carolina proprietor

WILLIAM DRUMMOND (fl.1664), first Governor of Albemarle County which later became North Carolina

SIR JOHN YEAMANS (1610?-1674), leader of South Carolina's Goose Creek faction

JOHN LOCKE (1632-1704), English political philosopher, who as Ashley Cooper's protégé helped to prepare the Fundamental Constitutions

JOHN CULPEPER (fl.1671-1680), leader of a rebellion against Albemarle's proprietary government in 1677

PHILIP LUDWELL (fl.1660-1704), first Governor of both Carolinas in 1691

EDWARD HYDE (c.1650-1712), first Governor of North Carolina independent of South Carolina

SIR FRANCIS NICHOLSON (1655-1728), first Royal Governor of South Carolina

## Summary of Event

The introduction of large-scale sugar production to Barbados in the early 1660's forced many small planters to consider emigration. When Sir John Colleton, a wealthy Barbadian, returned to England and gained a seat on the Council for Foreign Plantations, he conceived the idea of establishing a proprietary colony and recruiting Barbadians to settle it. For fellow proprietors he turned to seven powerful Englishmen who had been associated with colonial expansion: the Earl of Shaftesbury, Sir William Berkeley, John Lord Berkeley, the Duke of Albemarle (George Monck), the Earl of Clarendon (Edward Hyde), the Earl of Craven, and Sir George Carteret. On March 24, 1663, Charles II granted to the proprietors the land between latitude 36 and 31 degrees north and extending west to the South Seas, which they called Carolina. Required only to pay a nominal annual sum to the king,

132

the proprietors possessed vast powers—to fill offices, erect a government, establish courts, collect customs and taxes, grant land, confer titles, and determine military matters. They were obliged to guarantee the rights of Englishmen to their settlers, however, and could enact laws only with the consent of the freemen.

Having devised plans for the creation of three counties and begun negotiations with two groups of prospective settlers in Barbados and New England, the proprietors drafted a document, the "Declaration and Proposals to all that Will Plant in Carolina," which outlined a headright system of land distribution and a framework for participatory government. Sir William Berkeley received authorization to appoint a governor and council for Albemarle County (later North Carolina) and in October, 1664, he named William Drummond of Virginia Governor. A few months later, Sir John Yeamans was commissioned Governor of Clarendon County. As a further inducement to settlement, the proprietors in January, 1665, drew up the "Concessions and Agreements," which provided for a unicameral legislature including representatives of the freemen and insured religious toleration. Friction between new arrivals and the original settlers, combined with Indian hostility and news of better land to the south, led to the abandonment of Clarendon County in 1667.

Because the "Concessions and Agreements" proved unsatisfactory, the Earl of Shaftesbury in 1669 collaborated with his protégé John Locke to write "The Fundamental Constitutions of Carolina." An elaborate blueprint for government, it proposed a feudal system whereby two-thirds of the land would be held by a colonial nobility. Although a "parliament" consisting of the nobility and popular representatives would sit in the colony, the proprietors in England would constitute a Palatine Court which could veto the legislature's decisions. Certain provisions of the Fundamental Constitutions were implemented, but the proprietors never succeeded in winning the Assembly's approval of the system as a whole. Thus the actual government of Albemarle consisted of a powerful governor and council appointed by the proprietors and representatives elected by the freemen. After 1691, the popular branch of the legislature met separately and began to exercise parliamentary privileges. Until the establishment of a supreme court in 1700, the governor and council constituted the colony's highest court.

Since travel to Albemarle both by land and water was difficult, the area remained isolated and failed to develop. The proprietors, blaming the inhabitants for the region's slow growth, spent more time and money on South Carolina. The trickle of settlers to Albemarle County was due largely to uncertainty about the terms of landholding. To promote settlement of the region, the proprietors in 1668 signed the "Great Deed of Grant," placing landholding on the same basis as in Virginia, but because they themselves often violated its provisions, their efforts were unavailing. The failure of the proprietors to establish a stable, efficient government was also a great handicap to Albemarle's progress. Out of the proprietors' efforts to enforce the Navigation Acts, which were harmful to the colony's trade, there arose proprietary and antiproprietary factions. When Governor Thomas Miller of the proprietary faction attempted to assume the duties of customs collector in 1677, the opposing faction, led by John Culpeper, seized him and took control of the government. The rebellion failed, however, and the rebel governor was tried for treason in London. Shaftesbury magnanimously used his influence to bring about Culpeper's acquittal.

With the appointment of Philip Ludwell as "Governor of Carolina" in November, 1691, Albemarle's unfortunate history as a county ended. Ludwell was to reside in Charles Town, while North Carolina, governed by his deputy, was to retain a separate legislature. For the next fifteen years North Carolina enjoyed a peaceful and well-administered government. Huguenots from Virginia settled the area south of Albemarle Sound. In 1705 the Assembly incorporated Bath as the province's first town, and German Palatines and Swiss founded New Bern in 1710.

During the first decade of the eighteenth century, North Carolina was torn by religious dissension. Although toleration had prevailed from the beginning, and many dissenters had held positions of power, Anglicans were determined to establish the Church of England in the province. With the passage of the Vestry Act of 1703, Assembly members were required to take an oath of loyalty to the Church of England. In 1710 the proprietors appointed Edward Hyde Governor—the first Governor of North Carolina to be independent of the Governor of Carolina—and the legislature nullified the laws of the previous dissenter administration. The previous Governor, Thomas Cary, led an unsuccessful rebellion against Hyde.

In September, 1711, the Tuscarora Indians, seeking revenge for white encroachment on their lands, enslavement of Indians, and unfair trading practices, fell upon the already demoralized settlers from the Neuse to the Pamlico rivers. Two expeditions, aided by South Carolina and led by Colonel Jack Barnwell and Colonel James More in 1712 and 1713, finally broke the power of the Tuscarora.

Although the Indian war had placed the colony in dire financial straits, it drew the people together, and they entered a period of peace. The legislature of 1715 revised the laws in order to improve administration and avoid confusion. As the damaged towns were rebuilt, new ones were begun. Under the administration of Governor George Burrington in the mid-1720's immigration increased, and four new counties were formed. As part of the "royalizing" process throughout the colonies, the crown bought out the proprietors on July 25, 1729, and North Carolina became a royal colony.

Troubled as North Carolina's early years were, it had remained essentially a backwater, ignored by the proprietors who had taken a greater interest in its more prosperous sister to the south. After the abandonment of Clarendon County in 1667, Shaftesbury had convinced the proprietors that a larger investment was essential for success, and they decided to locate a settlement at Port Royal. Over one hundred settlers, led by Joseph West, left England in August, 1669, and in April, 1670, established Charles Town. Because the settlers were predominantly tradesmen ignorant of farming methods, a number got into debt and deserted the colony.

134

In response to recruitment efforts, large numbers of Barbadians immigrated to the colony, and by 1671 they contributed half its population. The new settlers soon learned agriculture, and Dr. Henry Woodward opened the way to trade with the Indians. Prosperity increased as the colonists developed a thriving trade in furs and naval stores with England, and in meat, lumber, and Indian slaves with the West Indies.

A powerful faction of Barbadians, known as the "Goose Creek men," gained control of the government and determined the colony's politics for nearly fifty years. Conflict between the proprietors and the settlers over debts, land distribution, and Indian slavery nearly brought an end to the colony late in its first decade. Attracted by the proprietors' promise of toleration, many dissenters came in, only to encounter the resentment of the conservative Anglican Barbadians, who resisted the proprietors' efforts at reform. When Governor James Colleton declared martial law in February, 1690, in an attempt to halt the abuses of the Indian trade and collect the quitrents, the Goose Creek faction ousted him and replaced him with Seth Sothel. In a revision of the government in 1691, the proprietors made Philip Ludwell Governor and declared that the freemen's representatives should meet as a separate house.

The decade of the 1690's was one of relative peace and prosperity. Rice became a staple crop, the Indian trade prospered, and Charles Town began to take on genteel trappings. By passing laws giving concessions to both sides, John Archdale, who became Governor in 1695, determined to reconcile the old factions. The Commons House of Assembly became the voice of the people and gained legislative prerogatives.

Factional rivalries were reviewed at the beginning of the eighteenth century. The selection of an Anglican governor in 1700 aroused the opposition of the dissenters to the establishment of the Church of England in the colony; in 1704, the parish vestries became seats of power. The popular division over religion was superseded by one over the issue of paper currency in 1712. As early as 1703, the colony had emitted its first bills of credit to pay for an expedition against the Spanish in Florida. Other emissions followed. The planters and tradesmen who did business solely within the colony favored the use of paper money, but the Charles Town merchants who had to pay their English creditors in specie bitterly opposed it.

The proprietors had never moved decisively to control the long-standing abuses of the Indian trade, and as a result, in 1715, the Yamasee War, the longest and costliest Indian war in the colony's history, broke out. During the conflict the people were driven from their homes to seek refuge in Charles Town. To end the abuses of the trade the Commons House of Assembly created a monopoly of the Indian trade under its own direction.

In 1718 the proprietors launched a strong attack upon some of the colony's most popular laws, disallowing measures providing for bills of credit and import duties, removing the monopoly on trade, and weakening the power of the legislature; consequently, antiproprietary sentiment crystallized in favor of royal government. All that lacked for rebellion was a final catalyst. It came in November, 1719, in the form of the rumor of an imminent invasion of the colony by the Spanish. When the Assembly convened in December, it declared itself a convention and petitioned the Board of Trade to be made a royal colony. The Privy Council assumed the administration of the colony and appointed Francis Nicholson the first Royal Governor.

Although Nicholson tried to reconcile the contending factions and establish local governmental institutions, the paper money controversy and problems caused by the Navigation Acts continued to plague the colony. By 1728 the government had ceased to function. The Crown bought out the proprietors in 1729, but internal strife remained.

## Pertinent Literature

Lefler, Hugh T. and Albert R. Newsome. *North Carolina: The History of a Southern State.* Chapel Hill: University of North Carolina Press, 1963.

In the preface to the first edition of this history of North Carolina, Hugh Lefler states that he and Albert Newsome were seeking to provide a comprehensive work for the general reader and the college student. Lacking a "pet theory of historical interpretation," the authors disavow any effort at revising history, preferring only "to present an accurate narrative." The resulting history is rich both in factual detail and interpretation. The chapters dealing with the proprietary period are for the most part objective in tone—critical of the proprietors, but by no means losing sight of the faults of factions within the colony.

The granting of the Carolina Proprietary Charter was Charles II's way of paying a political debt to some powerful countrymen who had supported him in the past and whose future support he wished to insure. Besides the furtherance of his personal ambitions, Charles had four motives in issuing the charter: the propagation of Christianity; the enlargement of the Empire; the promotion of English commerce; and an increase in the proprietors' fortunes. The discontent of the settlers and the ineffectiveness of the government during the colony's earliest years must be attributed, say Lefler and Newsome, to the vacillatory policies and lack of interest of the proprietary board. Shaftesbury's interest in experimenting with various forms of government served only to create instability, they charge. Crediting the Fundamental Constitutions to John Locke, the authors find it ridiculous that Locke and Shaftesbury should have considered imposing so complicated a scheme upon a wilderness environment. Yet they acknowledge the progressive features of the proposed system: registration of births, marriages, and deaths, and of land titles; bienniel parliaments; trial by jury; and religious toleration.

The authors manage to convey successfully the feeling of isolation and confusion experienced by the early North Carolina colonists through their geographical position and also because of their inept government. Blaming the unenterprising settlers for the slow growth of the colony, the proprietors neglected it and concentrated their efforts on the southern part of their territory. Lefler and Newsome assign much of the blame concerning North Carolina's backwardness to the proprietors.

136

The authors specifically mention their failure to establish consistent terms of landholding or to create a strong, stable, and efficient government. All too frequently governors appointed by the proprietors were turned out by public demand.

Culpeper's rebellion must be attributed at least indirectly to the proprietors since they should have recognized the inevitability of resistance to acts so harmful to the colony's trade. Obliged to support the Crown's position that the acts must be enforced, they were actually opposing their own economic interests. When the rebel governor came to trial, the proprietors acted opportunistically and minimized the rebellion, fearing that their charter would be abrogated.

The authors do not, however, reserve criticism solely for the proprietors; they also declare that, in dealings with Indians, the settlers were often de-ceitful and immoral. By encroaching upon Indian lands, cheating them in trade, and taking their people as slaves, the whites invited the massacre of 1711.

The instability of the government and the open flouting of laws, so vividly depicted by the authors, make it plain why the Crown desired to take over the colony. As early as 1706, the Board of Trade declared that the proprietary colonies had not only failed to accomplish their goals but had also violated England's laws, denied colonists their full rights as Englishmen, and shirked their obligations to the Mother Country.

Lefler and Newsome's chapters on the proprietary period furnish an excellent introduction to the history of the Carolinas and provide a sound basis for an understanding of the problems of the proprietary system within the context of English expansionist policy.

Sirmans, M. Eugene. *Colonial South Carolina: A Political History, 1663-1763.* Chapel Hill: University of North Carolina Press, 1966.

Eugene Sirmans undertook a revision of the political history of colonial South Carolina because he was dissatisfied with the failure of earlier historians "to relate the internal history of the province to other events in the British empire." Those writers had depicted the colony's early history "as a struggle between colonists who wanted only to defend their liberties and proprietors who alternated between despotism and greed."

Sirmans' view of the proprietors is generally charitable. Admitting that they expected the colony to yield a handsome return from a minimum investment, Sirmans nonetheless contends that the proprietors exhibited a practical knowledge of colonial affairs. For the much maligned Fundamental Constitutions and its architect, Shaftesbury, the author has high praise. Where other historians have condemned the scheme as ridiculously impractical for a primitive environment, Sirmans points out that the proprietors had no intention of implementing its provisions immediately. Rather, they viewed it as a long-term plan to be realized only after the wilderness period had passed. The Fundamental Constitutions contained nothing of vassalage or of the many anachronistic features of feudalism, concentrating instead upon a revised form of manorialism. Shaftesbury, in keeping with contem-

137

porary English political philosophy, hoped to develop a society in which aristocracy would balance democracy. Sirmans argues that both the establishment of a landed gentry and the policy of religious toleration had far-reaching effects upon the development of South Carolina.

Sirmans' most significant contribution to a proper understanding of the proprietary period is his analysis of the role of the "Goose Creek men" in the politics of South Carolina. A group of Barbadians who had settled in the Goose Creek region, this powerful faction consistently opposed proprietary policy and was contemptuous of newer, less-experienced colonists. They had no sympathy with Shaftesbury's plan to develop the colony but were interested only in building up their own fortunes by illegal trade. The dissenters who had been attracted to the colony supported the proprietors in return for religious toleration. Opposition to the staunchly Anglican Goose Creek faction on the part of the dissenters resulted in constant antagonism and unrest during the forty-two year period of largely Goose Creek dominance. When, in 1690, the proprietors attempted unsuccessfully to halt the abuses of trade with the Indians, the Goose Creek faction forced the Governor out, replacing him with their own man. Some historians have sought to characterize this rebellious action as a popular revolt against despotic proprietors. Sirmans, on the other hand, interprets it simply as an attempt to oust an unpopular governor in order to return power to the faction which had formerly been in control. The proprietors were finally forced to compromise with the dissidents so that order might be maintained.

After 1700, the proprietors launched a campaign to establish the Church of England and forced a realignment of the old factions. In response to the complaints of dissenters, however, the Crown directed the proprietors to disallow the more discriminatory provisions of the establishment act. During this period, Sirmans explains, the parish vestry became the real seat of political power in South Carolina.

Even after the religious controversy ended in 1712, new divisions developed between the merchants, who supported the proprietors, and the planters over the issues of trade abuses and paper currency. When the proprietors came under the influence of corrupt politicians and attacked laws favorable to the planters, the popular forces were driven to seek the stabilizing influence of royal government. Sirmans sees no revolt against tyranny in this action. Political rights were not in question, he maintains; the Assembly merely rebelled against the neglect and maladministration of the proprietors.

The account of the chaotic state of politics and constantly changing administrations during the proprietary period makes for rather difficult reading at times. Undoubtedly, the author's untimely death before he was able to condense to some extent the wealth of detail which he had assembled accounts for occasional confusing sections. On the whole, however, Sirmans has presented a profoundly revealing interpretation of a most complex political situation where others in the past have found only simplistic answers. — *W.M.B.*

## Settlement of the Carolinas

### Additional Recommended Reading

Andrews, Charles M. *The Colonial Period of American History.* Vol. III: *The Settlements.* Chs. 5 and 6. New Haven: Yale University Press, 1964. After describing the efforts of the proprietors to establish their colony, Andrews goes on to detail the political turmoil which racked the Carolinas under proprietary government.

Powell, William S., ed. *Ye Countie of Albemarle in Carolina: A Collection of Documents, 1664-1675.* Raleigh: State Department of Archives and History, 1958. Among this collection of twenty-eight documents are letters from the proprietors and instructions to various governors.

Craven, Wesley F. *The Southern Colonies in the Seventeenth Century, 1607-1689.* Ch. 9. Baton Rouge: Louisiana State University Press, 1949. Placing the settlement of Carolina within the context of British expansionist policy, Craven sheds light upon the economics of proprietary promotional efforts.

Salley, Alexander S., Jr., ed. *Narratives of Early Carolina, 1650-1708.* New York: Barnes and Noble, Inc., 1946. Among the original accounts included in this work are descriptions of the early explorations and life in the settlements.

Powell, William S. *The Proprietors of Carolina.* Raleigh: Carolina Charter Tercentenary Commission, 1963. In addition to biographical material, this small booklet includes an introduction which gives reasons for the granting of the charter.

Rankin, Hugh F. *Upheaval in Albemarle: The Story of Culpeper's Rebellion, 1675-1689.* Raleigh: Carolina Charter Tercentenary Commission, 1962. Views the rebellion as a reaction against the new colonial policies of Charles II.

# BRITISH CONQUEST OF NEW NETHERLAND

*Type of event:* Political: removal of the Dutch presence in North America
*Time:* August-September, 1664
*Locale:* Dutch colony in the New World

*Principal personages:*

PETER STUYVESANT (1592-1672), Dutch Governor of New Netherland until 1664

JAMES, DUKE OF YORK (Crowned KING JAMES II in 1685) (1633-1701), brother of Charles II and proprietor of New York after March, 1664

RICHARD NICOLLS (1624-1672), James's deputy and first Governor of New York 1664-1668

## Summary of Event

The restoration of the Stuart monarchy to the British throne in 1660 ushered in an era of colonial expansion allied with a more vigorous mercantilism and attempts to make colonial administration more unified. New Netherland's existence as an alien wedge between Great Britain's North American colonies impinged upon all three objectives. Charles II's supporters viewed land grants in America as a device for recouping their lost fortunes, and the region occupied by the Dutch enticed such land-grabbers. Furthermore, the Crown's attempt to unify colonial administration was frustrated by the situation of New Netherland, for its strategic geographic location impeded communications between the Chesapeake and New England colonies and made more difficult the task of defending those colonies from the French.

Charles II and his Parliament had designed the navigation system against their commercial rivals, the Dutch, but New Netherland's existence rendered enforcement of the Acts of Trade and Navigation ineffective. Great Britain's mainland colonies used New Netherland as a means of circumventing the

system, and the Dutch colony became a breeding ground for smugglers. Officials in the British colonies would not enforce the trade acts against the Dutch, and it was argued that the Crown lost ten thousand pounds annually in uncollected customs revenues.

The Crown concluded at length that the only effective remedy for these difficulties lay in wresting control of New Netherland from the Dutch. As early as 1663, the Council for Foreign Plantations, an advisory board of merchants and privy councillors, investigated the matter of Dutch power and examined the possibility of a military operation against New Netherland. Information from English residents on the eastern end of Long Island suggested that such a military undertaking would meet with little resistance from the Dutch garrison at New Amsterdam.

Based upon the council's recommendations, Charles moved swiftly. In March, 1664, he gave his brother James, Duke of York, a proprietary grant of all the land area between Delaware Bay and the Connecticut river, which included the Dutch colony. Parliament approved the grant, and in April the King nominated Colonel Richard Nicolls as Lieutenant-Governor of the proprietary, put him in charge of a small military force, and sent him on his way to America.

Nicolls and his squadron of four ships arrived off New Amsterdam in August, 1664. The Lieutenant-Governor immediately demanded the surrender of the colony, offering liberal terms as bait. Among the terms were guarantees to the inhabitants of all the rights of Englishmen, trading privileges, freedom of conscience, the continuance of Dutch customs and inheritance laws, and up to eighteen months for the settlers to decide whether to leave or not. At first, the Governor of New Netherland, Peter Stuyvesant, refused to surrender and began to make preparations for the defense of his colony. But the peg-legged Stuyvesant, having angered his people with his high-handed rule, received no support from the residents, who felt they would be no worse off under the British. Stuyvesant, therefore, on August 26, 1664, surrendered the town. A week later, the remainder of the colony fell into British hands.

In 1667, the Treaty of Breda, which ended the Second Anglo-Dutch War, confirmed the British conquest. Except for a brief loss of control during the Third Dutch War, the British retained a firm grip upon the former Dutch colony which they called New York.

Great Britain's conquest of New Netherland plugged the breach between the British colonies, thus forming a continuous English presence from Canada to the Floridas. It eliminated the Dutch as commercial rivals on the Continent and ultimately brought the British and the French into confrontation for continental supremacy.

## Pertinent Literature

Keesler, Henry H. and Eugene Rachlis. *Peter Stuyvesant and His New York.* New York: Harper & Row Publishers, 1959.

It is perhaps unfortunate that scholars of Early New York history have given so little attention to the British conquest of New Netherland. There is no study devoted exclusively to the questions of why and how the British set out to wrest New Netherland from their great commercial rivals. Consequently, one must turn to more general studies of early New York or to biographies of prominent colonists.

Such a course is not without its pitfalls, as is evident in Keesler and Rachlis' chapters on the fall of New Netherland. Since their work is a biography of Stuyvesant, the account of New Netherland's capture is seen through Stuyvesant's eyes, without regard to some of the larger implications of British interest in the Dutch colony. The book says almost nothing about British reasons for the attack. Unless a student was familiar with Charles M. Andrews' *The Colonial Period of American History,* his reliance upon Keesler and Rachlis would convey a false impression of British motives.

In Chapter XIII, which Keesler and Rachlis entitle "The Plot Against New Netherland," the authors interpret British designs as the product of a feud between the New Netherlanders and the British colonists in Connecticut over which government possessed ju-

141

risdiction in the largely-English settlements on eastern Long Island and over long-standing boundary disputes. These conflicts had existed since the founding of Connecticut in 1636, and they were sources of continual irritation between the two colonies, especially when the Indians took to the warpath; in Dutch minds the notion persisted that the British encouraged the Indians to raid Dutch settlements. Prior to 1660, Stuyvesant had been able to maintain an uneasy balance through diplomacy, but the restoration of the Stuarts complicated matters when Charles II put eastern Long Island under Connecticut's jurisdiction. Thus armed, the Connecticut government aimed at securing the whole of Long Island, thereby provoking a confrontation which the British home government sought to resolve by force of arms.

These disputes obviously generated friction between the two colonies. They probably played a role in the British government's decision to seize New Netherland, but the interpretation which Keesler and Rachlis advance obscures the major consideration which motivated the British, namely, the wish to eliminate the Dutch as commercial rivals.

These chapters do, however, provide insight into Stuyvesant's final years as governor and his understanding of the threat posed by British interests. Indeed, Stuyvesant is pictured as being more perceptive about the inherent dangers of New Netherland's situation than his superiors in Amsterdam.

Bancroft, George. *History of the United States of America, from the Discovery of the Continent.* 24th ed. Boston: Little, Brown, and Company, 1872.

George Bancroft's *History of the United States* is one of the classic works in American historiography. Begun at a time when the fires of American nationalism were being kindled, it gave new meaning to the great events in America's past when the United States was in the midst of a period of tremendous growth and intellectual flowering. One of the more obvious manifestations of this ferment was the advent of Jacksonian democracy, that *mélange* of men and ideas which sought to make America the most socially and politically democratic society in the world. Bancroft's view of the past seemed to buttress those ends.

The *History of the United States* is a general examination of the American past from Columbus' discovery to the end of the American Revolution, and most of the work is given over to consideration of the Revolution's causes.

The first three volumes, however, are devoted to a discussion of colonial origins. In the case of New Netherland, Bancroft picks up the colony's beginnings with the Dutch struggle for independence in the sixteenth century, which he discusses at length. He finds much to admire in the Dutch: they had overthrown their Catholic rulers; they had established a republic in which religious diversity was tolerated; and they had transformed a tiny portion of Europe's people and land mass into the world's premier commercial power. In short, the Dutch seemed to exemplify progress. Similarly, there were praiseworthy aspects about New Netherland. The colony's government tolerated all religious sects, even Jews, and it became a haven for Europe's dispossessed.

But New Netherland was not without its flaws, for there was "no distinct legislative power to the people." In Bancroft's view, much of the colony's history prior to 1664 was that of struggle between colonial authorities and the people, who, "without a teacher, had become convinced of the right of resistance." Bancroft has few kind words for Stuyvesant, since the Governor doubted "man's capacity for self-government." Given these considerations, Great Britain's conquest of the Dutch colony represented some progress, because "English liberties were to be added to the security of property." — *W.M.B.*

## Additional Recommended Reading

Andrews, Charles M. *The Colonial Period of American History.* Vol. IV: *England's Commercial and Colonial Policy.* New Haven: Yale University Press, 1964. Discusses Anglo-Dutch rivalry and relates the conquest of New Netherland to overall British efforts to create a self-contained colonial empire.

Raesly, Ellis L. *Portrait of New Netherland.* New York: Columbia University Press, 1945. Stresses the political and cultural aspects of the Dutch colony.

Wertenbaker, Thomas J. *The Founding of American Civilization: The Middle Colonies.* New York: Charles Scribner's Sons, 1938. Devotes more attention to social and cultural features of colonial life than to political matters.

Condon, Thomas J. *New York Beginnings: The Commercial Origins of New Netherland.* New York: New York University Press, 1968. A study of New Netherland emphasizing the role of the Dutch West India Company and stopping short of the British conquest of the colony.

# FRENCH EXPLORATION OF THE MISSISSIPPI VALLEY

*Type of event:* Socioeconomic: desire of the French to exploit and Christianize the West
*Time:* 1673-1740's
*Locale:* Mississippi River Valley

*Principal personages:*

JEAN BAPTISTE TALON (THE "GREAT INTENDANT") (1625?-1694), who sent the first expeditions to the Great Lakes

LOUIS JOLLIET (1645-1700), explorer and trapper to whom Talon entrusted the task of finding the Mississippi river

JACQUES MARQUETTE (1637-1675), Jesuit priest who accompanied Jolliet and whose journal is the only record of the journey

LOUIS DE BUADE (COMTE DE FRONTENAC) (1620-1698), known as the "Iron Governor," who sponsored the La Salle expeditions

RENÉ ROBERT CAVELIER (SIEUR DE LA SALLE) (1643-1687), French nobleman who first followed the Mississippi river to the Gulf of Mexico and who later made an abortive attempt to found a colony there

PIERRE LEMOYNE D'IBERVILLE (SIEUR D'IBERVILLE) (1661-1706), who in 1699 established Biloxi, the first French settlement on the Gulf of Mexico

ÉTIENNE DE BOURGMOUND (fl. 1714), Governor of Detroit and later Commandant of the Missouri, who extended French control into the Osage country near present-day Independence, Missouri

CHARLES CLAUDE DU TISNÉ (fl. 1714), the first Frenchman to explore the Kansas and Republican rivers

PETER MALLET (fl. 1739-1740), and

PAUL MALLET (fl. 1739-1740), brothers who first used the Santa Fe Trail in 1739

SIEUR DE LA VÉRENDRYE (PIERRE GAULTIER DE VARENNES) (1685-1749), who explored Manitoba and the Dakotas sixty years before the Lewis and Clark expedition

## Summary of Event

The exploration of the Mississippi River Valley was the logical result of France's desire to monopolize the fur trade of the St. Lawrence basin and extend its control to the rich fur-bearing rivers and lakes of the interior of North America. Expanding upon the explorations made by Samuel de Champlain in the early 1600's, Jean Nicolet opened the Ottawa river route to Lake Huron, Lake Michigan, and Green Bay in 1634. The trappers, or *"coureurs des bois"* (runners of the woods) as the French called them, were

144

forced to take this northern route to the western Great Lakes because of the constant enmity of the Iroquois Confederation. Living in upper New York, the Iroquois warriors hated the French partly because Champlain had helped Algonquin war parties to attack their villages, and partly because they wished to control the fur trade between the Europeans and the western tribes, which the French refused to allow.

The various Iroquois wars prevented the French from assuming control of the Great Lakes until 1671 when Nicholas Perrot guided Simon François Daumont, Sieur de St. Lusson, to Sault Sainte Marie where the latter formally took possession of the area for France and signed trade treaties with sixteen western tribes the following year. Perrot was the first man licensed to explore the Great Lakes by Jean Baptiste Talon, the intendant in charge of the judiciary and finances of the colonial government. Prior to Perrot's expeditions, Menard Chouart, Sieur des Groseillers, and Pierre Esprit Radisson had engaged in an illegal exploration and trade mission to Chequamegon Bay on Lake Superior from 1654 to 1660. The government, however, confiscated their sixty canoeloads of furs to discourage further unlicensed endeavors.

Talon, now wishing to extend French power, licensed two dozen traders and missionaries to go to Wisconsin. Two missions, St. Francis at Green Bay and St. Jacques on the Fox river, became the centers of French activity. Talon also engaged Louis Jolliet to explore the Mississippi river. In 1673, Jolliet, accompanied by Jacques Marquette, a Jesuit priest, left Michilimackinac and traveled across Green Bay and up the Fox river. They then made a portage from the headwaters of the Fox river to the Wisconsin river and descended the Wisconsin to its source. From there, they went down the Mississippi river in canoes as far as the mouth of the Arkansas. They identified and located numerous Indian tribes along the way. Becoming convinced that the Mississippi flowed into the Gulf of Mexico and not the Gulf of California, they turned around and ascended the Mississippi. On their return they discovered the mouth of the Illinois river and ascended it. From the Illinois they made a portage to the Chicago river through which they reëntered Lake Michigan at its southwestern end.

While Jolliet and Marquette were floating down the Mississippi, Talon was turning over the colonial government to Louis de Buade (Comte de Frontenac). Frontenac continued Talon's policy of exploration and trade, although he developed a few new concepts of his own. Frontenac's "Grand Plan" envisioned a series of forts west of the Appalachian Mountains to exclude the British from the Mississippi River Valley. He then hoped to tap the rich fur supply and ship it to France either through Quebec, or through a new city which he envisioned near the mouth of the Mississippi river.

The chief proponent of Frontenac's plan was René Robert Cavelier, Sieur de la Salle. Fluent in eight Indian languages, La Salle, like Jolliet, also believed that the Mississippi river flowed into the Gulf of Mexico. In 1669, his government authorized him to explore and prove his belief. For the next fifteen years, La Salle traveled throughout the West. First, he went down the Ohio

145

river to the falls at Louisville. Returning to France, he obtained a five-year trade monopoly from the crown. La Salle built his own sailing ship, the *Griffon*, to supply the several forts that he constructed near the Chicago portage.

Disaster haunted La Salle and delayed his actual exploration of the Mississippi until 1682. He lost several shiploads of supplies from France in the Atlantic Ocean, and the *Griffon* sank in one of the Great Lakes. In addition, La Salle was a martinet who lacked the finesse necessary to command a body of men without trouble. His arrogance and autocratic attitude caused several mutinies, the suppression of which also delayed his departure. On April 9, 1682, however, La Salle finally found the mouth of the Mississippi, and he claimed the whole area, which he named Louisiana after Louis XIV, for France.

In 1684, following Frontenac's original proposals, La Salle departed from France with four ships, one hundred soldiers, and three hundred settlers to establish a city in Louisiana. Unfortunately, he failed to find the river's mouth from the Gulf side, and Spanish raiders, shipwreck, and desertion plagued the colonists. La Salle and the survivors finally landed at Matagorda Bay, Texas, where they were stranded through the loss of their ships. Making a futile search for the Mississippi river by land, La Salle decided that the expedition's only hope for survival was to go overland to Illinois. In 1687, the party set out on the long journey. La Salle's authoritarian leadership caused much dissension and led to his murder near the Brazos river. The rest of the party struggled onward to Illinois

where they met a relief expedition led by Henri de Tonti, a one-armed Italian who was in charge of La Salle's Illinois operations.

Meanwhile, French control of the upper Mississippi tightened with the activities of Daniel Greysolon (Sieur du Lhut, or Duluth), who explored the western end of Lake Superior and discovered the Falls of St. Anthony where the twin cities of St. Paul and Minneapolis now stand. Other Frenchmen opened up the Galena lead mines, extracted some copper from Minnesota, and founded Cahokia in 1699 and Kaskaskia in 1700. La Salle's dream city in Louisiana was made possible by Pierre Lemoyne d'Iberville, who rediscovered the mouth of the Mississippi and was instrumental in founding Fort Maurepas, or Biloxi, in 1699. His brother, Jean Baptiste Lemoyne (Sieur de Bienville), established Mobile in 1702 and New Orleans in 1718; the latter became the gateway to the interior of North America.

French activities along the Mississippi river led to the exploration and exploitation of its major tributary, the Missouri river. Although others had preceded him, Étienne de Bourgmond, sometime Governor of Detroit, made the first extensive journey up the Missouri river in 1714. After traveling eight hundred leagues upriver, Bourgmond returned to write a book on his experiences. Bourgmond was followed by Charles du Tisné who explored the Missouri river as far as the Osage villages where he traded for furs and horses. He then advanced westward on the Kansas river to the Pawnee country, but only over the protests of the Osage, who forced him to leave most of his firearms behind. The Pawnee refused to grant Tisné permission to contact the Comanche farther west. Undaunted by Tisné's failure, Bourgmond, now Commandant of the Missouri, established Fort Orleans in Carroll County, Missouri, and through adroit diplomacy managed to contact the Comanche. In 1724 he made an impressive series of treaties with several plains tribes, and even took some of their chiefs to France to see the king.

The upper Missouri river was explored separately by several explorers going westward from the shores of Lake Superior. The principal man of importance there was Pierre La Vérendrye who, with his sons, Pierre II, François, and Louis Joseph, received a government fur trade monopoly for the region in 1730. Basing their operations at Fort La Reine on the Assiniboine river in Manitoba in 1737, the La Verendrye family traveled over much of the present-day Dakotas and Wyoming, searching for a water route to the Pacific and exploiting the Indian trade. In 1743, they buried a lead plate near Pierre, South Dakota, claiming the land for France. The plate was accidentally found by a fourteen-year-old schoolgirl in 1914.

At the same time that the La Vérendryes were exploring the upper Missouri river, two brothers, Peter and Paul Mallet, were journeying to New Mexico, the farthest west any Frenchman had ventured. Passing through the Osage, Pawnee, and Comanche lands along the route made famous by Americans one hundred years later, the Mallets reached the town of Santa Fe. The suspicious Spanish immediately jailed the brothers, but in 1740 they were released to return to Louisiana. Because of Spanish hostility and the decline of the French empire, the Santa Fe Trail was seldom used for the next eighty years.

The French exploration of the Mississippi River Valley is of great significance in American history. The French takeover of the interior valley led directly to the clash with Great Britain in the French and Indian War (1754-1763), which cost France its entire American empire and ultimately resulted in the American Revolution. Although the *coureurs des bois* erroneously believed that the Platte river was the main fork of the Missouri, by 1740 they knew much about the Trans-Mississippi West that would be utilized by the American mountain men and the British Hudson Bay Company nearly a century later. In addition, the French made a lasting contribution to the culture of the north woods and Louisiana that remains today.

## Pertinent Literature

Parkman, Francis. *The Discovery of the Great West: La Salle.* Edited by William R. Taylor. New York: Holt, Rinehart, and Winston Inc., 1956.

Francis Parkman is the first historian who comes to mind whenever one studies the rise and fall of New France. His works are classics in their field and have gone through numerous editions since they first appeared in the late nineteenth century. Parkman was a typical historian for his time, when most scholars were New Englanders who wrote in a literary manner, doing what they believed was a service to the nation by preserving its history. They were men of leisure who wrote history as a hobby and emphasized biography.

Most of Parkman's seven-volume history of New France was constructed around key persons, because he believed that great men molded events. The era between 1643 and 1689 revolved around La Salle because, to Parkman, he personified the extension of French power down the Mississippi river to the Gulf of Mexico. Other volumes focus on Samuel de Champlain *(Pioneers of France in the New World)*, the Jesuit fathers in the Huron country *(The Jesuits in North America)*, Frontenac *(Count Frontenac and New France under Louis XIV)*, and Louis Joseph, Marquis de Montcalm, and his British opponent, General James Wolfe *(Montcalm and Wolfe)*. The remaining two volumes in his history of New France, *The Old Regime in Canada,* and *A Half-Century of Conflict,* deal with the feudal nature of the French colonial government and Queen Anne's and King George's Wars.

Most historians write with a purpose or philosophy of history in mind, and Parkman is no exception. His main concern was with that nineteenth century demigod: progress. Parkman believed that progress was inevitable. He saw the struggle between France and Great Britain in America as a fight between the noble, progressive Anglo-Saxons and the decadent French; liberty and Protestantism versus absolutism and Catholicism.

Parkman believed that history was primarily a literary effort. Hence, his volumes make the events live again by emphasizing the romantic and heroic aspects of the past. In attaining his high literary effect, Parkman used methods considered unprofessional by more recent historians. He readily invents detail for his account, including dialogue and terrain descriptions, using his fertile imagination to fill in gaps if no actual accounts can be found. He sometimes plagiarizes other authors' works, reworking the original, but not indicating his sources. Parkman also rearranges the sequence of events to make the story more vivid and easier to follow. Throughout his work, he moralizes on events, which he sees with pro-British or American outlook.

*The Discovery of the Great West: La Salle* is typical of Parkman's style. He chose this explorer as his main character because La Salle was easily dramatized, not necessarily because he was historically significant. To Parkman, La Salle demonstrates gentility, veracity, disinterested patriotism, and supreme self-control. These factors together with his good breeding cause La Salle to achieve things in Parkman's eyes. Critics of Parkman, such as William R. Taylor, accuse him of distorting, suppressing contrary evidence, and quoting out of context to make a "half-crazed French explorer a tragic hero." Parkman suffered from a neurotic condition, says Taylor, which caused him to interpret La Salle, who was also neurotic, as a hero when, in fact, La Salle failed to accomplish much during his entire lifetime. Taylor implies that Parkman's history and La Salle's iron will are products of brilliant minds bordering on insanity.

Despite these shortcomings, Parkman's volumes remain among the most exciting and compelling historical works ever written. Some recent historians maintain that his work should be revised, but it would be difficult to retain Parkman's uncanny and envia-ble ability to make history interesting.

Steck, Francis B. *The Jolliet-Marquette Expedition, 1673.* Glendale, California: Arthur H. Clark Company, 1928.

The purpose of Steck's volume is to place the Jolliet-Marquette expedition in its proper historical perspective. The author discusses three major problems: did the French truly "discover" the Mississippi river? Was Marquette or Jolliet the leader of the exploring party? Was the narrative of the journey really written by Father Marquette?

As to the first question, Steck maintains that discovery involves obtaining knowledge or sight of something not previously known or perceived. Using this criterion, he denies that Jolliet and Marquette "discovered" the Mississippi river, because its existence was first noted by the Spanish explorer Alvarez de Pineda in the early 1500's. Steck finds that the French verb *"découvir"* has been too literally translated by Englishmen. Instead of "discover," the French meant a more subtle concept; *"découvir"* also means "to explore"—hence, the Jolliet-Marquette expedition explored something already known. Far from discovery, the French government commissioned Jolliet to ascertain if the Mississippi might yield the long-sought water route to the Pacific Ocean—the fabled Northwest Passage.

The leadership of the expedition, maintains Steck, was given to Jolliet, not Marquette. This problem arose after the 1673 journey and concerns relations between the Church and the state in New France. The Society of Jesus claimed that Marquette led the expedition, hoping that the French crown would give it a virtual monopoly of control in the new West, and exclude the Franciscans and the fur traders from their area. Being a Franciscan himself, Steck has a reason for criticizing the Jesuit plan, but he does make a convincing case for his position. The expedition, concludes Steck, was secular and was commanded by Jolliet. The author finds it ironic that Marquette's role, as amplified by the Jesuits, has been accepted without question by historians, and that Jolliet's role has been almost obliterated.

Finally, Steck asserts that the journal of the expedition, which was credited to Marquette, was not written by him at all. Using an analysis of the manuscript's handwriting, general tone, literary style, and contents, Steck charges that the document was probably written by Jolliet and amplified by others. Although Steck's account is sometimes laborious in detail, he presents an intriguing story of the Jolliet-Marquette expedition of 1673. — *W.L.R.*

### Additional Recommended Reading

Eccles, William J. *Canada and Louis XIV, 1663-1701.* New York: Oxford University Press, 1964. One of the best recent studies of early Canada, covering governmental, economic, and cultural aspects of New France.

Kellogg, Louise P. *The French Regime in Wisconsin and the Northwest.* Madison: The State Historical Society of Wisconsin, 1925. Concentrating on the discovery of the Great

Lakes and Wisconsin, Kellogg discusses early exploration, mining, and the fur trade in the Old Northwest.

Terrell, John U. *La Salle: The Life and Times of an Explorer.* New York: Waybright and Talley, 1968. A popular account of La Salle's exploration of the Ohio and Mississippi River Valleys.

Crouse, Nellis M. *Lemoyne d'Iberville: Soldier of New France.* Ithaca: Cornell University Press, 1954. A biography of the man who founded the first French settlements on the Louisiana and Mississippi Gulf Coasts.

Crouse, Nellis M. *La Vérendrye: Fur Trader and Explorer.* Ithaca: Cornell University Press, 1956. An interesting account of the La Vérendrye family who did much to further French interests in Manitoba and the Dakotas.

Nasatir, Abraham P. *Before Lewis and Clark: Documents Illustrating the History of the Missouri, 1785-1804.* St. Louis: St. Louis Historical Documents Foundation, 1952. 2 vols. Primarily a collection of documents, Nasatir's introduction to the first volume is a fine narrative of the French exploration of the Missouri river between 1673 and 1804.

# BACON'S REBELLION

*Type of event:* Military: uprising against royal authority
*Time:* April, 1676-January, 1677
*Locale:* Eastern Virginia

*Principal personages:*

NATHANIEL BACON (1647-1676), who commanded the rebel
forces against the Indians and the royal government

SIR WILLIAM BERKELEY (1606-1677), Governor of Virginia
1642-1652 and 1660-1676

SIR HENRY CHICHELEY (fl. 1677), Lieutenant Governor of Virginia, whom Governor Berkeley placed in command of a force
to pursue the Indians early in 1676 only to countermand the
order

JOSEPH INGRAM (fl. 1676-1677), Commander of the rebel forces
after Bacon's death

PHILIP LUDWELL (fl. 1660-1704), member of the Council of
State, and close adviser to Governor Berkeley

ROBERT BEVERLEY (fl.1675-1677), clerk of the General Assembly and Berkeley's chief lieutenant in the suppression of the
rebellion

SIR JOHN BERRY (fl. 1666-1667), and

FRANCIS MORYSON (fl. 1676-1677), two of the Royal Commissioners sent to investigate causes of the rebellion

HERBERT JEFFREYS (fl. 1676-1677), the third Royal Commissioner, who succeeded Berkeley as Governor

## Summary of Event

In the early spring of 1676, circumstances were ripe for rebellion in Virginia. Although the complex causes of
the rebellion are still being examined,
it is possible to identify three principal
causes for popular unrest: (1) the unstable political and social conditions
resulting from a rapidly changing society; (2) the severe economic depression; and (3) Governor Sir William
Berkeley's declining ability to govern
effectively.

Instability was inherent in the rapid
growth of population in Virginia after
1640. Competition for political power
and social position increased after 1660

as the earlier settlers entrenched themselves in local political offices. Where
a prosperous economy might have
counteracted unstable political and social conditions, Virginia's economy
stagnated after 1660. Chronic overpro-
duction of an inferior quality of
tobacco, aggravated by restrictive features of the Navigation Acts, drove the
price of tobacco down. Expensive experimentation with methods of diver-
sifying the economy and the need for
defense measures against the Dutch
and the Indians resulted in high taxes.
In 1674 the colonists were further
taxed to send agents to London to

151

lobby against the proprietary land grants to Lords Arlington and Culpepper. Circumstances conspired to exacerbate the planters' miseries, and Governor Berkeley's ineffectual leadership led to a general disaffection toward the government.

The events leading immediately to the rebellion grew out of a series of Indian raids which had begun in the summer of 1675. After forces of Virginians bent on revenge murdered numbers of friendly Susquehannocks on two separate occasions, the Indians increased the intensity of their raids throughout the fall and winter. Governor Berkeley angered the planters in the frontier settlements when he countermanded the order for a force to proceed against the marauding warriors. In keeping with Berkeley's overall Indian policy, the Assembly committed the colony to a defensive war, and the Governor ordered the erection of a chain of forts on the frontier.

In April an impatient group of upcountry planters persuaded one of their number, Nathaniel Bacon, Jr., to lead a band of volunteers against the Indians. Bacon, the ne'er-do-well son of an English gentleman, had not arrived in Virginia until 1674, but he had already been appointed to the Council of State. Governor Berkeley refused Bacon's request for a commission to raise volunteers and sent several letters warning him against becoming a mutineer. Unable to head off Bacon with his force of three hundred men, Berkeley, on May 10, 1676, declared him a rebel. On the same day, the Governor dissolved the "Long Assembly" and called for the first general elections in fifteen years, promising that the new Assembly would deal with the Indian threat

and any other grievances.

Bacon's success in killing some Indians prompted the residents of Henrico County to send him to Jamestown as one of their new burgesses, but the Governor ordered his capture before he could take his seat. Bacon confessed his error and received a pardon from the Governor. Several days later he slipped off to Henrico.

The June Assembly met for twenty days and passed a series of acts dealing with the prosecution of the Indian war and with various local problems, especially concerning the misuse of political power. Although Bacon has often been credited with pushing through reform legislation, he did not return to Jamestown until June 23, when the session was nearly over. Arriving with five hundred armed men, he terrorized the Governor and the burgesses into granting him a commission to fight the Indians.

As soon as Bacon marched toward the falls of the James river, however, Berkeley again proclaimed him a rebel and tried to raise a force against him. Failing in his attempt, Berkeley fled to the eastern shore, leaving Bacon in control of the western shore. Upon arriving in Middle Plantation, Bacon issued a manifesto, the "Declaration of the People," which accused the Governor of numerous offenses against the colonists and called for his surrender. While Bacon then proceeded to seek out and fall upon the friendly Pamunkey Indians, Berkeley returned to Jamestown, and having reached agreement with Bacon's garrison, took possession of the capital. Several days later, Bacon arrived with six hundred men and besieged the town. The faintheartedness of Berkeley's men forced

152

the Governor to concede the town. Bacon burned it on September 19. A little more than a month later, the rebellion fell apart at the news of Bacon's sudden death of the "Bloody Flux" and "Lousey Disease." Although Joseph Ingram made a bumbling attempt to lead the demoralized rebels, the last vestiges of rebellion were stamped out by February, 1677.

On January 29, the Royal Commissioners, John Berry, Francis Moryson and Herbert Jeffreys, arrived from England to investigate the uprising and restore order. Berkeley nullified the royal pardons which they brought for the rebels and ordered the execution of twenty-three men. His extreme cruelty was criticized by the commissioners, and Sir Herbert Jeffreys formally took over the government in April upon Berkeley's recall by the crown.

## Pertinent Literature

Wertenbaker, Thomas J. *Torchbearer of the Revolution: The Story of Bacon's Rebellion and Its Leader.* Princeton: Princeton University Press, 1940.

For Wertenbaker, Nathaniel Bacon was "the greatest figure of the first century of American history." Begun in 1914 with the publication of *Virginia Under the Stuarts,* Wertenbaker's life-long investigation of the rebellion resulted in the fullest statement of the "democratic" thesis about its causes. Although he employed a wide range of new sources, notably the official papers in the British Public Record Office and the British Museum, Wertenbaker's books bear the impress of the "progressive school of historiography." He views the first seventy years of Virginia history as a struggle for political, social, and economic power between democratic yeomen farmers and privileged aristocrats.

Wertenbaker's analysis of the origins of Virginia's population deals a severe blow to the long-standing notion that the colony had been peopled by Cavalier refugees from Cromwell's England. The great mass of immigrants to Virginia, according to Wertenbaker, were yeomen farmers who had escaped from oppressive conditions in England in order to gain the freedoms afforded by the New World. But by mid-century the door to advancement was closing for the humble immigrant, and the Navigation Acts were depriving him of a decent price for the tobacco he grew. Governor Berkeley had at first appeared as a friend to the colonists, supporting liberal reforms and aggressively fighting the hostile Indians. After his restoration to the governorship in 1660, however, he changed into a power-hungry despot bent on destroying representative government. In order to retain his clique of favorites in power, he refused to call new elections for fifteen years.

The man who came from England in 1674 to deliver the Virginians from oppression was, for Wertenbaker, a combination of George Washington, Thomas Jefferson, Sam Adams, Nathan Hale, and Robert E. Lee. The young Nathaniel Bacon, sentimentally idealized by Wertenbaker, was a lover of liberty and justice even as a child. Upon his arrival in Henrico County, he was immediately impressed by the suffering of the neighboring planters. Wertenbaker suggests that Berkeley,

# Bacon's Rebellion

suspecting Bacon's democratic tendencies, appointed him to the council in the hope of winning him over to his side.

The Indians depicted by Wertenbaker were by no means noble savages, but cruel devils who delighted in committing atrocities. Berkeley's refusal to allow the frontier settlers to deal with the Indians was but one more example of his willingness to sacrifice the colonists' best interests for his own profit. When Bacon agreed to lead the planter volunteers against the Indians, it was tantamount to the stand of the Minutemen at Lexington. Wertenbaker describes the rebels as "poor planters ground down by excessive taxes; hardy, weatherbeaten frontiersmen; ragged freedmen, some mounted, others trudging along on foot, all united by a common misfortune and by love for their youthful leader." Whether the rebels were attacking friendly Indians or holding loyalists' wives as hostages, Wertenbaker attributes their actions to noble motives. Although Bacon did not arrive with his men at the June, 1676, session of the General Assembly until it was nearly over, Wertenbaker credits the rebel with pushing through one liberal law after another.

The overt reason for the rebellion's failure, according to Wertenbaker, was the death of its indispensable leader. Even so, it was not without positive results. The rebellion put an end to Berkeley's corruption, fostered political reforms, and gave the English Privy Council a taste of what the colonists might do when driven to desperation. Most significantly, the uprising foreshadowed the American Revolution, showing that the forces which would one day result in Independence were active even in 1676.

Wertenbaker's extremely biased work is important both because it epitomizes the "democratic" tradition in scholarship and because it has served as a stepping-off point for later, more objective investigations into the rebellion's causes.

Washburn, Wilcomb E. *The Governor and the Rebel.* Chapel Hill: University of North Carolina Press, 1957.

The democratic thesis about the causes of Bacon's Rebellion espoused by Wertenbaker stood virtually unchallenged until this assault by Wilcomb Washburn appeared. Relying heavily upon the papers of the Marquis of Bath, Washburn reverses the molds in which Wertenbaker had cast the two principal antagonists. He absolves Governor Berkeley of major responsibility for the rebellion and places it instead upon Nathaniel Bacon and his Indian-hating followers.

Washburn finds no evidence to suggest that Berkeley was either unjust or dishonest. Disputing Wertenbaker's claim that the Governor favored his friends with large land grants, Washburn contends that Berkeley possessed no power to do so. During his administration, land was granted almost entirely under the headright system, whereby a settler received fifty acres for each immigrant brought in. Washburn's research reveals that Bacon's followers actually possessed landholdings comparable in size to those of Berkeley's supporters. Some of the rebels had records of antagonizing the Indians by scheming to cheat them out

154

of their rightful lands.

The colonists' principal complaints, as evidenced in the county grievances submitted to the Commissioners of Investigation after the rebellion, dealt with matters over which Berkeley had little control. Although the Governor was generally disliked in the period before the rebellion, he was not accused of graft or corruption. The severe economic depression caused by the low tobacco prices and the Navigation Acts so disturbed the planters that they centered their frustrations upon the Indian problem.

Berkeley hoped to maintain the peace with the Indians which had lasted since the 1640's. To counteract the antagonism aroused by white expansion onto Indian lands, he urged the Assembly to prohibit trade with the Indians and to authorize the building of frontier forts for defense. Washburn's thesis centers around the contention that the frontier planters hated Berkeley because he refused to wage war against basically benign Indians. Earlier historians had always overlooked the aggressiveness of the frontiersmen as a primary cause of the rebellion. Washburn argues that these planters, unlike Wertenbaker's fervent democrats, actually had no concept of the rights of others, and in fact expected to gain both privileged positions and estates when Bacon took control.

Since the "democratic" historians have always credited Bacon with pushing through the so-called reform legislation in the Assembly of June, 1676, Washburn undertakes an analysis of the laws passed there. He concludes that not only were most of the laws

passed in Bacon's absence, but also that the rebel, bent only upon obtaining a commission to fight the Indians, had no interest in reforms. Moreover, the laws were not particularly revolutionary. Other sessions of the Assembly had passed similar ones to remedy injustices; in fact, the very next session repassed the June laws after the crown had disallowed them.

Washburn suggests that historians may have been influenced in their indictment of the Governor more by his harsh punishment of the rebels after the rebellion than by his actions before it. The Royal Commissioners were generally sympathetic toward the rebels and critical of Berkeley's vengeful acts. Because Berkeley died before having an opportunity to see the King, he was deprived of the chance to defend his actions. Ironically, some of his supporters eventually became known as defenders of the people against arbitrary royal governors and commissioners.

*The Governor and the Rebel* is an important revisionist study, exposing many of the false assumptions made by ardent admirers of Bacon. Yet Washburn's identification of the root causes of the rebellion as the aggressiveness of the frontier planters and the conflict of alien cultures is somewhat simplistic. Since his study begins only with the Indian raids of 1675, it fails to investigate the possible effect of political and social instability and economic depression upon the planters. In his attempt to expose Bacon as a demagogue, Washburn is too willing to excuse the faults of Berkeley. — *W.M.B.*

# Bacon's Rebellion

## Additional Recommended Reading

Beverley, Robert. *The History and Present State of Virginia.* Edited by Louis B. Wright. Chapel Hill: University of North Carolina Press, 1947. Somewhat pro-Berkeley, this perceptive study emphasizes the economic difficulties and Indian troubles which led up to the rebellion.

Craven, Wesley F. *The Southern Colonies in the Seventeenth Century, 1607-1689.* Baton Rouge: Louisiana State University Press, 1949. Emphasizing the complexity of the rebellion, Craven's well-balanced account urges further research into its causes.

Morton, Richard L. *Colonial Virginia.* Vol. I: *The Tidewater Period, 1607-1710.* Chapel Hill: University of North Carolina Press, 1960. The most recent presentation of the "Progressive" school's interpretation, this study closely parallels Wertenbaker's works.

Andrews, Charles M. ed. *Narratives of the Insurrections, 1675 to 1690.* New York: Charles Scribner's Sons, 1915. Andrews includes three contemporary accounts of the rebellion, two by eyewitnesses and finally the official narrative of the Royal Commissioners of Investigation.

Wertenbaker, Thomas J. *Virginia Under the Stuarts, 1607-1688.* Princeton: Princeton University Press, 1914. This is an earlier, more balanced presentation of the views expressed by the same author in *Torchbearer of the Revolution.*

# FOUNDING OF PENNSYLVANIA

*Type of event:* Religious: desire of many Quakers to establish a colony
*Time:* 1681
*Locale:* Pennsylvania

Principal personages:
CHARLES II (1630-1685), King of Great Britain 1660-1685
WILLIAM PENN (1644-1718), Proprietor of Pennsylvania
WILLIAM MARKHAM (1635?-1704), Penn's personal agent in the colony and Deputy Governor 1681-1682 and 1693-1699
JAMES LOGAN (1674-1751), leader of the Proprietary Party
DAVID LLOYD (1656?-1731), leader of the Popular Party
THOMAS LLOYD (1640-1694?), president of the Council 1684-1686 and 1690-1691, Deputy Governor 1691-1692
ISRAEL PEMBERTON (1715-1779), leader of the strict Quakers in the 1740's and 1750's

## Summary of Event

On March 4, 1681, King Charles II of Great Britain granted to William Penn the colony of Pennsylvania. Named after his father Sir William Penn, an admiral who had aided Charles' accession, it was offered as payment of a debt of sixteen thousand pounds sterling which the King owed Sir William.

The charter given to William Penn made him Proprietor of the colony. It was similar to other proprietary charters in that it made Penn the owner and grantor of all land in the province and gave him authority to establish the form of government, appoint the governor, and initiate and promulgate laws with the advice and consent of the freemen in assembly. However, this particular charter was unique in its restriction of proprietary prerogatives. Three provisions assured the enforcement of the Navigation Acts passed by Parliament prior to the establishment of the colony: first, laws passed in the colony were to be submitted to the king for his

confirmation or disallowance, and the king retained the right to hear and decide appeals from the courts of the province; second, the Church of England was assured a place in the colony; and third, the charter contained a promise that the king would not impose taxes on the colony "unless the same be with the consent of the proprietary, or chiefe governour, or assembly, or by act of Parliament." These provisions implemented Great Britain's new colonial policy of limiting provincial self-government and centralizing the British Empire as a means of securing the commercial and defensive interests of the Mother Country.

Penn's avowed purpose in establishing a colony in America was to found a "holy experiment" based on Quaker doctrines. Pennsylvania was to be a holy commonwealth, characterized by peace, brotherly love, and religious toleration, which would serve as "an example . . . to the nations. . . ." At the same time, the colony offered a haven

157

to Quakers who were being persecuted in England for their nonconformist beliefs.

One month after receiving his charter from the King, Penn began advertising the new province to prospective settlers in England, Ireland, and Wales. *Some Account of the Province of Pennsylvania* was published in April, 1682, the first of eleven such publications designed to attract colonists. To the colony Penn dispatched his cousin William Markham, who was to serve as Deputy Governor until the Proprietor's arrival. Not until August 30, 1682, did Penn himself set sail for the colony in the ship *Welcome*, along with about one hundred colonists. Shortly before leaving England, he had obtained the Lower Counties (Delaware) from the Duke of York, an intimate friend, thereby gaining access to the Atlantic for his new colony.

Like other proprietors in the New World, Penn hoped to profit from the sale or rent of land in his colony, but his primary aim was a religious one. He was a member of the Society of Friends, or Quakers, founded by George Fox in the late 1640's. One of the many radical religious sects which emerged from the turbulence of the English Civil War, Quakerism embraced the Puritan social ethic but went beyond Puritanism in its rejection of formal creeds and worship. Quakers were mystics, believing that the Holy Spirit dwelled within each person, and that whoever yielded completely to the promptings of this divine presence, or "Inner Light," would be perfectly regenerated. Their ecclesiastical organization was based on the Puritan theory of congregationalism in that each congregation, or "meeting," was completely autonomous (though ultimately a hierarchy of meetings developed, similar in structure and purpose to that of the Presbyterians); it differed from Puritanism in its rejection of a national church. Like other sectarians, Quakers insisted on separation of church and state and viewed the meeting as a voluntary association composed only of believers. Two important social consequences of Quaker religious beliefs were equalitarianism and humanitarianism.

Before sailing to America, Penn had drawn up the "first frame of government" to serve as a constitution for the new colony. It provided for a governor appointed by the proprietor, a council of seventy-two members which was to be the source of all legislation, and an assembly of two hundred which had the power to accept or reject bills initiated by the council. Both the council and the assembly were elective bodies, with a property qualification for voting. The governor had a triple vote in the council but no veto over the actions of the council or assembly. When the two houses proved to be unwieldy, Penn issued a "second frame," or Charter of Liberties, in 1683, reducing the number of councilors to eighteen and assemblymen to thirty-six, and modifying the suffrage requirement. During the two years that Penn governed the colony, over 150 laws were passed by the legislature implementing the "holy experiment." In 1696, Governor William Markham issued a "third frame" which further modified suffrage requirements, reduced the council to twelve members and the assembly to twenty-four, and granted the latter body the right to initiate legislation. A "fourth frame," known as the

Charter of Privileges and drawn up by Penn in 1701, created a one-house legislature by vesting legislative power in the assembly, subject to the governor's veto, and limiting the council to executive and judicial powers. The council was appointed by the governor instead of being elected by the freemen.

Penn issued the Charter of Privileges in order to end almost twenty years of quarreling between council and assembly, the former asserting its superior status against the latter's demands for a greater share in the government of the colony. The assembly had considerably enlarged its power from 1692 to 1694 when the colony was under royal rule. Markham's "third frame," issued after the Crown returned Pennsylvania to Penn, also extended the prerogatives of the assembly, and the Charter of Privileges establishing a unicameral legislature represented a further triumph for that body.

With the council eliminated both as a legislative and also as an elective body, the assembly transferred its opposition to the governor. In the early eighteenth century, two parties dominated Pennsylvania politics: the Proprietary Party led by James Logan, which sought to centralize authority in the hands of the Governor and the council, and the Popular Party led by David Lloyd, which sought to expand the powers of the assembly. The main political issue was the Quaker principle of pacifism, which underwent a critical test in 1756 when warfare between Indians and Pennsylvania backwoodsmen erupted on the frontier. A declaration of war against the Delaware and Shawnee Indians by the Governor and the council resulted in the Quakers' decision to withdraw from the assembly rather than compromise their stand against war. This withdrawal ended almost seventy-five years of Quaker rule over the colony of Pennsylvania.

## Pertinent Literature

Tolles, Frederick B. *Meeting House and Counting House: The Quaker Merchants of Colonial Philadelphia, 1682-1763.* Chapel Hill: University of North Carolina Press, 1948.

The thesis of this volume on Quakerism in colonial Philadelphia was suggested by George Fox's admonition to the first Pennsylvania colonists: "My friends, that are gone, and are going over to plant, and make outward plantations in America, keep your own plantations in your hearts, with the spirit and power of God, that your own vines and lilies be not hurt." Tolles interprets the history of the Holy Experiment in terms of the tension between the inward and outward plantations, a tension symbolized by the two institutions of Quaker Philadelphia, the meeting house and counting house. The first seventy-five years of the Pennsylvania colony were concerned with the cultivation of the outward plantation. The withdrawal of the Quakers from politics in 1756 was the beginning of a shift to the inward plantation. As Tolles points out, the Quaker experience in the New World exhibits with striking clarity the transformation of sect into church; what was unique about the Quakers was their ultimate return to the sectarian posture, refusing to compromise with the world and insisting on purity and perfection.

159

Once established in Philadelphia, Quakers achieved economic preëminence, a fact which Tolles attributes not to their early arrival in Pennsylvania but to their pursuit of the Calvinist economic ethic which they had carried over from Puritanism into their own religious and social philosophy. The Quaker economic ethic "looked upon the material world of daily toil and daily bread as God's world in which men were called to do His will," and, like the Puritan code, adjured Friends to love the world with "weaned affections." The distinctiveness of Quakerism, according to Tolles, lay in its combining "the ethical position of the Anabaptists with the Calvinist attitude toward the material world. . . ."

The fortunes derived from commerce and manufacturing fostered the rise of a Quaker aristocracy in Philadelphia, which became the embodiment of the contradiction or tension inherent in Quakerism. With economic wealth went political hegemony. In turn, wealth and political power fostered "a subtle but constantly growing tendency, more noticeable among some Friends than others, towards conformity to the world against which the primitive Friends had so vigorously and persistently protested." Thus the Quaker economic ethic produced tendencies which worked directly against the perfectionist and separatist elements of the Quaker religion. The crisis of the 1750's and the retirement of the Quakers from politics produced a resolution of the contradiction. "After seventy-five years of preoccupation with the outward plantation, they turned their attention once again to cultivating the plantation within." The Quaker withdrawal marked the beginning of a reformation of the Society to root out the spirit of compromise and concession that had penetrated all phases of Quakerism in Pennsylvania.

In seeing the failure of Penn's Holy Experiment as a consequence of the contradiction inherent in Quakerism, Tolles in effect exonerates individual Quakers from blame for the gradual attenuation of the ideals of simplicity and spirituality on which the experiment was based. Daniel Boorstin, author of *The Americans: The Colonial Experience,* sees the history of Pennsylvania Quakerism in much the same terms as Tolles, but he is less restrained and indicts the Quakers for their "abdication of political power." Boorstin admits that the Quaker withdrawal "led them to look more closely into their own hearts and to preserve more strictly the tenets of their sect," but he contends that it also demonstrated "the unfitness of their dogmas for the larger tasks of building a new society in a new world." By contrast, Tolles is unwilling to pass judgment on the experience of the Pennsylvania Quakers. Instead he offers a balance sheet, conceding that the Quakers gained in "increased spirituality and humanitarian zeal" as a result of their withdrawal to the inward plantation, but noting that the price of their action was "the loss of immediate influence upon the world, the development of a narrowly sectarian mentality, and a liability to internal strife and tension."

## Founding of Pennsylvania

James, Sydney V. *A People Among Peoples: Quaker Benevolence in Eighteenth-Century America.* Cambridge: Harvard University Press, 1963.

*A People Among Peoples* is the story of the "new Holy Experiment" which emerged from the crisis of the 1750's. In contrast to Boorstin and Tolles, Sydney V. James maintains that Quakers did not immure themselves in "sectarian isolation," but became "active members of the civil community." After the middle of the eighteenth century Quakers turned increasingly to humanitarian concerns and enterprises as a way of making "participation in the affairs of the community compatible with membership among Friends."

James views the history of eighteenth century American Quakerism in terms of two seemingly antithetical tendencies: "the intensification of asceticism, sectarian exclusivity, and corporate solidarity, on the one hand, and a desire to use the church to improve the world around it, on the other." These two tendencies evolved simultaneously; they were combined by Quakers in the late eighteenth century to produce "a creative response to the ordeal of war and civil unrest."

Both tendencies had begun prior to the 1750's. A growing uneasiness over Quaker compromises with the world and a desire for reformation were intensified by the Great Awakening and the crisis brought on by the French and Indian War. Quakers in Pennsylvania split into two factions, compromising Friends and strict Friends, and it was the latter group, led by Israel Pemberton, that withdrew from the Assembly in 1756 in opposition to the proclamation of war against the Indians. But, according to James, though strict Quakers were concerned with purifying and unifying the Society, they did

not "desire to retreat into a sectarian shell" or to remove themselves completely from public affairs. As he demonstrates, Quakerism contained an element of utopianism, as seen in the Holy Experiment, an attempt to create a reformed society by making the government the agent of Quaker influence. After their withdrawal from government, Quakers increasingly looked to their religious Society, and to various benevolent institutions and private societies, as the means by which Friends could impress their ideals upon the world.

Thus the Quaker shift to humanitarianism, which coincided with an increasing sectarianism, involved an active concern with the world. As such, it revealed a transition within the Society of Friends from "charity," defined as "the members' mutual aid and surveillance," to benevolence, a concern for the welfare of all mankind. Humanitarianism, the focus of the "second Holy Experiment," offered Quakers a way of influencing a world from which they did not wish to withdraw completely, and a way of maintaining their inner purity and solidarity against contamination by the world. At the same time, it offered them a role in American society as "a people among people," a sect among sects, contributing "to the national welfare in ways which would preserve and express their distinctive views." In James's view, the Quakers did not fail "the test of significance" in the New World. "The idealism—the pacifism, humanitarianism, and public spirit which emerged from their eighteenth-century trials—remained an example of what Americans

161

can achieve, and to some degree per-    best exemplifies." — *A.C.L.*
vaded the estimates of what the nation

**Additional Recommended Reading**

Tolles, Frederick B. and E. Gordon Alderfer, eds. *The Witness of William Penn.* New York: The Macmillan Company, 1957. A collection of excerpts from William Penn's writings on religion and politics, which will appeal to both the general and scholarly reader.

Bronner, Edwin B. *William Penn's Holy Experiment: The Founding of Pennsylvania, 1681-1701.* New York: Temple University Publications, 1962. A detailed, well-documented, chronological study of seventeenth century Pennsylvania, this volume describes the religious and political conflicts as well as the economic pressures which compromised the idealism of the Holy Experiment.

Davidson, Robert L. *War Comes to Quaker Pennsylvania, 1682-1756.* New York: Columbia University Press, 1957. Davidson records the dissolution of the Holy Experiment under the impact of "profit seeking and politics" and "the clash of rival empires," attributing the survival of the experiment for over three quarters of a century to its isolation from the imperial struggle and its lack of conflict with the Indians, the two factors which ultimately brought about its downfall.

Tolles, Frederick B. *James Logan and the Culture of Provincial America.* Boston: Little, Brown, and Company, 1957. This biography of one of the most important figures of colonial Pennsylvania reveals much of the politics and personalities of his time.

Nash, Gary B. *Quakers and Politics: Pennsylvania, 1681-1726.* Princeton: Princeton University Press, 1968. Unlike earlier historians of colonial Pennsylvania, Nash approaches his subject not from a religious angle, but from the viewpoint of the sociology of politics. This monograph is a study of "the agonizing struggle for political stability and maturity" in which Quakers engaged during the half century after settlement.

# FORMATION OF THE DOMINION OF NEW ENGLAND

*Type of event:* Political: colonial resistance to British governmental policy
*Time:* June, 1686-April, 1689
*Locale:* New England colonies, New York, and the Jerseys

### Principal personages:

JAMES II (1633-1701), King of England from 1685 until his overthrow in 1689

WILLIAM III (1650-1702), who acceded with Mary to the throne of England in 1689 after the "Glorious Revolution" of 1688

EDWARD RANDOLPH (1632-1703), royal collector of customs and secretary of the Dominion of New England

SIR EDMUND ANDROS (1637-1714), Governor of the Dominion of New England

INCREASE MATHER (1639-1723), Puritan leader in Massachusetts

## Summary of Event

Only after the Restoration of the Stuart monarchy in 1660, when Great Britain recognized the advantages of bringing the American colonies into its expanding commercial system, did the lack of an adequate colonial policy become apparent; but by then it was too late. Great Britain had permitted its colonies a large measure of local self-government and had demanded little of them. The governments in the American colonies (which had never experienced direct royal control) had become accustomed to independence and wanted no interference, even from a relatively liberal Mother Country. Massachusetts, the most independent and rebellious of the colonies, not only violated the Navigation Acts and refused to coöperate with Edward Randolph (whom the Crown had appointed collector and surveyor of customs in 1678) but also usurped powers not granted by its corporate charter and denied that the laws of Parliament applied in the Massachusetts Bay colony. The Crown had no choice but to declare its charter null and void in 1684.

By this time it had become evident that revocation of the colonial charters was necessary for the development of Great Britain's commercial plans. The Lords of Trade issued writs of *Quo Warranto* ("by what authority?") to Connecticut, Rhode Island, the Jerseys, Pennsylvania, Maryland, the Carolinas, Bermuda, and the Bahamas in preparation for nullifying their charters. Because the establishment of royal governmental machinery in each colony would have been too expensive, a plan for three unions was devised: one for New England, one for the Middle colonies, and one for the South.

Only the New England union materialized. It began in the fall of 1685 as a provisional government for Massachusetts, Maine, New Hampshire, and the Narragansett Bay region, and it was to last until a royal governor could be commissioned and sent to America. On December 20, 1686, Sir Edmund Andros arrived to assume the

163

governorship and to organize the Dominion of New England. Rhode Island was incorporated into the union almost immediately, and Connecticut was brought in within a year. New York and the Jerseys entered in 1688. The commission and instructions drafted for Andros by the Lords of Trade provided for a governor and council appointed by the king, and a representative assembly chosen by the people, but James II had eliminated the provision for an assembly. The governor was empowered to appoint all officials, and with the council he was to legislate, levy taxes, establish courts, and sit as a supreme court. All laws were to be sent to England for approval.

Until a committee for codification could develop a uniform body of laws consistent with those of England, each colony was to operate in accordance with its old laws. In the absence of any revenue acts in effect in Massachusetts, the governor and council enacted increased customs, import and tonnage duties, excises, and land and poll taxes. The Puritans had habitually ignored or nullified laws which they disliked, and although the new taxes represented only a small increase, the selectmen of Ipswich led a revolt against them, claiming taxation without representation.

The matter of taxation was one of several areas of conflict between the Dominion government and the Puritans. In an effort to achieve conformity in the method of granting land and to make the new government self-supporting, the King had ordered that quitrents be collected on all new land granted, and that fees be charged for the compulsory confirmation of all old titles. The New Hampshire and Maine colonists welcomed the opportunity to ensure their titles, but the Puritans could not understand why the land was not theirs by right. Because Andros enforced the hated Navigation Acts, New England trade dropped off drastically. The continuing need for English manufactured goods created a drain on the colonies' hard money.

When the Dominion government attempted to make the administration of justice conform to English law, the Puritans resented the change. Jurors no longer had to be chosen from among the landowners, which meant that the leaders of the theocracy were robbed of some of their power. Even more alarming to the Puritans was the Declaration of Indulgence of April 4, 1687, granting liberty of conscience to all the King's subjects. No longer were the Puritan ministers and schools supported by the taxes of the entire population. When Andros appropriated one of Boston's Congregational churches for Anglican worship, the Puritans began to fear that the Church of England would become established in the colonies.

The Puritans regarded themselves as God's chosen people and interpreted the interference of Great Britain as a divine punishment for the younger generation's having slipped from the straight and narrow path. Thus they anticipated their eventual deliverance from their oppressors. In the spring of 1688, Increase Mather, the influential Puritan clergyman, traveled to England to petition for an assembly and other reforms. When James II was forced to publish a proclamation restoring rights to corporations, Mather and his fellow agents interpreted this concession to include colonial corporations. Mather gained the favor of the attorney-general, and the Lords of Trade agreed to promote a new charter granting more powers to the colonists.

The Glorious Revolution of 1688 and the accession of William and Mary in 1689 embodied the sign of deliverance that the Puritans had been expecting. The Lords of Trade recommended, however, that the Dominion be continued with two commissioners replacing Andros. In an effort to create the impression that the Puritans were allied with William and Mary against the Dominion and James, Mather suggested to the Massachusetts Puritans that they overthrow Andros in the name of the new sovereigns.

On April 18, 1689, when troops who had mutinied on the Maine frontier marched into Boston, insurrection broke out, and Andros was imprisoned. Within a month all the colonies had overthrown the Dominion government. On May 9, a convention of delegates from the colonies voted to restore the governments and laws of 1686.

Once back in power, the Puritan officials returned to their authoritarian policies, evoking many complaints from non-Puritans.

Both pro and anti-Dominion forces pleaded their cases before William and Mary on the question of New England's future government. Unfortunately, William was more concerned about gaining the Puritans' support for his war with the French than with colonial policy. Thus the new charter for Massachusetts was sealed on October 7, 1691. It allowed for a governor appointed by the Crown, but it also provided for an elected assembly and a council chosen by that assembly. New Hampshire became a separate royal colony, Maine and Plymouth were annexed to Massachusetts, and Connecticut and Rhode Island operated under their old charters. Massachusetts had gained a charter, but new policies insuring religious freedom and broadening the franchise had destroyed the Puritan oligarchy.

## Pertinent Literature

Barnes, Viola F. *The Dominion of New England: A Study in British Colonial Policy.* New York: Frederick Ungar Publishing Company, Inc., 1960.

The fall of the Dominion of New England was a pivotal event in American history. If Great Britain had managed to maintain the Dominion, "the most complete expression of [its] colonial policy in the seventeenth century," its relationship with the colonies in the eighteenth century might well have been entirely different. Viola Florence Barnes' thesis is an important one, for its implications are far-reaching. Her book, more than a study of the reasons for the rise and fall of the Do-

minion of New England, is an analysis of the effect of seventeenth century British colonial policy upon the movement for American independence.

Unlike "democratic" historians of the past, Barnes does not view the imposition of royal government upon New England as a tyrannical act. The Puritan oligarchy which held sway in Massachusetts before the revocation of the charter was actually more restrictive of the rights of the majority of the colonists than was the Dominion government. In fact, it was in part the refusal of the theocrats to grant non-Puritan colonists the rights of Englishmen that had made nullification of the charter inevitable. The moderate faction of Puritans realized that the Dominion government represented reform and attempted to gain a share of the power within the new system. In detailed chapters devoted to legislation and taxation, justice, liberty of conscience, trade, the land system, and defense, Barnes points out that the royal government tried consistently to achieve greater uniformity, efficiency, and fairness in the administration of government than had the Puritans.

That the Dominion failed was not the result of any fault in Great Britain's basic intention, but because of its lack of understanding of Puritan psychology and of a developing American consciousness. Confident that they were God's chosen people, the Puritans believed that their authority was divinely ordained. Ironically, they wanted the protection of the laws of England but refused to acknowledge that those laws applied to them. What Great Britain regarded as privileges granted to its colonies, the Puritans claimed as rights. Although Andros has been criticized severely for strict execution of his instructions and harsh dealing with the Puritans, Barnes argues that he had no choice if he was to break the Puritans of the habit of nullifying any law they disliked.

James II's decision to eliminate a popular assembly from the Dominion government was no mere exercise in Stuart absolutism, explains Barnes. If he had allowed an assembly, the Puritan theocrats would have retained control. Moreover, France with its more tightly popular assemblies had managed to govern without popular assemblies. But Great Britain's colonial policy—or rather, the lack of it—had encouraged decentralization, and James's decision was a fatal mistake. Had he listened to advisers who were aware of the situation in the colonies, the King would have realized that the colonists accepted self-government as a right. The Dominion's revenue acts were not oppressive, and the Puritans had never balked at taxing disfranchised nonchurch members, but now, because there was no assembly, taxation without representation became a *cause célèbre*. If James had preserved the assembly, basing the right to vote on an adequate property qualification, Barnes claims that he would have retained the support of the moderate Puritans against the theocrats. As it was, all the Puritans lined up against him. Because the moderates disliked Andros' trade and land policies, they made no effort to suppress the revolt against him.

William III understood the importance of colonial policy even less than James. Concerned only with winning the colonies' support to defeat Louis XIV, William unknowingly abandoned Great Britain's last hope for controlling its colonies when he granted Massachusetts a new charter. Fortunately, the charter represented a compromise between the old Puritan oligarchy and the Dominion, which had the effect of broadening participation in government.

Had Great Britain succeeded in forcing New England into its colonial system, Barnes theorizes, the colonists might never have considered independence. Because the Dominion of New

166

England collapsed, the colonies were free to develop their independent institutions more fully. By the eighteenth century, colonial institutions were too deeply rooted to change.

Adams, James Truslow. *The Founding of New England.* Magnolia, Massachusetts: Peter Smith Publisher, Inc., 1921. Also in paperback by Little, Brown, and Company.

James Truslow Adams views Great Britain's seventeenth century colonial policy in the perspective of the contemporary debate over the question of sovereignty and the divine right of kings. The reign of Charles II marked the end of religion and the beginning of commerce as the most important influence in national affairs. When Charles recognized the necessity for unity and administrative control within his commercial empire, he was unaware of the error of granting colonial charters free of royal control. According to Adams, the influence of the frontier environment was paramount in the shaping of individualism and the desire for self-government among the colonists. The Puritan theory that sovereignty had its source in a contract or covenant entered into by the governed conflicted directly with the concept of the divine right of kings.

One of the foremost debunkers of the Puritans, Adams contends that the defiant attitude of Massachusetts toward the laws of England forced the Mother Country to interfere in the colony's affairs. After the first generation of Puritan leaders died, the new leaders were native Americans who felt no strong ties with England. In their narrow, provincial environment, they developed narrow, unhealthy attitudes intent upon preserving discriminatory, intolerant policies; only force could have changed the Massachusetts government. Yet, Adams points out, the growth of factions within the Puritan leadership hastened the decline of theocratic control. The merchants and urban types tended to be more progressive and favorable to the Mother Country, while the rural farmers retained their narrow attitudes.

Like Barnes, Adams justifies many of the measures which the Dominion government employed to make New England conform to the English system. Likewise, he cites several fatal blunders which invited the colonists' protests. Had the royal officials considered the importance of land to the colonists, for instance, they would have realized the error of exacting fees for confirmation of titles. Many of the colonists had left England to escape the inequities of the land system and could not understand why the King should have any claim on their property. In the light of present-day American territorial policy, says Adams, Great Britain was not acting unreasonably in denying its colonies the privilege of self-government. Its policy was nevertheless unwise, because the colonists had come to accept a representative assembly as a right.

While Barnes assesses the administration of the Dominion of New England favorably and suggests that, had William III been more concerned with colonial policy, the Dominion might have been maintained as an integral part of the English commercial system, Adams argues that the inherent weaknesses of the system would have brought its end even without the Glorious Revolution of 1688. The very extent of the Dominion's territory, especially after the annexation of New York and the Jerseys, and the difficulty of communication all but rendered a centralized government impossible. Andros lacked able assistants to help control the distant reaches of the Dominion. The matter of taxation without the consent of the people created sufficient controversy by itself to wreck the royal government.

Adams pictures Massachusetts after the overthrow of Andros as a disaster area. Resentful of the Puritan government which drafted the men to defend the colony from the Indians but which had no funds to pay them, the people complained bitterly. Increase Mather, arguing in England for restoration of the old charter, resorted to reckless imputations and threats in the face of criticism.

The new charter which the King granted was more favorable than the old one which Mather desired to be restored. It freed Massachusetts from theological repression and opened the way for the development of liberal leadership. Whereas officeholding and the franchise had been based upon a religious test, it was now based only upon a property requirement which a majority of Massachusetts men could meet. The resulting movement toward the democratization of state and society was to provide a basis for the development of a common loyalty, a prerequisite for the movement toward independence. — *W.M.B.*

## Additional Recommended Reading

Andrews, Charles M. *The Colonial Period of American History.* Vol. IV: *England's Commercial and Colonial Policy.* New Haven: Yale University Press, 1964. This detailed study of Great Britain's commercial and colonial policy provides excellent background for understanding the significance of the Dominion of New England.

Beer, George L. *The Old Colonial System, 1660-1754.* Vol. II, chs. 11 and 12. New York: The Macmillan Company, 1913. Sees the Dominion as an instrument in Great Britain's effort to enforce the Navigation Laws and thus create a self-sufficient commercial empire.

Hall, Michael G. *Edward Randolph and the American Colonies, 1676-1703.* Chapel Hill: University of North Carolina Press, 1960. Focuses upon the role which the dedicated public servant who was England's foremost expert on the colonies played in the formation and government of the Dominion.

Harper, Lawrence A. *The English Navigation Laws.* New York: Octagon Books, Inc., 1964. Part Three, "Enforcement in the Colonies," explains the changes in English policy which brought about colonial resistance, thus necessitating the imposition of royal government.

Miller, Perry. *The New England Mind.* Vol. II: *From Colony to Province.* Cambridge: Harvard University Press, 1953. Discusses the decline of Puritan power in the years following the Restoration.

Andrews, Charles M., ed. *Narratives of the Insurrections, 1675 to 1690.* New York: Barnes and Noble, Inc., 1959. Included are descriptions of the revolt against Andros, Andros' report of his administration, and Increase Mather's account of his efforts to obtain the restoration of the old Massachusetts Charter.

# SALEM WITCHCRAFT TRIALS

*Type of event:* Legal: emotional upheaval resulting in persecution
*Time:* 1692-1693
*Locale:* Essex County, Massachusetts Bay colony

*Principal personages:*

SAMUEL PARRIS (1653-1720), Puritan pastor of Salem Village
NICHOLAS NOYES (fl. 1692), Puritan pastor of Salem Town
TITUBA (fl. 1692), West Indian slave in the Parris household
JOHN HATHORNE (fl. 1692), and
JONATHAN CORWIN (fl. 1692), assistants of the Massachusetts General Court who conducted the examinations of the accused witches
SIMON BRADSTREET (1603-1697), provisional Governor of Massachusetts after the fall of the Dominion of New England
SIR WILLIAM PHIPS (1651-1695), Royal Governor of Massachusetts (1692-1694)
SAMUEL SEWALL (1652-1730), Massachusetts magistrate and a judge at the witch trials
WILLIAM STOUGHTON (fl, 1692), Deputy Governor and presiding justice at the witch trials
INCREASE MATHER (1639-1723), pastor of the Boston Puritan church and President of Harvard College
COTTON MATHER (1663-1728), son of Increase, a Puritan minister interested in psychic research and author of *Wonders of the Invisible World*

## Summary of Event

Early in 1692, a circle of young girls began to meet in the home of Samuel Parris, the Puritan pastor of Salem Village. The minister's nine-year-old daughter Betty and her eleven-year-old cousin Abigail Williams were fascinated by the Voodoo-like tales and tricks of the family's West Indian slave, Tituba, and soon they began to invite their friends to share in the entertainment. Before long, some of the girls in the circle began to behave strangely, complaining of physical maladies, reporting visions, lapsing into trances, and trembling and babbling without restraint.

Among the Puritans, inexplicable afflictions were customarily attributed to the work of the devil, so most of the inhabitants of Salem Village believed the young girls when they charged that Tituba and two other village women of doubtful respectability were practicing witchcraft upon them. Two assistants of the Massachusetts General Court, John Hathorne and Jonathan Corwin, were called upon to conduct an examination of the accused women. Placing no store in lawyers, the Puritans were governed essentially by Old Testament law. When they found a statement in the Scriptures that witches must not be

169

allowed to live, their duty became clear. The two magistrates conducted their examination more like prosecuting attorneys than impartial investigators. They accepted the dreams and fancies of the young girls as positive evidence and concluded that a "strange tit or wart" on the body of one of the women was a "witches' tit," at which the devil and his familiars, or messengers, sucked the blood of the witch. When Tituba confessed her own connection with the devil, she implicated the other accused witches, and on March 7, all three were sent off to prison. Although many of the villagers were skeptical of the claims of the girls, the examiners, supported by Parris and Nicholas Noyes, his colleague in Salem Town, called upon other ministers of the area to consult with them.

More accusations—this time against respectable, pious women of the community—came almost immediately, and it seemed that the devil was carrying out his deception by possessing seemingly innocent persons. The panic soon enveloped not only the residents of Salem but those of neighboring towns as well. As the suspected witches confessed, they frequently accused others.

The devil's timing was faultless, for the Massachusetts Bay colony was still agitated over the loss of its charter in 1684 and the overthrow of the Dominion of New England in 1689. The weak provisional government, headed by the ailing governor, Simon Bradstreet, was merely awaiting the arrival of the new governor and did nothing to avert the crisis. When Sir William Phips, Royal Governor of Massachusetts, arrived in May, 1692, with the new Massachusetts Charter, he decided immediately that proper courts must be established for the trying of witches. On the last Wednesday in May, the Governor's Council set up a General Court, which promptly appointed seven judges to constitute a special court of Oyer and Terminer to convene on June 2. The witchcraft fever had continued to spread, but the accused were confident that the distinguished judges Bartholomew Gedney, Samuel Sewall, John Richards, William Sergeant, Wait Winthrop, Nathaniel Saltonstall (later replaced by Jonathan Corwin); and Presiding Justice William Stoughton, representing some of the best minds in the colony, would deal justly with the witchcraft problem. The court, however, accepted the testimony gathered at the examination as proven fact. At the trials the judges simply heard new evidence, and a jury decided the prisoner's fate. On June 8, the General Court revived an old law making witchcraft a capital offence. Two days later, Bridget Bishop, the first condemned witch, went to the gallows.

A schism among the judges over the validity of spectral evidence necessitated a delay in the proceedings while they sought the advice of the clergy of the Boston area. Although the ministers urged caution in the handling of spectral evidence, they praised the judges and encouraged further prosecution of the witches. As the summer brought more hangings, the remaining prisoners began to fear for their lives, and several managed to escape. The judges, as good Puritans, accepted confession as evidence of possible regeneration and were merciful to those who would confess their dealings with the devil and repent, but few of the staunch Puritans were willing to belie themselves even to save their lives.

By the time the last of the twenty victims had been executed on September 22, public opinion was ceasing to support the trials. There were numerous reasons for this change: several of those who were executed in August died calmly, forgiving their accusers and judges, and protesting their innocence to the end; the court's procedures seemed to be aggravating the witchcraft problem rather than alleviating it; and as the witch hunt spread, persons were being accused whom no one could believe guilty. The panic had been confined almost exclusively to Essex County, and ministers from outside the immediate area began taking a stand against continuing the trials. Increase Mather, the great Boston divine, warned against reliance on spectral evidence and traveled to Salem to investigate the method of obtaining confessions. A petition from Andover was the first among many to call for release of the remaining prisoners and to denounce the accusing girls. On October 29, Governor Phips dismissed the Court of Oyer and Terminer. Its end marked the end of the witch hunt.

By acts of the General Court of November 23 and December 16, special sessions of the Superior Court of Judicature were ordered to complete the trials. The new circuit court was composed largely of the same judges as the recently dissolved court, but it now held spectral evidence to be inadmissible. Fifty-two accused witches came to trial early in January, 1693, and forty-nine were released immediately for lack of evidence. The Governor soon reprieved the others, and by May all the remaining prisoners had been discharged.

While some people were disappointed to see the trials end, most were relieved to return to their long-neglected work. Blaming Parris for allowing the death of innocent relatives and friends, the congregation of the Salem church voted to void his salary. In the ensuing years, many of the accusers of the condemned repented, and in 1709 and 1711, the Massachusetts General Court restored to many of those who had been accused of being witches, as well as the children of the executed victims, their good names and awarded them compensation for financial losses. The names of some, however, were never cleared.

During the Salem witchcraft trials both Increase and Cotton Mather expressed their doubts about the proceedings, especially concerning the use of spectral evidence. It was Increase Mather who insisted that the special Court of Oyer and Terminer be terminated because it might be guilty of shedding innocent blood. Cotton Mather, acting as one of the "most" cogent critics of the court's methods" while it was sitting, afterward offered a strongly partisan defense of the judges. Because of this defense, historians have incorrectly presented Cotton Mather as the instigator of the witchcraft trials. He was in fact guilty of not opposing the trials vigorously enough.

Although the Salem trials were not the last, because of the Massachusetts authorities' actions in discovering, acknowledging, and disowning their errors, the Salem experience "helped put an end to witchcraft trials in Western civilization."

171

## Salem Witchcraft Trials

### Pertinent Literature

Starkey, Marion L. *The Devil in Massachusetts: A Modern Enquiry into the Salem Witch Trials.* New York: Alfred A. Knopf, Inc., 1949.

*The Devil in Massachusetts* reads more like a novel than a history book. Marion L. Starkey's talent for converting the records of the Salem witchcraft trials into dramatic dialogue invests the proceedings with an element of excitement. So deftly does she delineate the principal characters that they immediately evoke the sympathy or antipathy of the reader. Yet this work is by no means a shallow, popular account. Starkey has employed previously unused source materials and reviews the evidence in the light of modern psychological findings. In her preface she reports having investigated the works of Freud and Janet and studies of hypnotism and spiritualism, in addition to interviewing staff members and patients at a mental hospital. The psychological dimension contributes significantly to an understanding of the motives of the young girls who began the whole affair.

Starkey sees the witch trials against the background of the gray New England countryside and the drab existence of the Puritan colonists. The young girls, their appetites for the different and the unusual having been aroused by Tituba's stories, no doubt craved attention and excitement. It is not their antics, but the reaction of the community to them, that the author finds remarkable. Because the natural impulses of the Puritans were repressed, she suggests, they sought catharsis in the outpouring of vengeful fervor.

The Satan of Milton's "Paradise Lost" loomed large in the Puritan cosmology, so that the Salem villagers were ready to accept the smallest misfortunes as his doing. Starkey depicts them as "bewitched by a mad hypnosis," so convinced of the presence of evil among them that they refused to believe the confessions of two of the accusing girls, forcing them to remain within the crazed circle.

Democracy was not an acceptable political system to the Puritans, but ironically, the author points out, there was "democracy among witches." As the hunt for witches expanded throughout Essex County, it took in persons of various races, religions, and classes. The pious, church-going grandmother was condemned along with the village strumpet.

Massachusetts' unsettled political climate in 1692 served to prolong the witchcraft panic. In the period following the overthrow of the autocratic government of the Dominion of New England, the provisional government was too weak to exert a calming influence on the agitated colonists. The new Royal Governor was at first too preoccupied with the threat from the French and Indians to take matters in hand. The peculiar quality of the colonial judicial system, with its reliance upon Scriptural law, its lack of conformity to English legal practice, and its disregard for lawyers, likewise allowed for gross neglect of accepted legal rights. Because the judges willingly accepted spectral evidence while the defendants based their arguments upon the events of the visible world, the trials were conducted on two separate planes, with neither side being capable of understanding the other. Strangely enough, however, the judges were not without mercy for those who confessed practicing witchcraft. Good Calvinists, they believed that, since all men are sinful, salvation comes only through repentance. Then, too, the confessed witches were valuable informers. The author speaks with unbounded admiration for those condemned persons who refused to lie to save their own lives. The finest examples of the "indomitable Puritan spirit," they would surely have been beatified had they been Catholics, she contends.

The Puritan belief that the hand of God was in all events naturally extended to the conclusion of the witch trials. At first, many who had taken morbid delight in the prosecutions felt that God was punishing them—probably for accepting the new charter with its extension of the franchise to non-Puritans—by denying them the ability to ferret out the guilty ones among them. Cotton Mather's writings show that he had enjoyed the contact with the supernatural too much to learn something constructive from the horrible affair.

In keeping with her avowed purpose, the author presents a true Greek tragedy. In the classic pattern, good did come out of evil. The people of Massachusetts did, after all, possess the spiritual health to renounce error and to emerge from their tragedy with honor.

Kittredge, George Lyman. *Witchcraft in Old and New England.* Cambridge: Harvard University Press, 1929.

"It is easy to be wise after the fact,—especially when the fact is two-hundred years old." With this maxim George Lyman Kittredge concludes his list of theses about witchcraft. That the bulk of his study is concerned with the history of witchcraft in England prior to the Salem trials is significant to his defense of the Massachusetts Puritans. "The belief in witchcraft is the common heritage of humanity," he hypothesizes. Therefore, contrary to the assertions of earlier students of the subject, the outbreak in Salem cannot be attributed to some peculiarities of Puritan theology or to the accusers' colonial environment. On the contrary, Kittredge maintains, the affair was typical.

We of the present day, accustomed to thinking rationally, find it difficult to understand that seventeenth century man believed in witchcraft as a fact of experience, explains Kittredge. There had always been witches. Even the law recognized their existence. As evidence that belief in witchcraft was by no means confined to Puritans, Kittredge quotes some of the leading non-Puritan scholars and scientific thinkers of the seventeenth century. Misunderstanding on this point had developed probably because so many indictments of supposed witches occurred during the term of the Puritan Matthew Hopkins as "Witch-Finder General."

Several works denying the power of the devil appeared in the seventeenth century, but only the Dutch theologian Balthasar Bekker's *The Enchanted World* offered a complete theory on which a contemporary Christian could logically reject witchcraft. Whether Bekker's argument would stand or fall, however, depended upon the soundness of his Biblical exegesis, for the seventeenth century Christian accepted the Bible as absolute, divinely-inspired truth. Since many orthodox theologians who believed in witches were more correct in their interpretation of Scripture than were Bekker and his adherents, antiwitchcraft writings had little influence upon the general public.

Historians who have attempted to single out certain prominent individuals to bear the blame for the Salem affair have failed to perceive that responsibility for prosecution of witches frequently lay with the community. Prosecution, Kittredge asserts, also required a body of evidence concerning reputed witches and their causing strange occurrences over an extended period of time. Often, accused witches themselves believed they possessed supernatural powers, or they pretended to possess them in order to impress their neighbors.

Some suspicion of witchcraft existed around Salem before 1692. The "devil-worshipping" Indians provided a constant reminder of its dangers. Kittredge finds it remarkable, therefore, that the Salem outburst came so late. Europe and England had for many years experienced spasmodic episodes concerning witchcraft. That the Salem panic was slow in coming he attributes to the extraordinary steadiness of the Puri-

tans. Given the thesis that belief in witchcraft was almost universal at the time and the fact that outbreaks occurred regularly, what then triggered the Salem incident? Kittredge answers that such upheavals usually happen in times of political anxiety. Ever since the loss of its charter in 1684, Massachusetts had experienced division and unrest. Fear of Indian attack reinforced the feeling of insecurity.

In defense of the proponents of persecution at Salem, Kittredge argues that they held a scripturally stronger position than their antagonists, given the acceptance of the doctrines concerning supernaturalism by both sides. The admissibility of spectral evidence was an established legal principle in England. Kittredge, then, finds nothing abnormal in Salem's prosecution and condemnation of accused witches. What he does find remarkable is the rapid return to normalcy and the frank confession of error. The reversal of position by a judge and jury are without precedent in the annals of witchcraft. That the Puritans experienced only one short-lived outbreak in the century when England executed hundreds is much to the Puritans' credit, the author insists. Salem's repentance constituted a significant argument against maintaining the status of witchcraft as a recognized crime in England. — *W.M.B.*

**Additional Recommended Reading**

Hansen, Chadwick. *Witchcraft at Salem.* New York: George Braziller, Inc., 1969. This recent volume contains an excellent survey of the background and course of the Salem witchcraft hysteria.

Wendell, Barrett. *Cotton Mather: The Puritan Priest.* New York: Harcourt, Brace & World, Inc., 1963. This biography tells of the tragic consequences which the Salem incident had for the life of the determined minister who involved himself so deeply in the study of witchcraft.

## Salem Witchcraft Trials

Levin, David D. *What Happened in Salem?* New York: Harcourt, Brace & World, Inc., 1960. An excellent introduction precedes this collection, which includes selections from the trial evidence, contemporary writings relating to witchcraft, and two examples of historical fiction.

Miller, Perry. *The New England Mind.* Vol. II: *From Colony to Province.* Cambridge: Harvard University Press, 1953. In this excellent background work, Miller explains the witchcraft trials as a natural outgrowth of Puritan theology, but charges the Mathers with bringing the matter to a head.

Burr, George L. *Narratives of the Witchcraft Cases, 1648 to 1706.* New York: Barnes and Noble, Inc., 1952. Numerous selections from works of Cotton and Increase Mather are among this collection of seventeenth century writings relating to witchcraft in the colonies.

Upham, Charles W. *Salem Witchcraft.* New York: Frederick Ungar Publishing Co., 1959. Originally published in 1867, this detailed classic work is composed of three parts: a history of Salem Village, a history of witchcraft, and an account of the events of 1692-1693 in Salem.

Demos, John Putnam. *Entertaining Satan: Witchcraft and the Culture of Early New England.* New York: Oxford University Press, 1982. A historian uses the tools of the biographer, psychologist, sociologist, and historian to analyze witchcraft and culture in seventeenth century New England.

Silverman, Kenneth. *The Life and Times of Cotton Mather.* New York: Harper and Row, Publishers, 1984. A well-written biography that thoroughly illuminates the life and times of one of the most misunderstood figures in Colonial American history. Illustrated.

175

# THE GREAT AWAKENING

*Type of event:* Religious: desire of many people for a more pietistic faith
*Time:* 1730's and 1740's
*Locale:* American colonies

### Principal personages:

GEORGE WHITEFIELD (1714-1770), Anglican missionary and philanthropist whose visit to America in 1739 sparked the Great Awakening

JONATHAN EDWARDS (1703-1758), minister from Northampton, Connecticut, and principal defender of the Great Awakening; author of *A Treatise Concerning Religious Affections* (1746), which defined the doctrine of regeneration that formed the core of the theology of the Great Awakening

CHARLES CHAUNCY (1705-1787), minister of Boston's First Church and chief critic of the Great Awakening; author of *Seasonable Thoughts on the State of Religion in New England* (1743)

WILLIAM TENNENT (1673-1745), native of Ireland, pastor of the Presbyterian church at Neshaminy, Pennsylvania, and founder of the Log College

GILBERT TENNENT (1703-1764), son of William, educated at the Log College; pastor of Presbyterian church at New Brunswick, New Jersey; and leader of the revivalist party which organized the Synod of New York in 1745

SAMUEL DAVIES (1723-1761), organizer and propagator of Presbyterianism in Virginia, and founder of the Hanover Presbytery in 1755

### Summary of Event

Between 1739 and 1742 the American colonies experienced a quickening of religious faith that became known as the Great Awakening. The arrival of the young Anglican preacher George Whitefield probably sparked the religious conflagration. Whitefield, whose reputation as a great pulpit and open-air orator had preceded his visit, traveled through the colonies in 1739 and 1740. Everywhere he attracted large and emotional crowds, eliciting countless conversions as well as considerable controversy. Critics condemned his "enthusiasm," his censoriousness, and his extemporaneous and itinerant preaching, but his techniques were copied by numerous imitators both lay and clerical. They became itinerant preachers themselves, spreading the Great Awakening from New England to Georgia, among rich and poor, educated and illiterate, and in the backcountry as well as in seaboard towns and cities.

In the Middle colonies, Gilbert Tennent was the leader of the revival among the Presbyterians. His famous sermon, "The Danger of an Unconverted Ministry," was widely circulated throughout the colonies. Led by Jonathan Dickinson, Presbyterians of New England background joined in the revival. In New England, the most notorious evangelist was James Davenport, whose extravagances were even denounced by Tennent and other revivalists. Jonathan Edwards, Samuel Buell, and Eleazar Wheelock, less controversial than Davenport, were also instruments of the Awakening in New England. In the Southern colonies, the Great Awakening made greatest headway on the frontier. Samuel Davies preached revivalism among the Presbyterians of Virginia and North Carolina; Shubal Stearns and Daniel Marshall drew converts to the Separate Baptist fold; and Devereux Jarratt inaugurated the Methodist phase of the Awakening.

The colonists were not unprepared for the Great Awakening. Prior to 1739, there had been indications of a religious quickening among several denominations. In the 1720's the Dutch Reformed Church in New Jersey experienced a series of revivals led by Theodore Frelinghuysen, a native of Germany who had been influenced by the pietistic movement within the Lutheran Church. In the mid-1730's, a "refreshing" occurred among the Presbyterians of New Jersey and Pennsylvania as a result of the preaching of a group of Scotch-Irish ministers led by William Tennent and trained in his Log College. The revivals continued throughout the 1730's, coinciding with the "subscription controversy" within American Presbyterianism. New England was also the scene of religious excitement before 1739.

The "harvests" of Solomon Stoddard, known as the "pope" of the Connecticut Valley, and the Northampton revival of 1734-1735, led by his grandson Jonathan Edwards, foreshadowed the later, more general awakening. Thus Whitefield's tour provided the catalyst, not the cause, of the Great Awakening, which represented the culmination of impulses that were already beginning to transform colonial Protestantism.

At first the Great Awakening was celebrated as a supernatural work, the "pouring out of the grace of God upon the land." But controversy over the origins and effects of the revival soon displaced the earlier consensus. Prorevivalists continued to defend the Great Awakening as the work of God, but opponents criticized the excesses stemming from the religious "enthusiasm" fomented by the revival. At the root of their disagreement was a conflict over the source of religious faith. Opponents of the revival tended to emphasize reason as the basic ingredient of true religion. The defenders defined religion as a matter of the heart, not the head, or of the feelings or "affections," as Jonathan Edwards called them, not the intellect. The theology of the revivalists was Calvinist, which stressed the depravity of man and the sovereignty of God. They emphasized faith rather than good conduct as the means to salvation. Regeneration was defined as an emotional, even a physical, experience wrought by God, not man, and resulting in a "New Birth" or "Change of Heart"; the change in the convert's personality in turn would be manifested in his actions.

In many cases the controversy over the Great Awakening split denominations into opposing factions. The revival produced a temporary schism among the Presbyterians—between Old Sides who opposed the Awakening and New Sides who approved it. Congregationalism was split between Old Lights and New Lights. Some pro-revivalist New Lights became Separatists, withdrawing from the established Congregational churches and forming new churches of the regenerate; most of these Separate churches ultimately became Baptist, with the result that the majority of New England Baptists shifted from an Arminian to a Calvinist theology. No denomination entirely escaped the divisive effects of the Great Awakening.

There were numerous aftereffects of the Great Awakening. Despite the anti-intellectual bias of their theology, the revivalists founded a number of educa-tional institutions, including the College of New Jersey (later Princeton) and Dartmouth College. The Great Awakening stimulated social concern in other areas by virtue of its emphasis on "benevolence" as the outward sign of inner piety. Many revivalists encouraged philanthropic efforts to improve the condition of Negroes, Indians, orphans, and other unfortunates. Perhaps the most lasting effect of the Great Awakening was its encouragement of religious toleration and separation of church and state. Besides placing greater emphasis on the individual and his personal religious experience, the Awakening, by strengthening dissenting churches, such as the Methodists and Baptists, promoted the religious pluralism that helped to shape the distinctive character of American religion.

## Pertinent Literature

Heimert, Alan E. *Religion and the American Mind: From the Great Awakening to the Revolution.* Cambridge: Harvard University Press, 1966.

The relationship between the Great Awakening and the American Revolution is the subject of this study of the eighteenth century colonial mind. Heimert argues that the split in American Protestantism caused by the Great Awakening—between the "rationalists," or "Liberals," who opposed the revival, and the "evangelicals," or "Calvinists," who defended it—mirrored a "fundamental cleavage" in the American mind generally and became objectified in the politics of the colonies. Challenging the traditional view that the religion of the Enlightenment supplied the underpinning of the Revolutionary ideology, Heimert concludes that the stimulus to rebellion came chiefly from the evangelical religion of the Awakening. "Liberalism," he explains, "was profoundly conservative, politically as well as socially . . . Conversely, 'evangelical' religion . . . provided pre-Revolutionary America with a radical, even democratic, social and political ideology. . . ." In short, "What the colonies had awakened to in 1740 was none other than independence and rebellion." Indeed, Heimert suggests that after the American Revolution evangelical religion continued to play a considerable role in American intellectual and political development; he traces its influence in Jeffersonian and Jacksonian democracy, as well as late nineteenth century Populism.

Thus, in Heimert's view, the dispute between evangelicals and rationalists was "not so much a dispute between theologians as a vital competition for the intellectual allegiance of the American people." The two parties' conflicting conceptions of man, history, and the good society had profound political and social, as well as religious, implications. For example, Heimert argues that the view of man implied by the Calvinist doctrine of the "new birth" was eminently more egalitarian and democratic than the elitist and rationalist view of the Liberals. Similarly, the Calvinists' optimistic view of history and their belief in the coming of the kingdom of God reinforced the impulse toward independence from Great Britain, whereas the Liberals' "cosmic pessimism" persuaded them of the necessity of maintaining ties with the Mother Country. Heimert also contrasts the "radically communitarian" and highly moralistic political and social theory of the evangelicals with the

individualist and utilitarian premises of the rationalists. If the Liberals looked to John Locke for inspiration, it was the spirit of Rousseau that informed the views of the Calvinists. "The Calvinist political philosophy . . . centered finally not on the consent of the governed but on the will of the community," Heimert writes. In his view, the thrust of the evangelical impulse loosed during the Great Awakening was not only toward democracy but nationalism as well.

Heimert bases his analysis of the eighteenth century American mind on an extensive reading of the published literature of the period. His method, as he explains, is essentially that of "literary interpretation." In both its method and its thesis, *Religion and the American Mind* is a provocative and controversial work. If Heimert is correct, many of the earlier interpretations of the Great Awakening and its impact on American development stand in need of considerable revision.

Bushman, Richard L. *From Puritan to Yankee: Character and Social Order in Connecticut, 1690-1765.* Cambridge: Harvard University Press, 1967.

Like Alan Heimert, Richard Bushman considers the social and political consequences of the Great Awakening. However, his study of colonial Connecticut is only indirectly concerned with the relation between the religious revival and the American Revolution. His primary topic is the process by which Connecticut Puritans became Yankees, and the transformation of the social order which resulted from that change in character. In Bushman's view, the Great Awakening was one of the impulses which hastened the transition. The revival did in fact result in a "new birth," psychologically as well as

spiritually. "The converted were new men, with new attitudes toward themselves, their religion, their neighbors, and their rulers in church and state. A psychological earthquake had reshaped the human landscape."

The basic division between New and Old Lights was that of piety versus order. According to Bushman, "The revivalists undermined the social order . . . not by repudiating law and authority but by denying them sanctifying power." The external social order, which Puritans and Old Lights believed to be divinely authorized, no longer commanded the allegiance of

179

men who enjoyed a direct, personal relation with God as a result of regeneration. In this transfer of authority from the external order to an inward experience Bushman finds "the truly revolutionary aspect of the Awakening. . . ." Experimental religion not only diminished ecclesiastical authority and enlarged religious liberty. It also shaped the political behavior of New Lights. The loss of "faith in the divinity of earthly law and authority" accounted for the greater willingness of the New Lights to resist the Stamp Act in 1765, according to Bushman. In this willingness to resist authority lay the significance of the New Lights—and the political impact of the Great Awakening.

Bushman challenges a number of the theses advanced by Alan Heimert. Whereas Heimert treats the evangelicals as a unified group, Bushman argues that the New Lights were divided in their opposition to the traditional order. The majority were moderates whose views represented a compromise between order and piety. They disagreed with the other wing of the New Lights, radicals who advocated lay preaching and separation, though they shared their belief in the importance of the "new birth" and experimental religion. Nor does Bushman perceive so sharp a distinction between Old and New Lights as Heimert sees

between Liberals and Calvinists. For Bushman, the theological conflict between the two parties, like the debate between piety and order, was a matter of "emphasis and balance." Both Old and New Lights adhered to a Calvinist theology, though New Lights claimed their opponents were guilty of misinterpretation or outright heresy. Ironically, in some cases, as New Lights gained power, they threw off their role as defenders of dissent and religious toleration, and assumed the posture which had formerly belonged to the Old Lights, that of protecting orthodoxy.

Finally, in contrast to Heimert's contention that the cleavage between Liberals and Calvinists persisted into the Revolution, Bushman implies that political activity served to unite a society rent by religious schism. As early as 1765, the state had become "the symbol of social coherence, as once the Established churches had been." In turn, "concentration of community loyalties on the state intensified devotion to those principles on which all could agree. The contents of the social compact—liberty and property— became the rallying cry of the social order. When the opportunity to defend the common interests arose, men responded with religious fervor." — *A.C.L.*

## Additional Recommended Reading

Maxson, Charles H. *The Great Awakening in the Middle Colonies.* Chicago: University of Chicago Press, 1920. An account of the Great Awakening in New York, New Jersey, and Pennsylvania with emphasis on the Dutch Reformed and Presbyterian Churches, viewed as part of an international evangelical revival in reaction against the Age of Reason.

Trinterud, Leonard J. *The Forming of an American Tradition: A Re-Examination of Colonial Presbyterianism.* Philadelphia: The Westminster Press, 1949. In this study of

## The Great Awakening

colonial Presbyterianism, Trinterud demonstrates the process by which "an American understanding of Presbyterianism" emerged out of the theological controversy and spiritual quickening of the Great Awakening.

Gaustad, Edwin S. *The Great Awakening in New England.* New York: Harper & Row Publishers, 1957. This brief but compact study of the Great Awakening in New England combines narrative and analysis, describing the events and personages of the revival and assessing its long-range theological and institutional effects.

Gesehr, Wesley M. *The Great Awakening in Virginia, 1740-1790.* Durham: Duke University Press, 1930. In addition to narrating the Presbyterian, Baptist, and Methodist phases of the Great Awakening in colonial Virginia, Gesehr traces the influence of the revival on the rise of political democracy and the development of educational and humanitarian impulses in the Old Dominion.

Goen, Clarence C. *Revivalism and Separatism in New England, 1740-1800: Strict Congregationalists and Separate Baptists in the Great Awakening.* New Haven: Yale University Press, 1962. A study of the separatist movement in New England during the Great Awakening, and its relation to the Congregational establishment from which it withdrew and the Baptist fellowship with which it ultimately merged.

Miller, Perry. *Errand into the Wilderness.* Chs. 6-8. Cambridge: Harvard University Press, 1956. A brilliant and provocative analysis of Edwards' contribution to the Great Awakening, the political implications of the revival, and the continuity between Edwards' and Emerson's views of the universe.

181

# SETTLEMENT OF GEORGIA

*Type of event:* Socio-political: British desire to create a haven for debtors and also to establish a bulwark on the southern frontier
*Time:* June 20, 1732
*Locale:* Southeast Coast of North America

*Principal personages:*
JAMES EDWARD OGLETHORPE (1696-1785), British M.P. who proposed the founding of Georgia as a haven for imprisoned debtors and who served as its civil and military leader in its early days
SIR JOHN PERCEVAL (1683-1748), promoter of the Georgia venture
SIR ROBERT WALPOLE (1676-1745), Chancellor of the Exchequer of Great Britain
JAMES VERNON (fl. 1733), active Georgia trustee
BENJAMIN MARTYN (fl. 1733), secretary of the Board of Trustees for Georgia
TOMOCHICHI (1650-1739), Chief of the Yamacraw Indians who resided in the Savannah area

## Summary of Event

The founding of Georgia attracted more attention in England than that of any other colony. Because the project suited the purposes of both philanthropic and imperial interests, it drew support from all segments of society. Two unrelated sets of circumstances in England and North America combined in the early 1730's to augment the Georgia enterprise.

In England economic depression and unemployment had filled the prisons with hapless debtors. When the investigations of a Parliamentary committee under the chairmanship of James Edward Oglethorpe resulted in the freeing of thousands of debtors, they had no place to go. A philanthropic society begun by Thomas Bray, founder of the Society for the Propagation of the Gospel in Foreign Parts, determined to relieve the plight of the debtors. Led by

John Perceval, later Earl of Egmont, the "Associates of the Late Dr. Bray," at the suggestion of Oglethorpe, petitioned the Crown for a tract of land south and west of Carolina between the Savannah and Altamaha rivers with the intention of establishing settlement especially for debtors.

The request came at a propitious moment, for in addition to its social purposes, the proposed colony offered a possible solution to an increasingly serious imperial problem. Having claimed Florida more than a hundred years before the settlement of Carolina, the Spaniards had gradually expanded northward, establishing presidios and missions first on the Sea Islands and then on the mainland of Georgia. The grant by Charles II of land claimed by the Spaniards to the Carolina proprietors in 1663 marked the beginning of

182

the contest for the territory between Charleston and Saint Augustine. Not only did the British have to find means of protecting their frontier against the Spanish, but they also had to contend with the hostile Yamasee Indians. Settlement of the region between the Savannah and Altamaha rivers would create a buffer for the defense of Carolina. From an economic standpoint, a new colony could contribute raw materials for English manufacturers, provide a market for their goods, and ease the Mother Country's unemployment problem.

On June 20, 1732, the Crown conferred upon the twenty-one members of the Board of Trustees for Georgia a charter empowering them to found and to manage for twenty-one years the land between the Savannah and Altamaha rivers, stretching as far westward as the South Seas. Although the government took a calculated view of their enterprise, the trustees considered it the greatest philanthropic and social experiment of their age. Numerous churches, organizations, and individuals responded to their promotional campaign with contributions.

Since the settlers were to participate in a social experiment, they were individually selected from among applicants and imprisoned debtors. Each would receive free passage to Georgia, tools, seeds, provisions until his first crop could be harvested, and fifty acres of land. The colonists were also entitled to all the rights of British subjects.

By the fall of 1732, over one hundred settlers had been chosen, and Oglethorpe himself led the expedition to America. Disembarking at Charleston, South Carolina, in January, 1733, Oglethorpe soon chose a site for the town of Savannah and reached an agreement with Tomochichi, Chief of the Yamacraw Indians who resided there. On February 12, 1733, the colonists arrived in small boats. With the aid of William Bull, a Carolinian, Oglethorpe laid out an orderly town, and the settlers began building houses. Settlement was to proceed in an orderly fashion, not in the haphazard manner of the older colonies. So that compactness might be assured, no one was allowed more than fifty acres. The communal arrangement provided that each family own a town lot with a garden and a piece of farm land nearby. Settlers held their land through "tail male," meaning that tenure was for life, and only eldest sons could inherit land. The prohibition against sale or rental of property eliminated the possibility of unselected immigrants becoming part of the community. Hoping once again to make silk production a profitable colonial enterprise, the crown required each settler to clear ten acres and plant one hundred mulberry trees within ten years.

In addition to the "charity settlers," the trustees also admitted approved "adventurers," persons who paid their own passage to the colony. Persecuted Protestants from Europe, notably Lutheran Salzburgers and Moravians, were also welcomed. After a few years, the adventurers and foreigners far outnumbered the debtor element in the population.

Authority over Georgia's affairs was officially shared by the Board of Trustees and the British government, though in practice a smaller body known as the Common Council carried on most of the work. Among the most active trustees were Oglethorpe, Perceval, James

Vernon, the Earl of Shaftesbury (Anthony Ashley-Cooper), and Benjamin Martyn, the secretary. Although the trustees were to appoint the governor, his instructions came from the King. All laws passed by the trustees had to be reviewed by the king. While the trustees held the philanthropic and social goals to be of primary importance, the government was chiefly concerned with the economic and defensive advantages which Georgia might contribute to the Empire. The trustees came to distrust Sir Robert Walpole, the Chancellor of the Exchequer, and in order to evade the authority of the government, tried, as far as possible, to govern by regulations rather than laws. In the absence of local governmental institutions, Oglethorpe acted as an authoritarian, patriarchal leader.

Inevitably, Georgia took on the military character which the Crown intended it to have, and the colonists were distracted from the business of building a stable society. Georgia's most serious problems in the early years were caused by the conflicting purposes which she was expected to fulfill.

## Pertinent Literature

Coulter, E. Merton. *Georgia: A Short History.* Chapel Hill: University of North Carolina Press, 1933.

Coulter's work begins with the sixteenth century, for knowledge of the competition between Spain, France, and England for American territory is essential for understanding the situation which encouraged the founding of Georgia but which nearly destroyed it.

Coulter emphasizes the basic conflict between the idealism of the philanthropists and the pragmatism of the British government. The essential incompatibility of the two objectives made for the turbulent early history of Georgia.

In this book ample evidence is provided that Georgia bore a strong military tinge from the beginning. Oglethorpe concerned himself not only with fortifying Savannah, but also with establishing other strategic military posts. A considerable portion of his time was occupied with offensive as well as defensive expeditions against the Spanish.

Military duties were not the only concern that kept the settlers from the essential business of growing food. As in Virginia and South Carolina, the British government was determined to promote industries which would eliminate dependence on foreign markets for certain goods. So the Georgia settlers were required to plant mulberry trees with the intention of producing all the silk that England required. Again the government's efforts served only to divert the colonists from more practical and necessary activities.

Conflicting imperial interests were by no means Georgia's only problem. The trustees, who had so carefully screened the population and who had so thoughtfully planned the system of land tenure, had been sadly lacking in an understanding of human nature. By the early 1740's, dissatisfaction with the restrictions on landholding and the Indian trade, and with the prohibitions on the introduction of slaves and liquor, had resulted in a severe drop in the population and in vocal criticism

184

and widespread violations by the colonists. Realizing the impracticality of their plans, the trustees gradually relaxed the limitations on landholdings and allowed the importation of rum and slaves, thus destroying their dream of a controlled social environment. After the first ten years, many of the original disillusioned promoters lost interest in Georgia, and contributions for her support were no longer forthcoming. In actuality, Coulter contends, Georgia was never primarily a charitable enterprise. Less than half the immigrants came at the expense of the trust, and a large proportion of those who did were foreign Protestants rather than English debtors.

In Coulter's estimation, probably the greatest blunder of the trustees was their failure to establish adequate political institutions. Hoping to evade the King's veto, they governed when possible by regulations. Oglethorpe was never formally appointed Governor, but acted as a military, rather than a civil, leader much of the time. When he did set up a government, it consisted merely of three judges to try cases and a few minor law enforcement officials. The subsequent creation of a president and assistants, actually only a court of appeals, did little to advance the level of government. The colonists had no voice at all in their affairs. Only at the very end of their tenure did the trustees recognize the folly of expecting men to sit back and accept the will of an authority imposed upon them. In the year before they surrendered their charter, the trustees finally decided to experiment in the direction of popular government.

Reasons, both well-intentioned and selfish, for the failure of Georgia during the period of trusteeship become eminently clear to the reader through Coulter's analysis of factual data.

Ettinger, Amos A. *James Edward Oglethorpe, Imperial Idealist.* Hamden, Connecticut: Archon Books, 1968.

In an age not famous for social consciousness, Oglethorpe came to prominence as a proponent of humane treatment for the downtrodden. Ettinger portrays his subject as the "guiding genius" and "dominant force" behind reform of the corrupt English prison system. An unlikely candidate for distinguished service to his government, Oglethorpe was the son of ardent Jacobites. Although the family's political intrigues on both sides of the English Channel in the cause of the deposed Stuarts appear to have had little influence upon the young Member of Parliament, Ettinger relates them in some detail with obvious amusement.

Oglethorpe's parliamentary career was distinguished primarily by his leadership of the prison investigation, but he was a fairly consistent supporter of progressive causes. So enlightened were Oglethorpe's views on free trade and equality for all parts of the British Empire that, had they been realized, the author conjectures that there might have been no desire for American independence. Nonetheless, Oglethorpe's interest in the mercantilist and imperial spheres was sincere. As an advocate of military preparedness, he opposed the pacific tendencies of Walpole and the Whigs.

Combining the qualities of the social reformer, the mercantilist, and the military man, Oglethorpe seemed to be

## Settlement of Georgia

the ideal leader for a colony which was to serve a threefold purpose: philanthropic, economic, and defensive. The inaccessibility of the records of the "Associates of the Late Dr. Bray" at the time of Ettinger's research led him to underestimate the role of that society in getting the Georgia venture underway. It is true, nevertheless, that Oglethorpe was the dominant figure in the early period of settlement and the primary reason for its temporary success. Lacking any sort of political machinery, the colonists looked to him as a moral leader, planner, judge, and general. His diplomatic skill in winning the friendship and respect of the Indians, particularly of Chief Tomochichi, was of incalculable value to the colony.

Ettinger does not lose sight, however, of Oglethorpe's shortcomings in his management of Georgia's affairs. He pictures the general as headstrong and sometimes foolishly aggressive, marching his troops back and forth against the Spanish almost in comic opera fashion. Oglethorpe's irresponsible attitude toward the Board of Trustees no doubt proved a trial to Perceval, who had assumed the task of raising and administering the funds for Georgia. Oglethorpe not only neglected to inform the trustees of affairs in the colony, but also drew drafts on their funds without notifying them. In 1736, he was called to England over

three issues: the plight of the trust because of his failure to correspond, complaints by South Carolinians over restrictions placed upon their trade in Georgia, and the need for a stronger defense. With obvious admiration, the author recounts Oglethorpe's manipulation of the facts to work his way back into the favor of the trustees and the Crown to the discredit of Walpole.

Returning to Georgia with a newly-raised regiment, the general cleverly succeeded in saving the colony from the clutches of the Spanish, but only temporarily from the waning interest of the trustees. By the early 1740's, most of Oglethorpe's administrative powers had passed to far less able men. After his return to England in 1743, Oglethorpe's participation in Georgia affairs dwindled. His life from his forty-sixth year, though enlivened by association with Samuel Johnson's literary circle and by friendships with many of the famous figures of the age, was anticlimactic.

Because Oglethorpe exhibited at times seemingly paradoxical qualities, it is much to the author's credit that he manages to portray the various facets of his subject in a relatively unbiased manner. That this is a biography of scholarly importance is further evidenced by the nearly exhaustive assemblage of source materials which Ettinger consulted. — *W.M.B.*

## Additional Recommended Reading

Reese, Trevor R. *Colonial Georgia: A Study in British Imperial Policy in the Eighteenth Century.* Athens: University of Georgia Press, 1963. Georgia's internal affairs are subordinated to an examination of the colony's early history from the vantage point of British imperial policy.

McPherson, Robert G., ed. *The Journal of the Earl of Egmont: Abstract of the Trustees Proceedings for Establishing the Colony of Georgia, 1732-1738.* Athens: University of

## Settlement of Georgia

Georgia Press, 1962. An indispensable primary source, this private record of the meeting of the Georgia trustees was kept by Perceval in addition to the official minutes.

Tailfer, Patrick. *A True and Historical Narrative of the Colony of Georgia: With Comments by the Earl of Egmont.* Edited by Clarence L. VerSteeg. Athens: University of Georgia Press, 1960. Generally known as the "Tailfer Book," this famous polemic by three disgruntled Georgia settlers, published in 1741, roundly condemns the management of the colony.

Coulter, E. Merton, ed. *The Journal of Peter Gordon, 1732-1735.* Athens: University of Georgia Press, 1963. The author of this first-hand account of the establishment of Georgia occupied a position of authority in the local government and eventually became an agent of the malcontents.

Crane, Verner W. *The Southern Frontier, 1670-1732.* Ann Arbor: University of Michigan Press, 1956. A fine background study which provides a history not only of the beginnings of the Carolinas but also of the expansion of frontier trade with the Indians and of the contest for empire.

Church, Leslie F. *Oglethorpe: A Study of Philanthropy in England and Georgia.* London: The Epworth Press, 1932. Though less satisfactory than Ettinger's work as a biography, this book does portray the situation in Georgia in greater detail.

# TRIAL OF JOHN PETER ZENGER AND FREEDOM OF THE PRESS

*Type of event:* Legal: establishment of precedents for libel prosecutions
*Time:* August 4, 1734
*Locale:* New York

Principal personages:
JOHN PETER ZENGER (1697-1746), printer and publisher of the
*New York Weekly Journal*
WILLIAM COSBY (c.1690-1736), Governor of New York
ANDREW HAMILTON (?-1741), Zenger's defense counsel
JAMES ALEXANDER (1691-1756), lawyer and leader of the anti-Cosby faction
JAMES DE LANCEY (1703-1760), Chief Justice appointed by Cosby to the Supreme Court of the Province of New York
LEWIS MORRIS (1671-1746), Chief Justice removed by Cosby from the Supreme Court of the Province of New York
RICHARD BRADLEY (fl. 1734), attorney general of the Province of New York

## Summary of Event

John Peter Zenger's fame rests upon his role in what is perhaps the best known free speech case in American history. Born in Germany in 1697, Zenger emigrated to New York in 1710 and took up an apprenticeship with William Bradford, publisher of the *New York Gazette.* Bradford was then the only printer in New York and the printer for the colonial government. Upon completing his apprenticeship, Zenger traveled through the colonies and settled in Maryland during 1720-1722. He married and served for a time as the printer for the colonial administration. When his wife died, he returned to New York, where, in 1726, he established his own printing shop. Zenger later became the public printer for New York and New Jersey. He died on July 28, 1746.

Zenger's famous trial took place while he was living in New York, and grew out of a dispute between the Governor of New York and New Jersey, and the acting Governor. William Cosby was appointed Governor of the two colonies in 1731, but remained in England until 1732. During 1731-1732, Rip Van Dam, the senior member of the Governor's Council in New York, served as "acting Governor." Upon his arrival in New York, Cosby demanded that Van Dam turn over half of the stipend which he had received from the colonial legislature as "acting" Governor." When Van Dam refused, Cosby declared the colonial Supreme Court to be a court of equity and proceeded to sue Van Dam in that court. This tactic was an obvious ruse to evade the requirement of trying Van Dam before a jury of colonials hostile to the governor's authority. Two of the three justices of the Supreme Court coöperated with Cosby, but Chief Justice Lewis

Morris agreed with Van Dam's lawyers (who were later to serve as Zenger's original lawyers) that the governor had no authority to create the court of equity. Cosby was so angered by Morris' action that he removed him from office.

In the meantime, Morris and the leaders of the anti-Cosby forces began to plan the establishment of a newspaper which could counter the official *New York Gazette* in mobilizing public opinion in their favor. The paper they founded was the *New York Weekly Journal*, published by Zenger and edited by James Alexander, Morris' chief attorney and a leading figure in the opposition to Cosby. The first issue of the paper appeared in November, 1733.

Zenger's criticisms of Cosby and his actions soon brought him trouble. A few months after the journal began publication, Cosby condemned it, and in August, 1734, the Governor and his council ordered Zenger's arrest for libel. While Zenger was in prison, his second wife continued to publish the paper. After failing in their attempts to persuade a grand jury to indict him, the authorities secured from the attorney general of New York, Richard Bradley, a bill of information charging that Zenger had committed "false, malicious, and seditious, and scandalous libel" by printing two issues of his journal. One of these two issues, dated January 28, 1734, had asserted that the people of New York "think, as matters now stand, that their liberties and properties are precarious, and that slavery is likely to be entailed on them and their posterity . . . ." The second issue, dated April 8, 1734, contained a statement by a New York resident

which declared: "We see men's deeds destroyed, judges arbitrarily displaced, new courts erected without consent of the legislature by which . . . trial by jury is taken away when a governor pleases . . . ."

Zenger was given a jury trial in the colonial Supreme Court before Chief Justice James de Lancey and Justice Frederick Philipse. His first defense counsel, James Alexander and William Smith, challenged the validity of the entire proceedings on the ground that the commissions of the two judges were defective. This challenge provoked the court to disbar them, and they were replaced by Andrew Hamilton of Philadelphia as chief defense counsel. Seizing upon the bill of information's reference to the libel as "false," Hamilton first attempted to prove the truth of the assertions, but Chief Justice de Lancey ruled him out of order. The attorney then attempted to caricature the precedents relied upon by the prosecution as "Star Chamber" cases. A more successful tactic, apparently, was Hamilton's insistence that Zenger had merely exercised the "natural right" of "complaining and remonstrating," "that the restraint upon this natural right is the law only; and that those restraints can only extend to what is *false* . . . ." Accepting the defense argument, after a brief deliberation, the jury returned a verdict of "not guilty," and Zenger was released.

Zenger's case constituted a major innovation concerning the law of libel. Up to that time, the role of the jury had been limited to ascertaining whether or not the accused had in fact published the material in question. But two important new rules were derived from

189

this case: that juries in libel cases are competent to decide on questions of "law" as well as those of "fact"; and that truth is a defense in a libel prosecu- tion. These principles were not adopted into American law, however, until the enactment of the Sedition Act of 1798.

## Pertinent Literature

Buranelli, Vincent. *The Trial of Peter Zenger.* New York: New York University Press, 1957.

This study is considered by many to be the leading commentary on the Zenger trial because of its detailed examination of the trial's underlying social and political context. Buranelli aligns himself with those writers who see the persons around Zenger, specifically Alexander and Hamilton, as playing a more substantial role in the affair than Zenger himself. Although Buranelli tends to diminish Zenger's role, he nevertheless credits the overall movement with being "one of the most significant things that ever happened on this side of the Atlantic."

Buranelli states that the foundation for the Zenger affair was laid years before the trial took place by a savage feud between two of the most influential families in colonial New York, the Morrises and the de Lanceys. The de Lanceys, an emerging merchant family, sought to take away the political authority held by the traditional landowners' group as represented by the Morrises. As mercantile interests gained power, the influence of landowners in the colonial government declined. Year after year the conflict gained momentum until the Zenger affair precipitated an open confrontation of the two factions. From the beginning of his administration as Governor, Cosby sided with the commercial group and systematically replaced advisers, judges, and assemblymen who opposed him. Among Cosby's victims was Lewis Morris, who lost his position as chief justice to James de Lancey. The Morrisite faction, including Alexander, Van Dam, and Smith, clearly saw that their influence within the colony would be destroyed unless desperate measures were adopted. Their determination led them, Buranelli claims, to Zenger's print shop.

Buranelli credits Alexander with instigating the entire Zenger affair. Alexander was apparently convinced that the landowning interest could regain lost influence in colonial affairs if it could discredit the current colonial administration in the public mind. It was for this reason that the *New York Weekly Journal* was founded. It was, as Buranelli states, the first politically independent newspaper ever published on this continent.

Although the journal was known as "Zenger's paper," it was Alexander, according to Buranelli, who was actually its editor and who wrote most of its political editorials. Alexander had previously written political articles for the *New York Gazette.* Furthermore, the content of the paper, its witty and sarcastic tone, and its barbed innuendos were too professional for a man of Zenger's meager talents.

The journal was born not to gain a free press but to gain political influence. Buranelli believes that the overall importance of the *New York Weekly Journal* and the concepts which it embodied are to be found not only in its success in achieving its original goal but, more importantly, in its subsequent influence in political and legal reforms. It was an independent newspaper which not only printed news critical of the colonial government but also justified its right to do so. In defending the newspaper, Hamilton said that the people had the right to be informed on what their government was doing, and also the right to criticize their government when they had just cause.

Buranelli finds that Zenger's trial gave rise to two principles relative to a free press: "that truth may be used as a defense in libel cases" and "that the jury has a right to decide on both the 'fact' and the 'law'." These two propositions later became accepted legal principles both in America and in England.

Alexander, James. *A Brief Narrative of the Case and Trial of John Peter Zenger, Printer of the* New York Weekly Journal. Edited by Sidney N. Katz. Cambridge: Harvard University Press, 1963.

In his introduction, Katz questions the influence of Zenger's trial on the advancement of the free press. In his view, this development would have come about "with or without Peter Zenger." Katz believes that the most important aspects of Zenger's trial lay in the social and political forces surrounding the trial, which had been gaining impetus long before the Zenger affair. He implies that the Zenger case was used as a vehicle by which Zenger's associates, specifically James Alexander and Lewis Morris, hoped to regain their political influence by impeaching the colonial administration of Governor Cosby.

Katz points out that even Zenger's associates recognized the need of the state to restrain any speech which might endanger its security or tranquility. Katz doubts whether these men were "the radical exponents of free speech" that many writers have made them out to be. Their defense of Zenger consisted in assailing the jurisdiction of the judges and questioning the validity of their commissions on the grounds that they had not been approved by the State Council. It was not a legal defense resting on points of law, but rather a forthright accusation of maladministration leveled against Cosby.

Katz states that, although Zenger's first attorneys' defense argument was unsuccessful so that they were immediately disbarred and removed from the case, this action was significant because it allowed the entry of Hamilton into the case. Katz proceeds to use Hamilton's defense of Zenger to substantiate his contention that the real influence of Zenger's trial was not on the concept of a free press but on the political issues involved. Hamilton's defense of Zenger did not rest on law but on politics. His case was not based upon the legal question whether Zenger's editorials were to be considered libelous, but rather on the political issue whether the citizens had the right to criticize their government.

Hamilton's arguments for freedom of speech assumed that there existed a basic political difference between British and American government. Since

191

the Governors in America were only representatives of the Crown, they should not be allowed the same degree of freedom from criticism that the king enjoyed. Thus the colonists had the right to criticize their government even though their British counterparts did not have that right.

Finally, Katz states that, as Hamilton cited principles of government and not of law, his defense of Zenger was not meant to appeal to the legal sense of the judges. Rather, it was intended to appeal to the common men of the jury and their emotional involvement in the political issues of the time.

Katz concludes by stating that the influence of Zenger's trial on subsequent legal reform was not as great as some have considered. For example, Katz points out that the New York Assembly between 1747 and 1770 pressured the printers to exercise their freedom of the press cautiously under the threat of trial before the assembly for failure to do so. Although Zenger's

trial did assist in restraining the use of seditious libel as a weapon to restrict the press, it by no means guaranteed freedom of the press. It was not until passage of the Fox Libel Act in 1792 that juries were granted the power to give a verdict on the question whether or not certain writings were to be considered libelous. The substance of the libel law itself was not changed until more than a century after Zenger's trial when, with the passage of Lord Campbell's Act, it was stated that the truth of a written statement could be used as a defense in cases of seditious libel.

Although Katz presents a case which diminishes the measure of the Zenger trial's influence on freedom of the press and legal reform, he concludes that the most profound effect of the case was indirect. In his defense of Zenger, Hamilton articulated current colonial feelings concerning the proper relationship between government and citizens. — *J.J.B.*

## Additional Recommended Reading

Emery, Edwin. *The Press and America: An Interpretative History of Journalism.* 2nd ed. Englewood Cliffs, New Jersey: Prentice-Hall, Inc., 1962. In this detailed history of the growth of the American newspaper, the author presents some noteworthy comments on the legal aspects of the Zenger trial and questions the overall effect of the trial on the concept of the free press.

Kobre, Sidney. *The Development of the Colonial Newspaper.* Magnolia, Massachusetts: Peter Smith Publisher, Inc., 1960. This historical survey of the newspaper in colonial America provides some insight into the economic, social, and political temper of the 1730's which, combined with Zenger's trial, made possible the advancement of the free press in America.

Levy, Leonard W. *Freedom of Speech and Press in Early American History: Legacy of Suppression.* New York: Harper & Row Publishers, 1963. Levy follows Buranelli's lead in crediting James Alexander with being the architect of Zenger's defense; he also claims that the Zenger trial had little or no impact on the common law governing libel.

Mott, Frank L. *American Journalism: A History, 1690-1960.* New York: The Macmillan Company, 1962. The author, although sketchy on the historical details surrounding the trial of Zenger, is nonetheless firm in his belief that the trial did have an immense effect upon the development of the American press.

Rutherford, Livingston. *John Peter Zenger: His Press, His Trial, and a Bibliography of Zenger Imprints.* New York: Dodd, Mead & Company, 1904. Reprinted, Magnolia, Massachusetts: Peter Smith Publisher, Inc. Presents an account of the events leading to Zenger's trial and a reprint of the *First Edition of the Trial* written by Zenger and published in his *New York Weekly Journal.* The author tends to exaggerate the immediate effects of Zenger's trial on the legal and political environment of the colony.

# FOUNDING OF THE AMERICAN PHILOSOPHICAL SOCIETY

*Type of event:* Intellectual: desire to coördinate philosophical and scientific activities in the American colonies
*Time:* 1744
*Locale:* Philadelphia

*Principal personages:*
BENJAMIN FRANKLIN (1706-1790), editor, inventor, politician, diplomat, and founder of the American Philosophical Society
THOMAS JEFFERSON (1743-1826), author of the Declaration of Independence and third President of the United States
JOHN ADAMS (1735-1826), second President of the United States, political philosopher and theorist, author of *A Defence of the Constitutions of the United States*
THOMAS PAINE (1737-1809), British-born revolutionary, Deist, and author of *Common Sense, The Rights of Man,* and *The Age of Reason*
BENJAMIN RUSH (1745?-1813), physician and psychologist, one of the founders of the Pennsylvania Society for Promoting the Abolition of Slavery
CADWALLADER COLDEN (1688-1776), politician, scientist, and popularizer of Newton's theories
JOEL BARLOW (1754-1812), poet and author of *The Columbiad*
JAMES MADISON (1751-1836), fourth President of the United States and one of the authors of *The Federalist*
JONATHAN MAYHEW (1720-1766), pastor of Boston's West Church and author of *A Discourse Concerning Unlimited Submission and Non-Resistance to the Higher Powers*

## Summary of Event

In 1743 Benjamin Franklin proposed the establishment of an American Philosophical Society to be located in Philadelphia. "The first Drudgery of Settling New Colonies, which confines the Attention of People to mere Necessaries, is now pretty well over," he explained in the circular letter describing the organization, "and there are many in every Province in Circumstances that set them at Ease, and afford Leisure to cultivate the finer Arts, and improve the common Stock of Knowledge." The society was organized the following year, with its founder as secretary, but it soon lapsed into inactivity. In 1769 it merged with another organization, the American Society; the new organization was called the American Philosophical Society for Promoting Useful Knowledge. Its membership included the leading philosophers and scientists of America. As the focus of intellectual activity in the New World, it was an important agent in the shaping of the distinctive

194

pattern of thought known as the American Enlightenment.

Like their counterparts in Britain and on the Continent, the thinkers of the American Enlightenment accepted the Newtonian conception of the universe as a rational and harmonious machine operating according to natural laws which man, by the use of his reason, could discover. They believed that at the creation, all species of life had been arranged in a "chain of beings," ranging upward from the lowest form of life to man, a little lower than the angels; and that since that time no new species had come into existence and none had become extinct. Thus the harmony and variety of nature was matched by its economy. Believing that the universe was intelligible to man, eighteenth century Americans enthusiastically took up the task of studying nature. Thomas Jefferson's *Notes on the State of Virginia,* containing his observations on almost every aspect of the Virginia environment, suggested the wide-ranging interests and empirical bent of men of the American Enlightenment.

For Jefferson and other American thinkers, to study nature was to study God, who had created it. They worshipped God as the great architect of the universe and its laws, viewing him as an essentially rational and benevolent being to whom "the most acceptable service" was, as Benjamin Franklin declared, "doing good to His other children." Under the impact of Enlightenment ideas, Puritanism gave way to Arminianism and liberal religion. Boston's leading Arminians, Charles Chauncy and Jonathan Mayhew, preached the benevolence of God, the essential goodness of man, freedom

of the will, the primacy of reason in religion, and universal salvation. Deism, or natural religion, which appealed to those who shied away from organized religion, embraced similar doctrines, though it expressly repudiated the authority of Scripture and the divinity of Christ. But despite the efforts of Ethan Allen, Elihu Palmer, and Thomas Paine, Deism never made much headway in America; and outright atheism, which flourished among French *philosophes,* was rare indeed.

The "sensational" psychology of John Locke, which taught that all ideas come from experience, was the primary source of the environmentalism from which much of the thinking of the American Enlightenment emanated. Using the pseudonym J. Hector St. John, Michel Guillaume Jean de Crèvecœur wrote in his *Letters from an American Farmer* (1782): "Men are like plants; the goodness and flavor of the fruit proceeds from the particular soil and exposition in which they grow. We are nothing but what we derive from the air we breathe, the climate we inhabit, the government we obey, the system of religion we profess, and the mode of our employment." Americans of the Enlightenment used the theory of environmentalism to explain the great variety of minds and creeds in society, as well as racial differences. The theory also underlay the faith which eighteenth century men put in education as a means of individual and social improvement.

The thinkers of the American Enlightenment developed a view of human nature that was both optimistic and realistic. They emphasized man's capacity for goodness in contrast to the Puritan doctrine of innate depravity.

Man, they said, was endowed by his Creator with a moral sense, or faculty, which enabled him to choose right over wrong. Subscribing to a utilitarian system of ethics, they advocated the practice of virtue as the way to wealth and happiness. The belief in man's capacity for "benevolence," along with the doctrine of environmentalism, which attributed evil not to the sinfulness of man but to corrupt institutions which might be reformed, provided the impulse behind the humanitarian reform movement of the late eighteenth century.

Though they emphasized man's capacity for good, American thinkers also recognized his inherent selfishness. To check man's tendency to encroach upon his fellows, government was necessary. Its purpose was the promotion of security and happiness to society, by protecting the natural, and therefore inalienable, rights of life, liberty and property belonging to all men. But government, being the work of men, was itself inclined to infringe upon the rights and liberties of the gov-

erned by aggrandizing power at their expense. Therefore, the men of the American Enlightenment tended to agree with Thomas Paine that "Government even in its best state is but a necessary evil." As a result, they interpreted the functions of government in a negative, restrictive sense, and advocated the establishment of internal checks and balances to restrain what they believed was the natural tendency of government to assume power. They believed in government by consent of the governed. Should government fail to perform its duties, "it is the right of the people to alter or to abolish it, and to institute a new government, laying its foundation on such principles, and organizing its powers in such form, as to them shall seem most likely to effect their safety and happiness." Both the Declaration of Independence and the United States Constitution bear the lasting imprint of the political theory of the American Enlightenment and the assumptions about nature and human nature on which it was based.

## Pertinent Literature

Boorstin, Daniel J. *The Lost World of Thomas Jefferson.* New York: Holt, Rinehart and Winston, Inc., 1948.

Daniel Boorstin explains in his preface that his purpose is "to discover the dominant spirit of the Jeffersonian view of the world." He bases his analysis on the printed writings of the community of eighteenth century American philosophers and scientists whom he calls "the Jeffersonian circle": David Rittenhouse, Benjamin Rush, Benjamin Smith Barton, Joseph Priestley, Charles Willson Peale, Thomas Paine, and, of course, Thomas Jefferson him-

self, "the human magnet" who drew the others together and "gave order and meaning to their discrete investigations."

Boorstin agrees with other historians of the Enlightenment in emphasizing the Jeffersonians' worshipful attitude toward nature. Nature was apotheosized. Viewing nature "as the complete and perfected work of divine artifice," the Jeffersonians insisted that it supplied the standard by which to judge man and society. In addition, Boorstin emphasizes the naturalistic perspective from which Jeffersonians viewed man and his relation to the universe, noting that they commonly referred to man as "creature" to signify his "integration by the common Creator into the processes of nature."

Minimizing the influence of the European Enlightenment, Boorstin finds the keynote of Jeffersonian thought in what he calls "the American task," the business of carving a nation out of the wilderness. Thus the Jeffersonians worshiped God as "Architect and Builder" of the universe, the supreme embodiment of the talents which they themselves needed to fulfill their "continental task." The preoccupation with the American task also produced the Jeffersonians' sense of tension between man and nature. Though the Jeffersonians stressed man's adaptability, his capacity for adjusting to new environments, they also recognized that "the environment was in a sense master of man." In Boorstin's view, the sense of tension between man and nature was the most important source of the Jeffersonian vision of nature as a work of art. "It explains why the mere process of nature, the intricacy and smoothness of its operation, seemed to make the search for ends outside of nature superfluous. For the shaping, subduing and organizing of the material environment, in which the Creator had been so impressively successful, seemed itself the overwhelming task of the Jeffersonians."

The preoccupation with the American task also explains the profoundly activist temper of the American Enlightenment, which in turn influenced its political philosophy. Boorstin attributes the Jeffersonians' negative, restrictive view of government to their distrust of metaphysics. "A list of 'rights' substituted for a systematic theory of government." According to Boorstin the Jeffersonians saw no need to define the positive duties of government. "Such human definition was quite superfluous, for the ends had already been defined by the Creator and revealed in nature."

In effect, Boorstin has done what the Jeffersonians were unable to do because of their "antimetaphysical bias." He has systematized and synthesized their ideas about nature, God, and man, revealing the scientific and religious assumptions underlying the political and social theory of the American Enlightenment. At the same time, he exposes what he believes are the inadequacies of Jeffersonian thought—and of certain aspects of the American liberal tradition based on it—for the twentieth century. When the American task was completed at the end of the nineteenth century, Americans lost their earlier "sense of creaturehood"; they no longer felt a sense of tension between man and nature; they no longer saw nature as "a fixed point of reference." The intellectual world of the Jeffersonians had been annihilated. Moreover, the Age of the Robber Barons revealed the logical consequences of the Jeffersonian political philosophy once it had been stripped of the "prophetic spirit" that gave eighteenth century men "their sense of community, and prevented an emphasis on 'rights' from becoming anarchy, or from making society seem a hopeless jungle." Thus, in recreating the intellectual world of Jefferson and his friends, Boorstin reminds us at the same time of the extent to which the world of eighteenth century America, with its focus on the conquest of the wilderness, is indeed a "lost world."

Koch, Adrienne. *Power, Morals, and the Founding Fathers: Essays in the Interpretation of the American Enlightenment.* Ithaca: Great Seal Books, 1961.

*Power, Morals, and the Founding Fathers* is a collection of essays analyzing the political and social thought of Benjamin Franklin, Thomas Jefferson, Alexander Hamilton, John Adams, and James Madison—philosophers-statesmen whom Adrienne Koch considers "touchstones for the character of the American Enlightenment." Like Boorstin, Koch treats the American Enlightenment as a distinctive pattern of thought. But, whereas Boorstin emphasizes the activist temper of the Jeffersonian circle and its distrust of philosophical speculation, Koch argues that the thought of the founding fathers represents a conjunction of "supposedly contradictory" ideas and ideals: experience and theory, pragmatism and wisdom, power and morals. "Experimental humanism" is her term for "the central vision of the founding fathers and the temper of the Enlightenment in America . . . ."

Koch is primarily concerned with the political philosophy of the American Enlightenment and the way in which it conjoined the "two conditions necessary for successful free government," power and morals. In her view, the personal conflict between Jefferson and Hamilton and between Republicans and Federalists generally stemmed from different opinions as to the proper relation between the two elements. Whereas Hamilton and Adams tended to emphasize the necessity of power over moral concerns, Jefferson and Madison tipped the scales in the other direction, frequently advocating "moral restraints on the use of power." Jefferson's defense of the right of all men to pursue happiness and of majority rule were two such "moral restraints," both deriving from a belief in "the primacy of the human being," the purposes of which were to check the power of the government.

Koch argues that Jefferson and Madison were more successful than Hamilton and Adams in maintaining a balance between power and morals, and she implies that the two Virginians viewed power in a more positive light than has usually been thought. In Jefferson's conception of America as an "empire for liberty" she finds the two elements joined "in lifelike tension," the one term "symbolizing strength for self-preservation and growth, the other indicating the object for which that national strength, that power to resist outside manipulation and aggression, is to be sought: so that freedom, under the kind of benign government that values men and respects their natural rights, can be realized in fact." Because they saw the necessity of maintaining a "dynamic balance between power and morals," Jefferson and Madison were the true realists, according to Miss Koch, not visionary idealists as they have often been called. In contrast, Hamilton was a self-admitted political failure as a result of his "all-consuming passion for power," and at the same time something of an innocent because he remained unaware "that power is a runaway tiger, difficult to dismount."

Like Boorstin, Koch finds a lesson for the present in the thought of the American Enlightenment. In effect, she urges a revitalization of the "American philosophic tradition" formulated by the founding fathers. She believes that experimental humanism, with its recognition that "morals without power are weak, just as power without morals spells long-run destruction," can serve twentieth century Americans "as a strategic guide in meeting the future," particularly the exigencies of the Cold War. — *A.C.L.*

## Additional Recommended Reading

Becker, Carl L. *The Declaration of Independence: A Study in the History of Political Ideas.* New York: Harcourt, Brace & World, Inc., 1922. Analyzes the Declaration of Independence and the natural rights philosophy on which it was based.

Koch, G. Alfred. *Republican Religion: The American Revolution and the Cult of Reason.* New York: Holt, Rinehart and Winston, Inc., 1933. Reprinted in 1968 by Thomas Y. Crowell, as *Religion of the American Enlightenment.* A study of Deism and free thought in post-Revolutionary America, as revealed in the writings and activities of such men as Ethan Allen, Elihu Palmer, Thomas Paine, John Foster, and "Walking" John Stewart.

Kraus, Michael. *The Atlantic Civilization: Eighteenth Century Origins.* Ithaca: Cornell University Press, 1949. This study of the new civilization produced by the interrelationship of the New and Old World reveals the common fund of ideas shared by enlightened thinkers in both Europe and America. Kraus emphasizes the influence on America of eighteenth century concepts of political and religious freedom, economic opportunity, and humanitarianism.

Hindle, Brooke. *The Pursuit of Science in Revolutionary America, 1735-1789.* Chapel Hill: University of North Carolina Press, 1956. Describes the development of scientific interest and activity in the American colonies as a result of European influence and in response to indigenous needs.

Bailyn, Bernard. "Political Experience and Enlightenment Ideas in Eighteenth Century America," in *American Historical Review.* LXVII (January, 1962), 339-351. In this seminal article, based on his own research as well as recent revisionist interpretations of early American history, Bailyn sketches the broad outlines of a provocative new interpretation of the relation between the ideas of the Enlightenment and political developments in the American colonies.

Koch, Adrienne. *The Philosophy of Thomas Jefferson.* New York: Columbia University Press, 1943. A study of various aspects of Jefferson's philosophy in relation to European schools of thought.

# THE FRENCH AND INDIAN WAR

*Type of event:* Military: rivalry between the British and the French which culminated in the defeat of the French in America
*Time:* 1754-1760
*Locale:* The eastern half of North America

*Principal personages:*

BENJAMIN FRANKLIN (1706-1790), American statesman, scientist, and philosopher, whose Plan of Union was accepted by the Albany Congress but rejected by Great Britain and the colonies

WILLIAM PITT (THE ELDER) (1708-1778), Secretary of State of Great Britain and leader of the House of Commons with full control of foreign and military affairs 1757-1761

JOHN STUART (EARL OF BUTE) (1713-1792), Prime Minister of Great Britain 1762-1763 who negotiated the Treaty of Paris

WILLIAM SHIRLEY (1694-1771), Governor of Massachusetts 1753-1756 and British Commander in Chief in America 1755-1756

JOHN CAMPBELL (EARL OF LOUDON) (1705-1782), British Commander in Chief in America 1756-1757

JEFFREY AMHERST (1717-1797), British officer who commanded army against the French fortress of Louisbourg until it surrendered in 1758, Commander in Chief in North America in 1759, and Governor General of British North America 1760-1763

JAMES WOLFE (1727-1759), British army officer who served under Amherst at the siege of Louisbourg and who commanded the expedition against Quebec which routed the French in 1759

MARQUIS LOUIS JOSEPH DE MONTCALM DE SAINT-VÉRAN (1712-1759), Commander of French troops in Canada who fought heroically to save Canada from the British but who was defeated and mortally wounded in the Battle of Quebec in 1759

## Summary of Event

Before the 1750's, the rivalry between Great Britain and France in the New World had been incidental to their more significant conflicts in Europe. To thwart French territorial ambitions against the Austrian empire and the German states, Great Britain had formed and led coalitions to maintain the balance of power on the Continent. In the War of the League of Augsburg (1689-1697), and the War of the Spanish Succession (1702-1713), known in the colonies as King William's War and Queen Anne's War re-

200

spectively, neither antagonist felt any need to send large regular forces overseas. By the Treaty of Utrecht (1713), however, France acknowledged Great Britain's claim to the Hudson Bay country and gave up Nova Scotia. A later British conflict with Spain involving Georgia and the West Indies, the War of Jenkins' Ear (1739-1742), merged with the War of the Austrian Succession (1740-1748) and was called King George's War in the colonies. The British provincials, accomplishing relatively little in earlier wars against French strongholds to the north, successfully assaulted the fortress of Louisbourg on Cape Breton Island near the mouth of the St. Lawrence river; but the supposedly impregnable bastion, "the Gibraltar of the New World," reverted to France in the Treaty of Aix-la-Chapelle (1748) that restored the *status quo ante bellum.* Yet the colonists' achievement in capturing Louisbourg emphasized to both powers the increasing role that Great Britain's American subjects would have if, as was generally predicted, the shaky settlement of 1748 failed to last.

Events in America, not in Europe, brought about a resumption of hostilities in the early 1750's. The British settlers, numbering more than a million by mid-century and "multiplying like rattlesnakes," were pushing westward; already they were trickling through the mountain passes and looking toward the fertile bottom lands of the Ohio river country, a region claimed by both France and Great Britain. The French, with their small and diffused population in Canada (called "New France"), strengthened their claim by cementing their traditional Indian alliances and by erecting forts in the Ohio River Val-

ley. Initially, the British numerical advantage failed to bring positive results. Colonial disunity was demonstrated through the rejection, by both Great Britain and the colonies in general, of Benjamin Franklin's Plan of Union in 1754 even after it had been accepted by the Albany Congress. Likewise, the defeat of Washington's Virginia militia near the forks of the Ohio on July 3, 1754, and the tragic failure of the British expedition under General Braddock against Fort Duquesne on July 9, 1755, all foretold a long and difficult war for Great Britain and its American colonists. Braddock was succeeded by William Shirley, Governor of Massachusetts, as Commander in Chief of British forces in America from 1755 to 1756, who was succeeded in turn from 1756 to 1757 by John Campbell, Earl of Loudon, and until 1759, by James Abercrombie. During their tenures, expeditions against Fort Niagara, Crown Point, and Fort Ticonderoga sputtered and failed, and their French adversaries seized Oswego and Fort William Henry. Inadequate generalship and the inability of the British and Americans to galvanize their impressive advantages in human and material resources played a decisive part in the string of reversals between 1754 and 1758. Moreover, the French pursued the policy of a strategic defense, which compelled Anglo-American forces to cope with formidable obstacles in advancing men and supplies over hundreds of miles of dense, unsettled country. The French also were fortunate in that their own movements were greatly facilitated by the St. Lawrence river, providing them with a continuous waterway from Louisbourg to Niagara. In Europe, too, the French seemed to have the upper hand; their "diplomatic revolution" made an ally out of a former enemy, Austria, while England was driven into the arms of Prussia. On the high seas, a French victory over the British fleet in the Mediterranean led to the capture of Minorca.

Great Britain needed a sound logistical system and better leadership, both at home and in America, in order to win. Actually, the discredited Loudon, who was replaced by Abercrombie, had recognized the first essential requirement and had put in motion plans to build roads, create supply stations, and utilize colonial manpower—not on the battlefield but to transport supplies for armies advancing into positions from which to mount attacks against French outposts. Leadership, the second necessary ingredient, came from William Pitt, the Elder, who after 1757 was Secretary of State of Great Britain and leader of the House of Commons with full control of foreign and military affairs. Vigorous and resourceful, unmindful of tradition or military seniority, Pitt elevated younger officers over their elders and dipped lavishly into the Treasury to subsidize both the hard-pressed Frederick the Great of Prussia on the Continent and the American colonies in order to encourage greater participation of the latter in the War. Two of Pitt's hand-picked officers, Jeffrey Amherst, a former lieutenant colonel who had never before had an independent command, and thirty-one-year-old James Wolfe, took Louisbourg on July 26, 1758, the first major British victory of the War. Cut off from the mouth of the St. Lawrence river,

the French lost control of the other end of that river a short time later when Lieutenant Colonel John Bradstreet captured Fort Frontenac. Its seizure cut French supply lines to Fort Duquesne and forced the evacuation of that post, which the British occupied and renamed Fort Pitt.

The campaign of 1759—the culmination of Pitt's grand strategy for America—saw pincer movements directed at Quebec and Montreal. Quebec fell to the brilliant Wolfe, who, fatally wounded, as was the French commander, Marquis Louis Joseph de Montcalm de Saint-Véran, did not live to witness the surrender on September 18, 1759. As French efforts to recapture the city failed, a second British force was driving northward and overcame Montreal on September 8, 1760. The war for North America was over, but the international phases of the conflict continued as Great Britain inflicted crushing defeats on France's ally, Spain, at Manila and Havana. The temperamental Pitt, who lost political support once victory was assured and who was not close to the new King, George III, was out of office before the peacemaking began. John Stuart, Earl of Bute, the new Prime Minister and an intimate of the young monarch, did not share Pitt's desire to strip the Bourbon enemies of all their possessions. Even so, as a result of the Treaty of Paris, he vastly extended the British Empire by taking Canada from France and Florida from Spain, and by carving up French possessions in India. Great Britain in 1763 stood unrivaled as the foremost power in the world.

## Pertinent Literature

Parkman, Francis. *Montcalm and Wolfe.* 2 vols. Boston: Little, Brown, and Company, 1884.

*Montcalm and Wolfe* is probably the most famous of Francis Parkman's historical works. It forms a part of his eight-volume series on *France and England in North America,* an account of the struggle between the two great European powers for supremacy in the New World, which was written over a period of more than forty years between 1851 and 1892. "The plan of the work," writes Parkman, "was formed in early youth." He "visited and examined every spot" connected with his history of the French and Indian War, which drew its title from the two famous generals who opposed each other at the Battle of Quebec. "In short, the subject has been studied as much from life and in the open air as at the library table." Born into a family of Boston patricians and educated at Harvard, Parkman possessed the financial means and the intellectual background to accomplish his long-term objective of chronicling the duel for empire between Great Britain and France; the fact that he suffered long periods of semiblindness was really a virtue, for he had to master his materials completely before beginning composition.

The devoting of his life to a gigantic undertaking, the development of a grand theme, and the use of bold, descriptive prose, make Parkman's work rank with the best historical writing of the nineteenth century, such as that of Lord Macaulay in England and of William H. Prescott, John L. Motley, and George Bancroft in the United States. Parkman, in the fashion of his period, presents detailed vignettes of the personalities who figured largely in his story. If he unabashedly favored the British cause, he admired many of the French as individuals, including Frontenac and La Salle in the early volumes and Montcalm in his treatment of the French and Indian War. The reader sees both the public and the personal sides of his characters. Parkman often, in moving prose, bids farewell to one of his heroic personalities, as with the dead Montcalm at Quebec in 1759: "Montcalm lay in his soldier's grave before the humble altar of the Ursulines, nevermore to see the home for which he yearned, the wife, mother, and children whom he loved, the olive-trees and chestnut-groves of his beloved Candiac. He slept in peace among triumphant enemies. . . ." Even the Jesuits, whose religion Parkman abhorred, aroused his admiration for their hardships and suffering, and for their bravery in the face of unbelievable torture from the Iroquois. For the Indians, however, the author had nothing but contempt, considering them treacherous, murdering fiends rather than "noble savages." Although Parkman had observed the Plains Indians firsthand on a journey resulting in his classic, *The Oregon Trail,* he never saw the red men as fighting to save their own lands or to maintain their way of life.

If Parkman's history has its serious weaknesses stemming from ideas of race, religion, and nationality current in his own day; if he and other literary craftsmen of the last century were overly imbued with the concept of history as a guide to the present and shaper of the future, his work still towers majestically over almost all the literature of American history. It endures not merely because of the rare narrative power or his prodigious research, but, more important, because he addressed himself to the fundamental question inherent in the century-long conflict for supremacy in North America: Why did the English-speaking people win? Their victory was explained, in the final analysis, by the superiority of British society in America. The absolute government, religious repression, economic restrictions, and restraints on immigration that characterized New France and retarded its growth and development, were absent from British America. The English settlers, for the reasons mentioned above, were more numerous than the French inhabitants to the north and had greater incentive. They fought to maintain the freedom they already possessed. One may question many of Parkman's details, and object that he somewhat neglected to give credit to British naval power and other European factors that helped to shape the outcome, but his overview is still reflected strongly in the writings of American historians. The most recent one-volume synthesis of the subject by a leading authority (Howard H. Peckham's *The Colonial Wars, 1689-1762*), agrees largely with Parkman.

Gipson, Lawrence H. *The British Empire Before the American Revolution.* Vol. VI: *The Years of Defeat, 1754-1757: The Great War for the Empire.* New York: Alfred A. Knopf, Inc., 1949.

Gipson, Lawrence H. *The British Empire Before the American Revolution.* Vol. III: *The Victorious Years, 1758-1760: The Great War for the Empire.* New York: Alfred A. Knopf, Inc., 1949.

Lawrence H. Gipson, who like Parkman, was an indefatigable researcher, spent the most productive years of his long life in the preparation of his own magnum opus: *The British Empire Before the American Revolution.* Gipson is concerned with a shorter time span than Parkman, roughly the quarter century before the Declaration of Independence, but Gipson's history is more broadly conceived, devoted to a detailed examination of the whole of the British Empire in the eighteenth century, including Africa, India, and the West Indies, and their administrative and economic relationships with the Mother Country. While Parkman gives his readers a glamorized picture of the final Anglo-French conflict before the American Revolution, Gipson covers the ground in the role of a dispassionate analyst, laying stress upon France's lack of seapower and her debilitating involvements on the Continent of Europe.

Gipson believes that our nationalist tradition has led us astray concerning various truths about the war. Even the name which Americans gave to the struggle, "the French and Indian War," arose from hostility to Great Britain during the American Revolution. Among the revolutionists, Thomas Paine did most to destroy the notion of Great Britain's fighting to protect the colonies after 1754; among historians, George Bancroft is the chief culprit. According to Gipson, the na-

tionalist tradition has several compo-
nents: that Great Britain's rivalry with
France involved the colonists in wars
of no vital interest to them; that what-
ever Great Britain contributed to the
successful outcome, "the unlimited ex-
panses of North America were predes
tined to be the heritage of the Americans . . . the war in question was but
a somewhat incidental thing"; and
that Great Britain's motive was only
self-interest, and that its troops, un-
schooled in wilderness warfare, were
more of a handicap than an advantage.

In striving to disavow these concepts, Gipson insists that the stakes in
the war were exceedingly high. The
outcome determined whether British
or French civilization would prevail in
North America and whether the Appalachians would be a permanent bar-
rier to westward expansion. As for the
myth of the supremacy of colonial militia over redcoats, Gipson shows that
the provincial assemblies begged for
royal regiments; the Americans "had
much greater faith in the performances
of troops trained in the regular method
of warfare than in irregulars fighting in
Indian fashion." Gipson also contends
that this final conflict, begun by the
French and directed at the Ohio River
Valley, initially "had nothing to do
with the old animosities of Europe." It
was a peculiarly American war, as the

Duke of Newcastle maintained when
he said, "Let Americans fight Americans." Instead of following Newcastle's
pronouncement, the Mother Country
provided massive aid, its primary purpose being to preserve its empire, not
to enlarge it. Thus it was not "the
French and Indian War," but "the
Great War for the Empire," a name the
author employs throughout, as have
later writers sympathetic to his viewpoint.

Critics, though sometimes finding
fault with the author for his occasional
criticism of Pitt's leadership and
Wolfe's tactics at Quebec, among other
things, have generally accepted Gipson's contention that orthodox military
science and tactics predominated in a
struggle that increasingly resembled "a
European conflict in a New World setting." But not all specialists subscribe
to his claim that Great Britain acted
primarily from a spirit of altruism in
hastening troops and monies to
America; after all, it was British colonies that were threatened, and Britain
had much to lose by their defeat or
dismemberment. Certainly Pitt viewed
the war as one of territorial gain for
Great Britain. Whether it was a war for
the British Empire or a war to acquire
empire, the outcome had momentous
consequences for both Great Britain
and America. — *R.D.H.*

### Additional Recommended Reading

Pargellis, Stanley M. *Lord Loudon in North America.* New Haven: Yale University Press,
1933. A sympathetic portrait which contributes significantly to our knowledge of supply
and logistics.
Freeman, Douglas Southall. *George Washington.* Vol. V: *Victory with the Help of France.*
New York: Charles Scribner's Sons, 1948. 2 vols. An excellent narrative of the first three
years of the war on the Virginia frontier.
Stacey, C. P. *Quebec, 1759: The Seige and the Battle.* New York: St. Martin's Press, 1959.
The bicentennial of Wolfe's victory marked the appearance of three good books on the

subject, but Stacey's is the best.

Cuneo, John R. *Robert Rogers of the Rangers.* New York: Oxford University Press, 1959. A sprightly, well-documented life of a New Hampshire frontier leader whose commando-like tactics against the French have been studied in recent years by the United States Army.

Schutz, John A. *William Shirley: King's Governor of Massachusetts.* Chapel Hill: University of North Carolina Press, 1961. A perceptive biography of a popular and successful colonial administrator who met with failure upon assuming the position of Commanding General early in the French and Indian War.

Peckham, Howard H. *The Colonial Wars, 1689-1762.* Chicago: University of Chicago Press, 1964. A readable synthesis of existing scholarship.

Leach, Douglas Edward. *Roots of Conflict: British Armed Forces and Colonial Americans, 1677-1763.* Chapel Hill: University of North Carolina Press, 1986. A history of relations between British armed forces and Colonial Americans during the century of Anglo-French colonial wars.

# PROCLAMATION OF 1763

*Type of event:* Political: desire to avoid further Indian wars by retarding colonial expansion
*Time:* October 7, 1763
*Locale:* London, England

*Principal personages:*

EARL OF HALIFAX (GEORGE MONTAGU DUNK) (1716-1771),
president of the Board of Trade 1748-1761

WILLIAM PETTY (EARL OF SHELBURNE, MARQUIS OF LANS-
DOWNE) (1737-1805), president of Board of Trade 1763 and
Secretary of State for the Southern Department 1766-1768,
who opposed the British government on its American policy.

EARL OF EGREMONT (CHARLES WYNDHAM) (1710-1763),
Secretary of State for the Southern Department 1761-1763

EARL OF HILLSBOROUGH, MARQUIS OF DOWNSHIRE (WILLS
HILL) (1718-1793), president of the Board of Trade 1763-1765
and 1768, and Secretary of State for the Colonies 1768-1772

JEFFREY AMHERST (1717-1797), British Commander in Chief
in North America from 1759, and Governor General of British North America 1760-1763

SIR WILLIAM JOHNSON (1715-1774), superintendent of Indian
Affairs 1755-1774

## Summary of Event

How would Britain, victorious in the French and Indian War, control the vast domain between the Appalachians and the Mississippi after 1763? The answer to this question was awaited by Indians, French Canadians, and British colonial administrators as it was by American fur traders, merchants, and land speculators. The West had increasingly occupied the attention of British and colonial officials since the Albany Congress. During the ensuing war, the Crown appointed superintendents to coördinate Indian affairs, Sir William Johnson for the Northern Department and Edmund Atkin (succeeded by John Stuart in 1762) for the Southern Department, but exigencies of the moment made the new arrangement inadequate. In the eyes of White-

hall officials, the old policy of leaving control of the frontier to the individual colonies had been chaotic and ruinous. The line of English agricultural settlement had steadily edged westward with scant regard for Indian land claims or the red man's way of life. Repeatedly, royal governors, Indian superintendents, and British military men had complained of the disregard of Indian treaties by the colonists as well as fraudulent land purchases by them, and of the mistreatment of the aborigines at the hands of white traders.

The necessity of reaching an accord with the Indians was underscored by Pontiac's Rebellion of 1763-1764. The red men, already uneasy over the defeat of their French allies, encountered repeated insults from the British Com-

207

mander in Chief, General Jeffrey Amherst, who also refused to court them with guns, ammunition, and other gifts, as was the French custom. The storm broke early in May, 1763. Striking first in the remote West and later on the Pennsylvania frontier, roving parties of Ottawas, Chippewas, Delawares, and Senecas overran one British-occupied post after another until, by the end of June, only Forts Detroit, Pitt, and Niagara still held out against the warriors. Amherst, who was soon recalled under a cloud, dispatched relief expeditions to his remaining garrisons, and several colonies raised troops to repel the invaders. The prospect of fire and sword, the diplomatic skills of William Johnson, and the breakup of the coalition of tribes, never united as to ultimate objectives, explain the restoration of peace in 1764. The Indians, treated generously, paid no penalty for Pontiac's Rebellion.

During the uprising, the government announced its new policy for the West, one that had evolved from British experience in the French and Indian War. It was the work of no single minister or subminister, although the Earl of Egremont (Charles Wyndham, Secretary of State for the Southern Department 1761-1763), William Petty, the Earl of Shelburne, President of the Board of Trade in 1763 and later Secretary of State for the Southern Department), and the Earl of Hillsborough (Wills Hill, President of the Board of Trade from 1763 to 1765 and later Secretary of State for the Colonies) were keenly interested in the matter. On October 7, 1763, King George III signed the edict known today as the Proclamation of 1763. By its terms, the recently acquired territories of Canada and East and West Florida became Crown colonies, and their inhabitants became entitled to the same rights as Englishmen at home. All colonial claims to territories west of the crest of the Appalachians were nullified, those lands, "for the present, and until our further Pleasure be known," being set aside for the Indians. Trade with the tribesmen was to be "free and open," although traders were to be licensed and were to obey such regulations as might be prescribed. Since the Proclamation of 1763 contained no provision for law enforcement in the area beyond provincial boundaries, an *ad hoc* system developed, with the trade confined to certain posts or towns under the supervision of the Indian superintendents, assisted by fort commanders whose regular troops were to enforce the trade regulations.

In the long run, this "Western policy" of Great Britain failed. Land-hungry settlers spilled over into the Indian country in defiance of the Proclamation of 1763. British troops could not guard every mountain pass, nor could they and Crown Indian agents confine white traders to specified locations. Moreover, the maintenance of Western garrisons was expensive, especially when American revenues for the army's upkeep failed to materialize and when the redcoats did not accomplish their mission. In 1768, the British government, beset by these problems and colonial rebelliousness in the East, adopted a policy of retrenchment in the West. Control of the Indian trade reverted to the individual colonies, and British troops received orders to abandon all the interior posts except Niagara, Detroit, and Michilimackinac. Almost simultaneously, the government bowed to pressure for pushing the Indian boundary westward. This shift was accomplished in the Treaty of Fort Stanwix (1768) with the Iroquois and the Treaties of Hard Labor (1768) and Lochaber (1770) with the Cherokee. No longer did the West loom uppermost in British imperial thinking.

## Pertinent Literature

Alvord, Clarence W. *The Mississippi Valley in British Politics.* Glendale, Calif.: The Arthur H. Clark Co., 1917. 2 Vols.

Clarence Alvord was the first scholar to write an in-depth study of British Western policy between the final colonial war and the American Revolution. Throughout the years in question, maintains Alvord, the foremost concern of the home government was not the revolutionary agitation on the Eastern seaboard; it was rather the development of the tramontane region acquired from Great Britain's vanquished enemies. Alvord's examination of successive ministries and the relationships between leading political personalities resulted in his conclusion (reached before most scholars) that British politics revolved around factions instead of easily defined parties bearing the Whig and Tory labels. However, with the debate over the Peace of Paris in 1763, especially the question of whether to retain Canada or Guadeloupe, there emerged a "clear-cut issue": those who favored retaining Canada committed themselves to a program of westward expansion, while their opponents, who favored annexing the French West Indian Guadeloupe Island, generally opposed the opening of the North American interior. To state the matter another way, as does Alvord, the struggle involved whether or not to stand rigidly behind mercantilist principles. The mercantilists, believing that the greatest value of colonies was as markets for finished goods or as sources of raw materials needed by the Mother Country, favored the retention of the valuable sugar island of Guadeloupe over the barren wastelands of Canada. "Thus it may be said with approximate truth that all future issues concerning the Mississippi Valley were formed and the trend of partisan opinion determined during the critical period of the peace negotiations."

According to Alvord, the key to understanding the various proposals for controlling the interior before the American Revolution is to be found in the Proclamation of 1763. Of all the politicians who figure in the story of the West, Lord Shelburne, President of the Board of Trade in 1763, emerges as the most enlightened and far-seeing. Writes Alvord, "To name Lord Shelburne is to name the man who has exercised greater influence on the development of western America than any other British statesman, not excepting even William Pitt." Responsible for the more admirable features of the Proclamation of 1763, Shelburne later, as Secretary of State for the Southern Department, proposed to deal with Indian relations and colonial growing pains by creating two new colonies, one in the Illinois country and the other in the area around Detroit, which the author calls "a wise, conciliatory, and statesmanlike measure." If the book has a

209

villain, it is Lord Hillsborough, holder of various ministerial posts before the American Revolution, a man who crossed swords with Shelburne repeatedly, who opposed new colonies in the West, and who, in the opinion of Benjamin Franklin and the author, favored a hard, uncompromising position in dealing with the colonies on all matters. The fall of Shelburne in 1768 and the ascendancy of Hillsborough ushered in the British policy of retrenchment in the interior, and ideas of systematic expansion were permanently discredited. The Quebec Act of 1774, the final ministerial effort to organize and administer the country between the Ohio and the Mississippi, denied the colonists the opportunity for attaining their legitimate aspirations in the West, as Lord Shelburne pointed out, although that part of the act was not designed with malice in mind. "If historians would interpret rightly the causes of the American Revolution," writes Alvord in bringing his work to a close, they must extend their vision beyond the East to include "the occurrences beyond the mountains, where the British ministers experimented in imperialism and sought a basis for their future colonial policy in the administration of the West."

Sosin, Jack M. *Whitehall and the Wilderness: The Middle West in British Colonial Policy, 1760-1775.* Lincoln: University of Nebraska Press, 1961.

For many years historians in piecemeal fashion have worked over the terrain covered by Alvord. They have not always agreed with the old master; nor, for that matter, have they always found unanimity among themselves. In his monumental history of the *British Empire Before the American Revolution,* Lawrence H. Gipson stresses the temporary nature of the Proclamation of 1763 that was designed to safeguard the welfare of the Indians; it did not, as Alvord contended, contain serious weaknesses which were incorporated in its final form after Shelburne had stepped down as President of the Board of Trade. On the other hand, Bernhard Knollenberg has more recently, in *Origin of the American Revolution,* resurrected the specter of British selfishness in addition to a concern for the Indian. He sees a desire on the part of certain British leaders to keep the colonists economically and politically subservient to the Mother Country by confining them to the territory east of the Appalachians. In any case, another scholar, Robin Humphreys, shows conclusively that the constructive features of the proclamation were not the brain child of one man, Shelburne, whose originality and authority Alvord exaggerated.

In 1961, Jack M. Sosin published the first comprehensive account of British Western policy since Alvord's pioneer undertaking. Sosin's conclusions are strikingly different. Discounting the significance of the Canada versus Guadeloupe debate, the author observes that many of the sixty-five pamphlets on the subject appeared after the ministry had made its choice of Canada. The Crown's ministers seldom, if ever, inaugurated programs for the interior on the basis of abstract mercantile principles. They "were primarily administrators who arrived at particular solutions for specific problems as they arose. . . ." Indeed, Sosin believes that we have put undue emphasis upon the roles of prominent personages in the creation of laws and pronouncements for the back country. A host of second-line bureaucrats, such as ex-governors and subministers in the Colonial Department, exercised no small influence in decision making, as did military officers and Indian agents in America.

So it was with the Proclamation of 1763, which the ministry began to formulate before Lord Shelburne entered the picture. Sosin sees the Proclamation as an outgrowth of efforts on the part of royal officials in the colonies during the French and Indian War to win the Indians' allegiance and to maintain peace on the frontier. In fact, the British military establishment had by the early 1760's already put into practice the basic features later incorporated into the Proclamation. Sosin also disputes Alvord's contention that considerations relating to the West dominated the thinking of Whitehall policy-makers throughout the period 1763-1775. Although the ministry always sought peace and stability in the back country, the late 1760's witnessed the West's declining importance as the government shifted its primary attention to meeting the American challenge on the Eastern seaboard.

On these points Sosin's revisionist views appear to be sound and sensible. But critics have raised questions or objections to certain of the author's additional interpretations. Lord Shelburne receives rough handling from Sosin, who contends that his thinking on extending the frontiers and creating new colonies was not always consistent or enlightened. A final estimate of Shelburne as an imperial statesman will have to await extended monographic treatment of the man who has hitherto been treated sympathetically by most historians. We may also need to look more fully into the career of Lord Hillsborough, whom Sosin defends in his unwillingness to give in to the American expansionistic ambitions. American land speculators, traders, and other expansionists are seen in these pages as generally irresponsible in their lust to roll back the frontiers at the expense of the Indians and the best interests of the British Empire; but, as one reviewer remarks, we need a clearer picture of the colonists' point of view. Only when we understand the Americans' thinking can the full story emerge; only then can we say with precision the degree to which British Western policy was a factor in the origins of the American Revolution. — *W.D.H.*

**Additional Recommended Reading**

Abernethy, Thomas P. *Western Lands and the American Revolution.* New York: D. Appleton-Century Co., 1937. Broad in scope, Abernethy's work is now outdated in some respects.

Alden, John R. *John Stuart and the Southern Colonial Frontier: A Study of Indian Relations, War, Trade, Land Problems in the Southern Wilderness, 1754-1775.* Ann Arbor: University of Michigan Press, 1944. Alden's exhaustive study of the wilderness of the South between 1754 and 1775 is definitive.

Peckham, Howard H. *Pontiac and the Indian Uprising.* Princeton: Princeton University Press, 1947. An excellent monograph, this work invalidates part of Francis Parkman's older treatment of the same subject.

Gipson, Lawrence H. *The British Empire Before the American Revolution.* Vol. IX: *New Responsibilities Within the Enlarged Empire, 1763-1766: The Triumphant Empire.* New York: Alfred A. Knopf, Inc., 1956. Gipson sees British Western programs as more flexible than do some writers.

Knollenberg, Bernhard. *Origins of the American Revolution, 1759-1766.* New York: The Macmillan Company, 1961. Knollenberg is much less sympathetic than Gipson to the British point of view.

Philbrick, Francis S. *The Rise of the West, 1754-1830.* New York: Harper & Row Publishers, 1965. Philbrick presents a broad survey, but at times he injects fresh interpretations.

Middlekauff, Robert. *The Glorious Cause: The American Revolution, 1763-1789.* New York: Oxford University Press, 1982. Drawn largely from secondary sources, this work contends that the American nation and its republican ideology were fundamentally shaped by the War for Independence.

# CAROLINA REGULATOR MOVEMENTS

*Type of event:* Military: clashes arising from abuses in government in North Carolina and the absence of government in South Carolina
*Time:* 1765-1771
*Locale:* The back country of the Carolinas

*Principal personages:*

WILLIAM TRYON (1729-1788), British Governor of North Carolina 1765-1771

SAMUEL JOHNSTON (1733-1816), conservative leader in the North Carolina assembly

HERMON HUSBANDS (1724-1795), pamphleteer who stated the case for the North Carolina back country

EDMUND FANNING (1739-1818), Justice of the Peace and Recorder of Deeds of Orange County who was hated by the North Carolina Regulators

WILLIAM BULL (1710-1791), Lieutenant Governor of South Carolina who was friendly to the back country

CHARLES WOODMASON (fl. 1770's), Church of England clergyman who wrote a petition of grievances for the South Carolina frontiersmen

CHARLES GARTH (fl. 1770's), South Carolina agent in London who sought legislation to cope with the colony's interior

MOSES KIRKLAND (fl. 1770's), aggressive planter and businessman who emerged as leader of the South Carolina Regulators

## Summary of Event

Conflicts between the East and the West, between old established societies and new bucolic settlements of the frontier, have been recurring phenomena of American history. The breadth and depth of these sectional antagonisms have varied sharply according to time and place. The Regulator Movements of the 1760's and 1770's in the Carolinas illustrate the complexity of the subject.

In Maryland and Virginia the frontier folk harbored no deep-seated grievances against the East. The legislatures, though dominated by tidewater aristocrats, had established counties—with courts, justices of the peace, sheriffs, and representation in the assemblies —and had enacted statutes to build roads and bridges for facilitating trade. In North Carolina, where the same political institutions made their appearance in the piedmont, there was nevertheless serious regional discord because of the malpractices of local officials, and, to a lesser extent, because of high quitrents, inadequate arteries of transportation, and underrepresentation in the legislature. Sheriffs, by failing to publish the tax rate, collected far more than the law permitted and lined their own pockets in the process; if a taxable person could not pay—and cash was ever in short supply—they

213

seized his property and sold it, rigging the auctions in favor of insiders. Here the sheriffs acted in collusion with other county officials; these "courthouse rings" moreover charged exorbitant fees for performing routine legal services. The symbol of the people's unhappiness was New York-born, Yale-educated Edmund Fanning ("by his civil robberies, He's laced his coat with gold"), Justice of the Peace and Recorder of Deeds of Orange County.

Although violence erupted as early as 1759 in the Granville District, the initial pattern of the Regulators (a name which the aroused victims of these discriminatory practices borrowed from a simultaneous but separate reform movement in South Carolina) was to lodge formal protests with the governor and the assembly. Humble in tone and legalistic in concept, these petitions were largely ignored or condemned on the seaboard. Only then, after rebuffs, did the Regulators broaden their goals to include dividing western counties and instituting secret voting so as to increase their representation in the colonial legislature. New elections, however, strengthened the hand of the Regulators and their sympathizers. James Iredell, a conservative, declared that a majority of the lower house was "of regulating principles." But the modest reforms concerning officers' fees and court costs in litigation which were enacted were inadequate without the means of enforcement at county level. Violence increased, and in September, 1770, Regulators invaded the Orange County court at Hillsborough, drove out the justices, and tried cases themselves. Fear of rebellion led the assembly to abandon its "regulating prin-

ciples" by enacting the repressive Johnston Act against unlawful gatherings and by backing Governor William Tryon in sending a militia army against the Regulators. Near the banks of the Alamance Creek, twenty miles from Hillsborough, a motley throng of a thousand farmers gathered to oppose Tryon's force of equal size. After desultory firing and ludicrous field movements on both sides, the Regulators fled, each side losing nine dead. The Regulation ended at Alamance, but subsequently justices and sheriffs in the Piedmont appear to have paid stricter attention to the law in performing their duties, for patriot leaders saw the need to placate the West to achieve unity in the face of the challenge from Great Britain in the middle 1770's.

The "back country" of South Carolina was settled somewhat later than that of the Tarheel colony, and its chief grievance was the absence of government rather than the abuses of government that plagued frontier North Carolina. In the 1760's, newcomers flooded into the back country, which was a region suffering from the aftermath of the Cherokee War of 1759-1761. Life in the "up country" (a South Carolina expression), precarious at best, threatened a total breakdown before rising lawlessness and social and economic maladjustment. The parishes of South Carolina, the units of political and ecclesiastical authority, were only theoretically extended to the back country. There were, it is true, justices of the peace, but their authority was limited to minor civil cases. The absence of courts meant a visit to Charleston if one desired to transact any form of important legal business, and the journey entailed a week on horseback or two weeks by wagon from distant stations, such as Ninety-Six. In 1767, as roving bands of outlaws terrorized the region while Charleston authorities looked the other way, leading citizens with the support of respectable elements formed an "association" for "regulating" the back country. Dedicated to law and order and to the protection of property, the Regulators, by 1768, had dealt harshly and effectively with the criminal part of the population. But many honest men felt the Regulators had gone too far by punishing immorality as well as lawlessness. An anti-Regulator group, the Moderate movement, brought the excesses of the extremist Regulators to an end so that the restoration of control by respectable property owners was completed. A direct confrontation between the Regulators and constituted authority in Charleston never took place, partly because Lieutenant Governor William Bull and others in authority recognized the need to bring tran-

quility to the interior. In addition, the Commons House of Assembly finally endeavored to solve back country problems, including more legislative representation and the establishment of schools. These well-intentioned undertakings ran afoul of British policy and the emerging Anglo-American conflict, but a major grievance terminated following passage of the Circuit Court Act of 1769, which created four back country courts with full jurisdiction in civil and criminal matters, and contained provisions for jury trials and the strict regulation of legal fees.

Despite obvious differences, the broad objectives of the two Regulator movements in the Carolinas were the same. Eschewing theoretical political innovations or radical social leveling, the Regulators asked principally for a redress of specific grievances, for government that was just and responsible, for the political and legal rights to which freeborn Englishmen were everywhere entitled.

## Pertinent Literature

Bridenbaugh, Carl. *Myths and Realities: Societies of the Colonial South.* Baton Rouge: Louisiana State University Press, 1952.

"Too much has been made of the supposedly primitive, semibarbaric condition of the Southern back country between 1730 and 1776," writes Carl Bridenbaugh in a lengthy essay surveying the various levels of society in that region. Easy generalizations do not come readily regarding the quarter of a million Germans, Scotch-Irish, and English who settled the interior from Maryland to Georgia before the American Revolution, and who for the most part streamed down from Pennsylvania, many over the seven hun-

dred-mile-long Great Wagon Road, which Bridenbaugh claims should be as well remembered today as the Lancaster Pike and the Santa Fe and Oregon Trails. To be sure, there was an abundance of poverty, crudity, and immorality; life was hard, ministers of the gospel few, and schoolteachers a rarity, as one can tell from reading the fascinating journal of the Reverend Charles Woodmason *(The Carolina Backcountry on the Eve of the Revolution).* As would be true in the future, the West seemed an inexorable "safety

215

valve" for shiftless lawbreakers from the East. But men could go up the ladder, just as others could go down. Daniel Morgan, a youthful pugilist and rum-drinker involved in countless scrapes with the law, who lived with his wife-to-be for ten years before marrying her, rose to be a general in the American Revolutionary Army and a leading citizen of the Valley of Virginia. The solid core of back country society consisted of small planters who owned at most a few hundred acres. By their labors they might climb, like Daniel Morgan, to become leading men. Indeed, from the beginning there were always some inhabitants who occupied positions of prestige and influence in their rural surroundings. For, as Bridenbaugh remarks, there came along with the simple folk country gentlemen, soldiers, lawyers, land speculators, merchants, and men of culture. The only resident peer in America was Thomas, the sixth Baron Fairfax, and he built his home, Greenway Court, in the Southern interior near Winchester, Virginia, in 1752.

The author reminds us that just as settlement of the back parts of each colony took place at different times, so it was that developments within each province followed their own patterns. Here Bridenbaugh sheds light on why Maryland and Virginia escaped the Regulator troubles of the Carolinas. The interior of the Chesapeake colonies was settled early, and partly by influential aristocrats from the tidewater counties; the ideals and attitudes of the East were quickly implanted there, just as were its political institutions, and its inhabitants sometimes sent tidewater planters, such as George Washington, to represent them in the assemblies. "I have searched fruitlessly," says Bridenbaugh, "for evidence that before 1776 political sectionalism—western resentment of eastern overrepresentation and rule—was an issue, either open or covert, in Maryland or Virginia." Even the rise of Patrick Henry, as the author indicates, is no longer considered a sign of western radicalism but rather a readjustment within the ruling Virginia aristocracy.

By the time of the American Revolution, the back country had witnessed the growth of towns, the rise of commerce with the North and East, the accumulation of wealth, and the growth of slavery. If the interior had taken on certain characteristics of the other two "Souths," those the author terms "the Chesapeake Society" and the "Low Country Society" (and discusses in detail in separate chapters), the back country remained "a land of sharp contrasts and amazing antitheses." "Not until 1790 was the back country ready to crystallize into a definite society, and by that time much of its old colonial character had been modified by the exigencies of the new age, or had disappeared forever."

Brown, Richard M. *The South Carolina Regulators*. Cambridge: Harvard University Press, 1963.

This splendid monograph is the only lengthy account of either group of Regulators to appear in many years. Fortunately, Richard M. Brown chose to examine the movement in South Carolina, for less was known about the convulsions there. Brown reveals that the Regulators were the "have's" and not the "have not's" of the back country. They were upstanding citizens concerned with protecting property rights and restoring order in a region devastated by Indian warfare and overrun by outlaws and "lower people." Are responsible men in such circumstances entitled to go outside the law, or become law unto themselves, in order to maintain their liberty? The question itself is contradictory, but so has been the reality of men's plight on several frontiers in American history. The South Carolina Regulators were among the first to face up to this predicament with a successful plan of action. Here was no East-West schism cut from traditional cloth, for the greatest opposition to the Regulators was never in Charleston, where ultimately the seriousness of back country turbulence prompted the governor and legislature to seek ways of satisfying Regulator demands. It was in the back country itself that the Regulation stirred dissatisfaction by overseeing morals, family life, and debt collections, all scarcely comparable to the criminal activity that had initially caused the Regulators to take the field. The "Moderates," themselves of the better sort, might have clashed seriously with the extreme Regulators except for a truce arranged in 1769, also the year of the Circuit Court Act that met the Regulators' deepest grievances. "The Moderate movement checked the Regulation when the latter had outlived its usefulness." Even so, as Brown demonstrates, "the larger objectives of halting the demoralization of the Back Country had been attained, a result

which the Moderates did not even desire to reverse."

The author amasses a wealth of information from which he makes careful estimates as to the ages, wealth, and geographic distribution of the Regulators. They were "a coalition of small planters and leading men" who endeavored to establish "a society in which they themselves were to prosper," who took the law into their own hands "for conservative social purposes." According to the standard histories, the Regulators out of bitterness against the low country supported the British during the Revolutionary War. The conclusion is deflated in Brown's pages: "There was little genuine resentment (only a bit of 'rhetoric') directed at the Charleston ruling circle by the identifiable Regulators, of whom only five percent can definitely be classified as Tories."

Not the least of the book's virtues is the placing of the South Carolina Regulators within the framework of American vigilante movements. The Carolinians, in fact, served as "the prototype" of such undertakings, and similar organizations in the first half of the nineteenth century in Texas, Illinois, and elsewhere used the term "Regulator" and employed South Carolina precedents. If the celebrated San Francisco vigilantes of 1851 eclipsed the older name of "Regulator," the South Carolina movement, thanks to Richard M. Brown, is restored to its significant niche in the story of the search for law and order on the American frontier. — *R.D.H.*

## Carolina Regulator Movements

### Additional Recommended Reading

Bassett, John S. "The Regulators of North Carolina, 1765-1771," in *Annual Report for the Year 1894.* Pp. 141-212. Washington, D.C.: American Historical Association. Still useful though limited in scope.

Meriwether, Robert L. *The Expansion of South Carolina, 1729-1765.* Kingsport, Tenn.: Southern Publishers, 1940. A piece of meticulous scholarship by a leading authority on South Carolina history.

Alden, John R. *John Stuart and the Southern Colonial Frontier: A Study of Indian Relations, War, Trade, Land Problems in the Southern Wilderness, 1754-1775.* Ann Arbor: University of Michigan Press, 1944. Contains valuable information on the Cherokee War and white-Indian relations.

Woodmason, Charles. *The Carolina Backcountry on the Eve of the Revolution: The Journal and Other Writings of Charles Woodmason, Anglican Itinerant.* Edited by Richard J. Hooker. Chapel Hill: University of North Carolina Press, 1953. An itinerant Church of England clergyman who sympathized with the Regulators, Woodmason paints a vivid and sometimes amusing picture of life in the up country.

Dill, Alonzo T. *Governor Tryon and His Palace.* Chapel Hill: University of North Carolina Press, 1955. A readable and informative study of the Governor who put down the North Carolina Regulators, and of his times.

Gipson, Lawrence H. *The British Empire Before the American Revolution.* Vol. XI: *The Rumbling of the Coming Storm, 1766-1770: The Triumphant Empire.* New York: Alfred A. Knopf, Inc., 1965. Gipson devotes two chapters to what he calls "The Struggle for Political Equality" in the Carolinas.

# STAMP ACT CRISIS

*Type of event:* Constitutional: British and American friction
*Time:* 1765-1766
*Locale:* America and Great Britain

*Principal personages:*

GEORGE GRENVILLE (1712-1770), head of the ministry, 1763-1765, and chiefly responsible for the program of American taxation

THOMAS WHATELY (fl. 1765), Treasury official who prepared the Stamp Act and who maintained Americans were virtually represented in Parliament

DANIEL DULANY (1722-1797), Maryland lawyer who wrote the most significant pamphlet attacking the Stamp Act and the concept of virtual representation

PATRICK HENRY (1736-1799), led the Virginia House of Burgesses in adopting resolutions against taxation that influenced other assemblies to do likewise

BENJAMIN FRANKLIN (1706-1790), colonial agent in London who told Parliament that Americans objected only to internal taxes

CHARLES WATSON WENTWORTH (MARQUIS OF ROCKINGHAM) (1730-1782), succeeded Grenville as first minister and secured the Stamp Act's repeal

## Summary of Event

In 1763, the British national debt had soared to a level double its prewar figure. Besides finding revenues to meet the interest on this war debt, George Grenville, first minister, needed additional funds to administer a greatly enlarged empire. Although Parliament had never before placed direct taxes on the colonies, Grenville persuaded that body to approve the Sugar Act of 1764 and the Stamp Act of 1765. The decision to tax America was momentous in its consequences. The intensity of the colonists' opposition shocked most Englishmen, and on both sides of the Atlantic the crisis produced an atmosphere of tension and mistrust that influenced all subsequent Anglo-American relations before the War of Independence.

Grenville, a narrow-minded financial expert, amassed impressive statistics to show that the prosperous colonists were lightly taxed compared to Englishmen at home. The Sugar Act grew out of Grenville's discovery that the American customs service was costing the government more to maintain than it was collecting in revenues. The colonists were evading payment of the import duties—sixpence a gallon—on foreign molasses, which was required under the Molasses Act of 1733. Grenville revamped the customs service and ordered the Royal Navy to guard against smuggling. The Sugar

219

Act itself cut the molasses duty to threepence a gallon, a sum Grenville believed would be enforceable without ruining the New England rum industry. It was clear that colonial rum distillers needed more molasses than the British West Indian sugar islands could provide. The new statute placed additional duties upon colonial imports, increased restrictions upon colonial exports, and added further to the difficulties of smugglers by strengthening the system of Vice-Admiralty Courts. But the preamble to the Sugar Act, unlike the Molasses Act, made it clear that the law of 1764 was not designed primarily to regulate trade: it stated "that a revenue be raised" in His Majesty's dominions. Subsequently, Grenville introduced his Stamp Act, passed by Parliament and signed by the King on March 22, 1765—to be effective on November 1. Taxes fell on every kind of legal document and on playing cards, dice, and almanacs, each item to carry a stamp indicating payment of the tax. Offenders were to be tried in Vice-Admiralty Courts (without trial by jury), which formerly had jurisdiction only over affairs relating to the sea and commerce. New taxes meant payments in cash, but money, always scarce in the agriculturally oriented colonies, became tighter than ever because Grenville, in 1764, had persuaded Parliament to adopt the Currency Act that forbade the provincials to continue making their own paper money as legal tender.

The colonists found much to displease them in Grenville's program. Merchants thought the rum industry would not be able to stand the threepence duty on molasses, and they found the new customs procedures complicated and difficult, just as the currency restrictions would make silver in shorter supply than ever; nor did it seem fair to try Stamp Act offenders in courts devoid of juries and possessing authority beyond that permitted them in England. Even more important to Americans, Parliament's direct taxes seemed to deprive them of their rights as British subjects to be taxed only by their elected representatives. They were, of course, represented in their own assemblies but not in the House of Commons. They vigorously approved the pamphlet written by Maryland lawyer Daniel Dulany, who denied the contention of Englishman Thomas Whately that all residents of the empire were, in effect, represented in Parliament, which allegedly looked after the interests of all, regardless of whether one had the opportunity, as many local Englishmen did not, to vote for members of the House of Commons. American writers quoted John Locke, political philosopher of the "Glorious Revolution" of 1688, who said that the most esteemed right of people was the right of property, without which both life and liberty were endangered. The Virginia House of Burgesses, prodded by young Patrick Henry, took the lead in drafting remonstrances against Parliamentary taxation. Soon afterward the Massachusetts legislature issued a call for a congress from all the colonies to meet to consider ways of securing relief. The Stamp Act Congress, meeting October 7 to 27, 1765, at New York and attended by delegates from nine colonies, acknowledged Parliament's authority to regulate trade (to legislate) for the welfare of the whole empire while rejecting its right to tax America. By

November 1, the date the stamps were to go on sale, none were available. The Sons of Liberty had "persuaded" almost every designated stamp distributor to resign. Colonial merchants also aided the cause by curtailing imports from Britain until the oppressive Stamp Act was repealed.

In 1766, Grenville was out of office (for reasons unrelated to America), and the ministry was under the Marquis of Rockingham, who had opposed the Stamp Act and who now listened to the outcries of British merchants suffering from the colonial economic boycott. By stressing the disruption of trade and ignoring American rioting, and by employing Benjamin Franklin's erroneous testimony that the colonists opposed only internal taxes (the Stamp Act), Rockingham secured repeal of the Stamp Act—after Parliament passed the vaguely worded Declaratory Act, a bill that affirmed Parliament's right to "make laws and statutes . . . to bind the colonies . . . in all cases whatsoever." Americans rejoiced at the outcome without knowing the Declaratory Act's precise meaning.

## Pertinent Literature

Morgan, Edmund S. and Helen M. Morgan. *The Stamp Act Crisis.* Chapel Hill: University of North Carolina Press, 1953.

The turn of the twentieth century gave rise to the so-called "imperial school of American historiography," which endeavored to sweep away nationalistic stereotypes and to examine objectively the British Empire prior to the American Revolution. Products of the new graduate schools, these historians were trained and disciplined in their craft. They looked askance at George Bancroft, the most influential student of the Revolution in the previous century, a patrician scholar who had gazed on the Anglo-American rupture through patriotic glasses. The imperialists contributed impressively to our understanding of the intricate workings of "the Old Colonial System," as George L. Beer described it. Writing sympathetically of British administrators' manifold problems, the imperialists saw the Navigation Acts— designed to regulate and control imperial trade—as a sensible and equitable means of strengthening both the colonies and the Mother Country. Thus it was difficult, contrary to Bancroft's nineteenth century free trade principles, to argue that a restrictive mercantilistic policy in the eighteenth century had severely damaged the colonial economy and had driven the Americans to revolt. Broadly speaking, the imperialists explained the clashes of the 1760's and 1770's as not so much over different theories or principles as over conflicting interests. The matter of colonial rights, wrote Charles McLean Andrews, a distinguished scholar and the "dean" of the imperial school, was a "subject of more or less legal and metaphysical speculation," which had relatively little impact on the vast majority of Americans. Thirty years later Andrews' most prolific student, Lawrence H. Gipson, in his monumental *The British Empire Before the American Revolution,* also passed lightly over constitutional issues. According to Gipson, when the colonies were no longer threatened by the French in Canada after 1763, they shirked their imperial responsibilities in rejecting Parliamentary taxation. They were eager to pursue their own ends without interference from the home government. Gipson apparently sees the Revolution as an inevitable development, with growing American nationalism as the prime cause.

Revisionism is surely the life blood of historical study, and in time the fashionable opinion is cast aside or severely modified. The American Revolutionary field has witnessed the rise of the neo-whig, or neo-conservative school in the years since World War II. Deterministic histories have been replaced by articles and monographs that attempt to pinpoint the significance of individual actions and immediate controversies. The Revolution no longer appears predestined, not in the third quarter of the eighteenth century at least, especially if the Mother Country displayed more enlightened leadership. Ideas, particularly American constitutional arguments, receive careful scrutiny.

The most influential member of the neo-whig school is Edmund S. Morgan, a successor to the Early American history post at Yale University once held by Charles Andrews. None of Morgan's numerous writings has had such a vital impact as *The Stamp Act Crisis,* written with the assistance of Helen M. Morgan. The blame for the first imperial controversy is placed squarely upon George Grenville, who, although pretending otherwise, made no real effort to allow the colonies to raise revenues on their own to aid in the upkeep of the empire; in fact, the first minister discouraged Massachusetts and the agents of various colonies in London from devising means to acquire needed revenue in America. Consequently, the Americans in Morgan's pages appear less irresponsible in facing up to their imperial obligations than they are depicted in accounts by the imperial school. Believing the actual stamp tax would have been a small expense to almost all the colonists, Morgan considers the crux of the American opposition a matter of the constitutional principle of no taxation without representation. Moreover, Morgan parts company from previous historians by demonstrating that Americans objected not only to internal taxes (the Stamp Act) but also to external taxes (the Sugar Act) as well in 1765-1766. During the following decade they consistently adhered to this constitutional principle, at the same time that they continued to recognize the need for Parliament to legislate (but not for revenue) in the interest of harmonizing the trade and commerce of the empire for the welfare of all its parts. Morgan stresses American unity in still another way by revealing that the Sons of Liberty were not, as often claimed, simply groups of lower-class men who wished to wrest control of the patriot movement from the aristocratic leaders who traditionally dominated political office. The "better and wiser" element of society was active in the Sons, working hand in glove in many cases with the artisans and mechanics who directed the street gangs. Subsequent books by the present generation of early American historians show the profound impact of *The Stamp Act Crisis* in reorienting the study of the Revolution's origins.

# Stamp Act Crisis

Knollenberg, Bernhard. *Origins of the American Revolution, 1759-1766.* New York: The Macmillan Company, 1960.

Knollenberg's *Origins of the American Revolution* complements and amplifies Edmund Morgan's account of the first imperial crisis. Knollenberg discovers little evidence of colonial unhappiness with the British empire as it existed before the Seven Years' War. He finds no reason to doubt the colonists' sincerity in opposing taxes by Parliament on principle. The British, reasonable in asking Americans to contribute to the cost of imperial affairs, nevertheless went about exacting American cash in the wrong way: "to act unilaterally, to change a constitutional relationship established for over a century without prior effort to negotiate a settlement and without any offer of compensation or assurance against future exploitation was highhanded, reckless and unjust." But Knollenberg does modify slightly Morgan's picture of Americans consistently opposing all forms of British taxation. At any early point in the controversy, Massachusetts implicitly and Connecticut explicitly distinguished between external and internal taxes; but Americans generally did adhere to the position outlined by Morgan. There would likely have been no program of American taxation in the first place, speculates the author, had William Pitt, in 1761, and the Duke of Newcastle, in 1762, not retired from the ministry; for the two most powerful ministers were well versed in colonial affairs and opposed to controversial schemes upsetting to imperial trade and harmony. The men responsible for the plan of taxation, as Knollenberg observes, were inexperienced in colonial matters and preoccupied with domestic distractions at the conclusion of the Seven Years' War.

Even so, there was colonial discontent prior to 1763 that did not stem from taxation. Here Knollenberg develops his most original and significant thesis: beginning in 1759, when the war was all but won and there was no further need to placate the colonists, various crown officials inaugurated certain measures that angered many colonials. The disallowance of the Twopenny Act in Virginia, the stipulation that judicial tenure in New York and New Jersey should be at the Crown's pleasure instead of during good behavior, the disallowance of an election law in South Carolina, the issuance of writs of assistance in Massachusetts to combat smuggling, the needless exploitation of white pines in New England for the Royal Navy, and the endeavors of Archbishop Thomas Secker to create an Anglican bishopric in America, when taken together, explain much of the violent reaction in the colonies at the time of the Stamp Act episode. If the Stamp Act remains the foremost issue that drove Americans to the verge of open revolt in the mid-1760's, we now know that other factors heightened the vehemence of the American opposition. — *R.D.H.*

## Additional Recommended Reading

Bancroft, George. *History of the United States of America, from the Discovery of the Continent.* 6 vols. New York: Appleton-Century-Crofts, Inc., 1888. For all of Bancroft's faults, no one since his time has been so familiar with the sources and no one has attempted a history of the Revolution in such comprehensive fashion.

Beer, George L. *British Colonial Policy, 1754-1765.* New York: The Macmillan Company, 1907. One of several volumes that Beer devoted to "the Old Colonial System"; the others cover the earlier colonial period.

Andrews, Charles M. *The Colonial Background of the American Revolution: Four Essays in American Colonial History.* New Haven: Yale University Press, 1924. This thoughtful monograph consists of four essays that provide a good starting point for a study of the origins of the Revolution.

Gipson, Lawrence, H. *The Coming of the Revolution, 1763-1775.* New York: Harper & Row Publishers, 1954. Gipson's book, a part of the *New American Nation* series, is a useful condensation of themes treated in more detail in volumes IX and X of his *The British Empire Before the American Revolution.*

Malone, Joseph J. *Pine Trees and Politics: The Naval Stores and Forest Policy in Colonial New England.* Seattle: University of Washington Press, 1964. Malone now offers the full story of the white pines controversy in New England.

Bridenbaugh, Carl. *Mitre and Sceptre: Transatlantic Faiths, Ideas, Personalities, and Politics, 1689-1775.* New York: Oxford University Press, 1962. Bridenbaugh believes that American fears of an Anglican establishment throughout the colonies were a factor in the growth of American nationalism and a hitherto neglected cause of the American Revolution.

# REVENUE ACT OF 1767 AND THE TOWNSHEND CRISIS

*Type of event:* Economic: attempt by Parliament to impose new regulations and taxation on the American colonists
*Time:* June 29, 1767-1770
*Locale:* North America and Great Britain

### Principal personages:

WILLIAM PITT (THE ELDER) (1708-1778), Prime Minister of Great Britain 1766-1768

CHARLES TOWNSHEND (1725-1767), Chancellor of the Exchequer 1766-1767

GENERAL THOMAS GAGE (1721-1787), British Commander in Chief in North America

JOHN DICKINSON (1732-1808), Philadelphia lawyer whose *Letters from a Farmer in Pennsylvania* denied the constitutionality of the Townshend duties

EARL OF GUILFORD (LORD FREDERICK NORTH) (1732-1792), former Chancellor of the Exchequer who became Prime Minister of Great Britain in 1770

## Summary of Event

When the Rockingham Ministry followed its repeal of the Stamp Act in 1766 by imposing fresh taxes at home, it was replaced by a coalition of diverse politicians under the ailing William Pitt, who had been elevated to the House of Lords as Lord Chatham. Pitt's prolonged absences because of bad health enabled his ministers to pursue their own individualistic ends. The Chancellor of the Exchequer, "Champagne Charlie" Townshend, dealt with the financial crisis, which became considerably worse after Parliament appeased its constituents by slashing the land tax, depriving the government of over £400,000 in yearly revenue. Seizing upon Benjamin Franklin's testimony, preceding the Stamp Act's repeal, to the effect that Americans opposed on principle only internal taxes, Townshend declared that if the colonists adhered to such a foolish dis-

tinction, then they should be saddled with external duties on tea, lead, paper, paints, and glass. The danger to Americans in the subsequent Revenue Act of 1767 containing these proposals was not in the quantity of cash to be extracted from their pockets. That sum annually, by Townshend's own admission, would be only £40,000, less than a tenth of the money lost by Parliament's cutting the land tax. The danger, as Americans saw it, was that Parliament persisted in its efforts to destroy their constitutional rights, not only by taxing them without their consent but also by a provision in the act stating that part of the amount collected was to be used of necessity to pay the salaries of judges and governors in America, thus making them independent of the financial jurisdiction of the colonial assemblies. These legislatures had developed impressive powers in

225

the eighteenth century because of their control of the purse; it was a means of keeping the Crown's appointed officials in line, of making them responsive for the most part to the will of the people they served.

The assemblies believed themselves threatened on still another front by the Quartering Act of 1765; when barracks were unavailable British troops in the colonies were to be lodged in taverns and other public houses at the expense of provincial authorities, who were also responsible for furnishing redcoats with firewood, candles, bedding, and other items. Here Parliament seemed to be taxing Americans indirectly by ordering their assemblies to levy monies for the upkeep of royal regiments. Although the American legislatures after 1765 usually provided for the army's needs, they were careful to maintain their constitutional integrity by avoiding a precise compliance with the letter of the law. But when New York (because of its location the colony most frequently called upon for support) enacted a billeting measure which the military deemed to be inadequate, Parliament suspended the colony's legislature until it bowed to the letter of the British Quartering Act. New York was not cowed, nor were the other assemblies, and when a compromise on military appropriations for New York was reached with local leaders, the ministry secured a lifting of the ban, but not before Americans realized that a dangerous precedent had been set in temporarily depriving citizens of the British Empire of their political representation.

For the colonists there were other ominous straws in the wind. Townshend brought about a reorganization of the customs service in America to guarantee collections of the new taxes as well as to achieve greater compliance with the older Navigation Acts. Previously controlled from Great Britain, customs officers in the colonies were now under a special board sitting in Boston; they would predictably be zealous in the handling of their assignment, for a third of all fines received in the Vice-Admiralty Courts went to the customs men. For that matter, additional courts were established the following year, where many merchants faced charges of violating the exceedingly complicated provisions of the Sugar Act.

If these various British measures prompted a less violent reaction in the colonies than the Stamp Act, they collectively represented an even larger threat to American rights. The point was brought home when, in response to the customs collectors' appeal for protection, the Secretary of State for the colonies, the Earl of Hillsborough (Wills Hill), ordered General Thomas Gage, British Commander in Chief in North America, to station regular troops in Boston. Even before then, however, American opinion was mobilizing in response to lawyer John Dickinson's *Letters from a Farmer in Pennsylvania,* which became popular reading throughout America. What Dickinson lacked in originality he made up for by expressing with vigor and clarity the colonists' constitutional opposition to all forms of taxation by a Parliament in which they were not represented. Other writers joined the battle, as did the assemblies with their remonstrances and petitions against the unpopular doings of the British government. The Massachusetts legislature with its so-called circular letter led the way with a bitter denunciation of Parliamentary taxation and the scheme to pay judges and governors from funds other than those appropriated by the colonial assemblies. Once more merchants formed nonimportation agreements, just as the Sons of Liberty reappeared to lend a hand with violators. Once more Englishmen saw that Parliament had created a storm without producing the intended revenue. With Townshend dead and Pitt retired from office, the ministry of Lord North, in 1770, convinced Parliament to repeal all the Townshend duties except the one on tea, a symbol of Parliament's authority to tax. North was a practical man whose way out of the crisis seemed to herald a *rapprochement* in Anglo-American relations. For the time being, the remaining tax was all but forgotten, as were other grievances, as Americans celebrated their second victory over Parliament in four years.

## Pertinent Literature

Namier, Lewis B. *The Structure of Politics at the Accession of George III.* 2 vols. London: Macmillan & Company, Ltd., 1929.

Namier, Lewis B. *England in the Age of the American Revolution.* London: Macmillan & Company, Ltd., 1930.

While dedication to principle and growing unity are popular themes in our current historical literature about the American Revolution, the trend in Great Britain today is to view the eighteenth century history of the island kingdom as a time when issues counted little and ideas counted even less. Compared to a scholarly trend in vogue a half century and more ago, the change in Great Britain has been profound, for the "Whig interpretation" of the years between the revolutions of 1688 and 1776 is now *passé.* Thus it is considered erroneous to portray the Whigs as the sole defenders of Parliamentary supremacy and the Bill of Rights, as juxtaposed with the Tories in a symmetrical two-party system, while the Crown occupies a subordinate role in such political affairs as the selecting of ministers and the influencing of policy. Nor can one confidently take the next step, as did older writers, such as W. E. H. Lecky and George Otto Trevelyan, and assert that in 1760 the new monarch, George III, was out to wreck the constitutional settlement of 1688-1689; with the support of the previously discredited Tories, he allegedly tried to destroy the Whig party and to institute virtually one-man rule at the expense of his subjects on both sides of the Atlantic. He was opposed in these designs by a small but undaunted band of heroes: William Pitt, Rockingham, Edmund Burke, Charles James Fox, and their followers, men united with the American patriots in a common struggle against tyranny.

The Whig interpretation of eighteenth century British politics has received devastating blows from Sir Lewis Namier and the historical school that has grown up around him. Born a Polish Jew, Namier was an outsider looking in at the British aristocracy, an object of fascination to a man who himself lacked deep roots. Basing his research heavily upon a detailed structural analysis of constituencies, elections, and family relationships, Namier published *The Structure of Politics at the Accession of George III* in 1929, followed the next year by *England in the Age of the American Revolution.* At the time of his death in 1960 Namier and his students had launched a coöperative series that took the title of Namier's book of 1930: *England in the Age of the American Revolution, (1750-1784),* several volumes of which are now in print. To his chief lieutenant, John Brooke, Namier also left the task of completing the first three volumes of the monumental *History of Parliament;* they appeared in 1964 and cover the period 1754-1790.

Namier tells us there was no party system in the age of the Hanoverians, only factions and family groups that coalesced to obtain favors and office. It could scarcely have been otherwise when local rather than national or imperial considerations dominated men's thinking and when ideas and principles scarcely mattered. To avoid chaos and to bring about some order to the political scene, kings inevitably had to play a stabilizing role. Ministers were responsible to the monarch, and they led Parliament in his behalf. George III produced no constitutional revolution, nor did he desire one. The difference between the young George III and the first two Georges was primarily a matter of not relying on the old-line politicians, such as the Duke of Newcastle who had managed affairs for his predecessors; George III used his legitimate powers himself. Interested in the country, high-minded and hard-working, he hired and fired ministers who were personally responsible to him in the absence of a modern cabinet sys-

tem. His own handling of patronage guaranteed him the dominant voice in much that Parliament did. If the King was attacked by the "Old Whigs" (really the displaced political henchmen of George II) in the years after 1760, the explanation is not that ideas and issues were at stake as they claimed, but rather that now they were the "outs" instead of the "ins."

Such an interpretation vindicates George of usurping the constitution but does not necessarily absolve him of the traditional charges of being obstinate and short-sighted. While the stature of the King rises, the luster of the American Revolution diminishes, indirectly at least. The Rockinghams and the other opponents of the post-1763 imperial policies appear to have been mainly disgruntled office-seekers after a means of bringing down the ministry. Certainly the zigs and zags of British measures between the Sugar Act and the opening shots of the American Revolution are more understandable owing to the labors of the Namierists. The absence of parties, the shifting of factions, and the involvement with internal concerns reveal why inconsistency was the rule and not the exception in handling the American problem. For yet another reason, but related to the absence of parties with programs, it would have been virtually impossible to institute a comprehensive plan for the colonies, be it repressive or enlightened; the prime function of government in the eighteenth century was to administer, not to legislate. Hence, a series of measures, often unrelated and adopted in hit-and-miss fashion, managed to inflame the colonies without bringing any benefit to the Mother Country.

The confusion and the contradictions notwithstanding, some men were fairly consistent in the way they viewed the American problem. Indeed, Herbert Butterfield has expressed a common complaint against the Namierists, reminding us that men do not live by bread alone, that principle may not have been completely absent in the age of the American Revolution. Whether the Namierists' microscopic research techniques tend to take "the mind out of history" is perhaps debatable, but some historians point to a discernible consistency in Rockingham and his followers. They opposed the taxing of America and most other harsh measures directed toward the colonies, believing such schemes disruptive and harmful to imperial unity; and for the most part during their long years on the outside, they gained absolutely no political mileage from their stand —usually contrary to the position of the King, who dispensed "the loaves and fishes."

Namier, Lewis B. and John Brooke. *Charles Townshend.* New York: St. Martin's Press, 1964.

Other men could also be consistent; by advocating the bringing of the mature and supposedly headstrong colonists to heel, as Namier himself shows in his biography of Charles Townshend, which was completed after Namier's death by John Brooke. A man of rare charm and eloquence, gay and amoral, Townshend was brilliant but erratic. Of his "champagne speech" Horace Walpole cried, "Nobody but he could have made that speech, and nobody but he would have made it if they could." His theatrics and instability aside, Townshend was one of a growing number of British administrators who desired to limit colonial self-government and to bolster royal authority throughout the British Empire. As early as 1753, he revealed aspects of the program he pushed through Parliament fourteen years later. A junior minister on the eve of the French and Indian War, he drafted instructions for the Governor of New York, Sir Danvers Osborn, that were designed for the local assembly to make permanent arrangements for salaries of the governor, judges, and other officials. The Crown-appointed executives and judges would have become financially independent of the New York legislature had Townshend's dispatch been acted upon. His "Townshend duties" of 1767 were pushed through Parliament in spite of the opposition of Pitt, the Duke of Grafton, and Lord Shelburne. They were not in fact the result of Parliament's lowering the land tax and leaving no alternative other than once again to prime the American pump. The Revenue Act of 1767, worked out a month before the government's defeat on the land tax, had nothing to do with that setback. As much as anything else, Townshend's legislation was the realization of his earlier design to bolster British control at the expense of the colonies.

Thanks to the Namierist school we know how the game of politics was played in the days of the Hanoverians. But we may wonder whether, in the third quarter of the eighteenth century, the players were capable of managing a far-flung empire, immersed as they were in factional and other parochial issues of a domestic nature. Indeed, it was not until 1774, with the passage of the Coercive Acts, that Parliament cast aside the irresolution that had marked its actions toward America since 1763. Then it pursued in earnest the imperial approach of Townshend. From that point, if not earlier, the days of the first British Empire were numbered. — *W.D.H.*

## Additional Recommended Reading

Pares, Richard. *King George III and the Politicians.* Oxford: The University Press, 1953. A brilliantly written account of the Monarch's place in the political and constitutional picture, reflecting the Namierist point of view.

Brooke, John. *The Chatham Administration, 1766-1768.* New York: St. Martin's Press, 1956. This first volume in Namier's series on *England in the Age of the American Revolution* mirrors the approach and conclusions of the author's mentor.

Butterfield, Herbert. *George III and the Historians.* New York: The Macmillan Company, 1957. In this historiographical monograph, Butterfield finds serious fault with some of the conclusions of Namier and Brooke concerning parties and principles.

Ubbelohde, Carl. *The Vice-Admiralty Courts and the American Revolution.* Chapel Hill: University of North Carolina Press, 1960. According to the author of this carefully researched work, "the Vice-Admiralty Courts were a minor, but persistent, cause of the American Revolution."

Jacobson, David L. *John Dickinson and the Revolution in Pennsylvania, 1764-1776.* Berkeley and Los Angeles: University of California Press, 1965. A useful narrative of Dickinson's political ideas and activities.

Gipson, Lawrence H. *The British Empire Before the American Revolution.* Vol. XI: *The Rumbling of the Coming Storm, 1766-1770: The Triumphant Empire.* New York: Alfred A. Knopf, Inc., 1965. A detailed investigation of the second imperial crisis which deals sympathetically with Charles Townshend.